THE SUPREME COURT
from Taft to Burger

OTHER BOOKS BY
ALPHEUS THOMAS MASON

Organized Labor and the Law, 1925
Brandeis and the Modern State, 1933
The Brandeis Way, 1938
Bureaucracy Convicts Itself, 1941
Brandeis: A Free Man's Life, 1946
The Fall of a Railroad Empire
(with Henry L. Staples), 1947
Free Government in the Making, 1949, 1964
*The Supreme Court: Vehicle of Revealed Truth
or Power Group,* 1953
American Constitutional Law
(with William M. Beaney), 1954, 1978
Security Through Freedom, 1955
Harlan Fiske Stone: Pillar of the Law, 1956
The Supreme Court: Palladium of Freedom, 1962
William Howard Taft: Chief Justice, 1965
The States Rights Debate, 1972
American Constitutional Development
(with D. Grier Stephenson, Jr.), 1977

THE
SUPREME COURT
FROM TAFT TO BURGER

Alpheus Thomas Mason

Third Edition, Revised and Enlarged
Originally published as
The Supreme Court from Taft to Warren

LOUISIANA STATE UNIVERSITY PRESS
BATON ROUGE AND LONDON

Portions of Chapter 8 appeared in the January, 1979,
Review of Politics.

1980 printing

LIBRARY OF CONGRESS CATALOGING IN PUBLICATION DATA
Mason, Alpheus Thomas, 1899–
    The Supreme Court from Taft to Burger—originally published as
The Supreme Court from Taft to Warren.

    Includes index.
    1. United States. Supreme Court. I. Title.
KF4748.M37   347'.74'26   78–19084
ISBN 0–8071–0468–X
ISBN 0–8071–0469–8 pbk.

To Hilary
Winsome Lady of Nine

Hardly any question arises in the United States that is not resolved sooner or later into a judicial question

. . . DE TOCQUEVILLE

Contents

Illustrations

Preface to the Third Edition

Now IN its third edition, this book illustrates Justice
Holmes's colorful image of the Supreme Court as a
"storm center." The first edition was published in
1959, five years after Chief Justice Warren initiated a momentous revolution. The second edition coincided with
Richard Nixon's Presidential campaign drive to restore
"law and order" by packing the Court with "strict constructionists." History is repeating itself. As this edition goes to
press in the spring of 1978, angry marchers have gathered
around the Marble Palace, protesting the counter revolution they fear is in the offing—a ruling in favor of the embattled Allan Bakke.

From academe comes a more reasoned, but scarcely less
impassioned attack. In late 1977, under the prestigious im-
print of the Harvard University Press, Raoul Berger, bor-
rowing Louis Boudin's title of 1932, *Government by Judiciary,* lashed out fiercely, equating judicial usurpations with
those of President Nixon. Although Harvard's legal scholar
centers his fire on the Warren Court, he does not spare,
much less condone, the sins committed by its successor. At
no time during the twenty-year life span of this book was it
amiss to echo Holmes's candid confession: "We are very
quiet here, but it is the quiet of a hurricane."

Every Court is the product of its time, reflecting the solemn views of fallible men in black robes. While wearing

the magical habiliments of the law, Supreme Court Justices take sides on controversial issues. Thus judicial activism, whatever its orientation, involves a paradox at the heart of constitutional orthodoxy—the Supreme Court considered as the mouthpiece of self-interpreting, self-enforcing law.

In a moment of judicial candor, Justice Robert H. Jackson shattered this beguiling myth: "We are not final because we are infallible, but we are infallible only because we are final." Even those inclined to think of the Supreme Court as "brushed with divinity" do not accept constitutional theology at face value. Few Americans were shocked in 1968 when the GOP Presidential candidate made the Court a major political issue and bluntly announced his determination to restore "law and order" by changing judicial personnel. Presumably the President, given an opportunity, can mold the Constitution simply by a discriminating choice of Supreme Court nominees.

More than any President in this century, perhaps more than any in our history, President Nixon made nominations with an eye to politics and ideology rather than to merit or professional distinction. Even the staid American Bar Association deplored his narrow, political approach.

Nixon was not, however, the first President to recognize that the judicial function is unavoidably political. As a counterweight for his successor, Thomas Jefferson, President Adams named Jefferson's arch political antagonist, John Marshall, Chief Justice of the United States. When Marshall died in 1835 after thirty-four years on the supreme bench, soothsayers and politicians, mindful that President Jackson would choose Marshall's successor, predicted disaster. President Taft rated his six Supreme Court appointments during four years in the White House a signal achievement, glorying in the fact that President Wilson made only three appointments in twice that time. In the 1920 Presidential campaign, former President Taft spoke out emphatically. Like Nixon in 1968, Taft underscored the major domestic issue—appointment of judges who would maintain the Supreme Court as the "bulwark" of property. Thanks to Warren G. Harding's landslide election, Taft himself as Chief Justice translated political conviction into Supreme Court decisions.

President Eisenhower's most noteworthy act during eight years in the White House was the appointment of Earl Warren as Chief Justice of the United States. Under Warren's leadership the Court spearheaded a revolution. Looking back dourly on the unforeseen consequences of his choice, Ike called it "the biggest damn fool mistake I ever made."

It fell to President Nixon, Vice-President during Eisenhower's administration, to attempt reversal of the Warren Court's revolutionary decisions. Four Justices in the Court headed by Warren Earl Burger were appointed to halt the activist drive. Commentators, by and large, lament the erosion of major decisions protecting civil rights. Still others deplore continuing judicial activism, charging that the Court is still "the nation's paramount policy maker, usurping the amending power under the guise of interpretation."

In certain respects the judicial *supremacy* that marked the years 1900–37 may be considered less presumptive than that of the Warren and Burger Courts. The former negated state and national attempts to regulate the economy; the latter have formulated policy on the most emotionally charged issues. Are we headed for another showdown with the Supreme Court? "How long," Raoul Berger asks in a resounding denunciation of the Supreme Court of the past twenty-five years, "can public respect for the Court survive if the people become aware that the tribunal which condemns the acts of others as unconstitutional is itself acting unconstitutionally?" (*The New York Times*, October 29, 1977).

One thing seems certain: never before has the Supreme Court put its constitutional fingers in so many social, cultural, and political pies. The irony is that four of its present members were selected as "strict constructionists."

A.T.M.

Princeton
May 5, 1978

THE SUPREME COURT
from Taft to Burger

CHAPTER 1

The Cult of the Robe

CONSTITUTION making was rendered difficult by the framers' elusive goal. They tried to combine in a single system called *free government* the opposite, sometimes complementary, values of liberty and restraint. In *Federalist* No. 37, Madison noted that "among the difficulties encountered by the Convention a very important one must have lain in combining the requisite stability and energy in government with the inviolable attention due to liberty and the republican form." The search for this dichotomous objective involved allocating and separating power between the national government and the states and among the three departments of national authority, and drawing the precious line between government at all levels and individual rights.

The difficulties were compounded, Madison wrote, "by indistinctness of the object, imperfection of the organs of conception, inadequateness of the vehicle of ideas. . . ." Underscoring the problem, Madison observed: "When the Almighty himself condescends to address Mankind in their own language, his meaning, luminous as it must be, is rendered dim and doubtful by the cloudy medium through which it is communicated."

Ironically, the Supreme Court, faced with these manifold

complexities, has compounded constitutional interpretation by resorting to penumbral labels. Not infrequently
the result has been to enlarge judicial power at the expense
of the political organs of government.

In 1895, Chief Justice Fuller fashioned the "direct and
indirect effects" formula to undermine the national commerce power, and the Court thus permitted a 98 per cent
monopoly in the manufacture of sugar, allowing itself what
it denied to Congress—the power to regulate commerce.[1]
The doctrine of "dual federalism" cut two ways, defeating
both national and state power to regulate the economy. To
dilute the state police power, defined as the authority "to
govern men and things," the Court invoked a penumbral
right not mentioned in the Constitution—"liberty of contract."[2] Scores of state statutes, including hours-of-labor
and minimum-wage laws for women, fell under this judicial
creation. In its heyday, liberty of contract meant liberty of
business. The phony "separate but equal" formula kept
public schools racially segregated for half a century.[3] A
newcomer in the ever-lengthening list of penumbras is
"executive privilege,"[4] one of the foggiest labels in the lexicon of constitutional interpretation.

---

[1] *U.S.* v. *E. C. Knight,* 156 U.S. 1 (1895). Dissenting Justice Harlan
(the elder) declared that denial of Congress' power to regulate this
monopoly meant that "the Constitution has failed to accomplish one
primary object of the Union, which was to place commerce among
the states under the control of the common government of all the
people, and thereby relieve or protect it against burdens or restrictions imposed, by whatever authority, for the benefit of particular
localities or interests" (pp. 24, 44).

[2] *Allgeyer* v. *Louisiana,* 165 U.S. 578 (1897); *Lochner* v. *New York,*
198 U.S. 45 (1905); *Adkins* v. *Children's Hospital,* 261 U.S. 525
(1923).

[3] *Plessy* v. *Ferguson,* 163 U.S. 537 (1896).

[4] Raoul Berger, *Executive Privilege: A Constitutional Myth* (Cambridge, Mass., 1974).

Less esoteric are the terms "preferred freedoms" and "judicial activism." Both have recently gained widespread currency, yet both denote values and procedures going back to the beginning of judicial history. "Preferred freedoms" appeared in a 1942 Supreme Court opinion to describe constitutional values entitled to special judicial scrutiny.[5] Thereafter it was used to identify the priority accorded speech, press, religion, and certain other Bill of Rights imperatives. Previously property and contract rights were "preferred," but that term was not used to identify them.

The Revolutionary Fathers had an abiding concern for

[5] Justice Stone dissenting in *Jones* v. *Opelika*, 316 U.S. 583, 600, 608 (1942). Justice Rutledge (*Thomas* v. *Collins*, 323 U.S. 516, 529–30 [1945]) speaks of "the preferred place given in our scheme to the great, the indispensable democratic freedoms secured by the First Amendment. . . . That priority gives these liberties a sanctity and sanction not permitting dubious intrusions. And it is the character of the right, not of the limitation, which determines what standard governs the choice."

In *Lloyd* v. *Tanner*, 407 U.S. 551 (1972), 568, Justice Powell refers to "a special solicitude" which the "courts properly have shown for the guarantees of the First Amendment." In 1972 (*Lynch* v. *Household Finance Corp.*, 405 U.S. 538), Justice Stewart, speaking for the Court, argued that this is a distinction without a difference:

"The dichotomy between personal liberties and property rights is a false one. Property does not have rights. People have rights. The right to enjoy property without unlawful deprivation, no less than the right to speak or right to travel, is in truth a 'personal right,' whether the 'property' in question be a welfare check, a home, or a savings account. In fact, a fundamental interdependence exists between the personal right to liberty and the personal right in property. Neither could have meaning without the other. That rights in property are basic civil rights has long been recognized."

See Madison's "Essay on Property," quoted in Alpheus T. Mason and William M. Beaney, *American Constitutional Law* (6th ed.; Englewood Cliffs, N.J., 1978), 339. The dichotomy Justice Stewart adumbrated is increasingly evident in the Burger Court. See *Lloyd* v. *Tanner*, 405 U.S. 551, and *Pittsburgh Press Co.* v. *Commission on Human Relations*, 413 U.S. (1973). The author's views are explored elsewhere in this book.

property. Eighteenth-century Americans warmly endorsed John Adams' deep-seated conviction that "property is as sacred as the laws of God."[6] The Founding Fathers, recognizing that life, liberty, and property are basic, rejected legislative supremacy. The Constitution embodies a variety of written and institutional restrictions on all organs of government, harnessing these with the peculiarly American auxiliary device—judicial review. In England the fate of property depends primarily on the legislature; in America until 1937 it depended on courts.[7]

During a good part of our history, especially between 1890 and 1937, courts, including the supreme bench, gave property priority. Supreme Court decisions in the 1920's reflect this ranking. While resisting legislative encroachments on economic rights, the justices often upheld government restrictions on freedom of thought.[8] Since 1938, Supreme Court Justices have tended to rank traditional individual freedoms and assign a larger degree of constitutional protection to one rather than another, depending on judicial preference.

Of recent vintage is another caption—"judicial activism." Some observers would have us believe that this phenomenon, so conspicuous in decisions of the Warren Court, has no antecedents. The fact is that all Courts have been activist in one way or another.[9]

John Marshall was an activist whose Court focused on

---

[6] Quoted in Mason, *Free Government in the Making* (New York, 1965), 179.

[7] See Edward S. Corwin, review of B. F. Wright's *Growth of American Constitutional Law*, in *Harvard Law Review*, LVI (1942), 484, 487.

[8] See Felix Frankfurter, *Mr. Justice Holmes and the Supreme Court* (Cambridge, Mass., 1938), 62.

[9] See Mason, "Judicial Activism: Old and New," *Virginia Law Review*, LV (1969), 385–426.

nation building. Under his leadership, national power was expanded and state power was curtailed. Property and contract rights ranked high in Marshall's scale of constitutional values.

Roger Brooke Taney was an activist. His Court wrestled with sectionalism, asserting for the states a power-generating doctrine called "police" and fashioning at the national level the power-hampering theory of "dual federalism."[10] The Taney Court's misguided activism in *Dred Scott*[11] helped to precipitate the Civil War.

The Court headed by Chief Justice Fuller, preferring an unregulated economy, read the laissez faire dogma into the Constitution, carrying judicial activism to unprecedented heights. After 1900 judicial *review* became judicial *supremacy*.

The Taft, Hughes, and Stone Courts tried to reconcile conventional "hands off" attitudes with a popular legislative mandate for government regulation of the economy. In the 1930's judicial activism in defense of property led to a crucial impasse between President Franklin D. Roosevelt and the Supreme Court. To break that deadlock F.D.R. threatened Court-packing. Within an incredibly short time —one year—the Justices first vetoed and then legitimatized the New Deal. The capricious element in the judicial process was starkly revealed. In 1935–36 judicial activism in defense of property had been the Court's posture. A year later, without a single change in judicial personnel, "self-restraint" became the order of the day.

Ironically, use of penumbral devices had not rendered the Constitution's meaning less "cloudy" and "doubtful." In 1936, when "direct and indirect effects," "dual federal-

[10] Edward S. Corwin, "The Passing of Dual Federalism," *Virginia Law Review*, XXXVI (1950).
[11] 19 *Howard* (1957), 393.

ism," and "liberty of contract" had carried the Court's "proud preeminence"[12] to unprecedented heights, Justice Stone, dissenting, tried to teach his colleagues an elementary lesson on the nature and scope of their role vis-à-vis the political organs of government. He wrote:

> The power of courts to declare a statute unconstitutional is subject to two guiding principles of decision which ought never to be absent from judicial consciousness. One is that courts are concerned only with the power to enact statutes, not with their wisdom. The other is that while unconstitutional exercise by the executive and legislative branches of the government is subject to judicial restraint, the only check upon our own exercise of power is our own sense of self-restraint. For the removal of unwise laws from the statute books appeal lies not to the courts but to the ballot and to the processes of democratic government.[13]

After nearly two hundred years, judicial decisions still turn not so much on specific issues as on differences among the Justices concerning the function the Court may legitimately exercise and the probable consequences of one decision rather than another.

Since 1937 the justices have left protection of property to what Madison called the primary control on government— "dependence on the people," the ballot box.[14] Judicial activism old style was dead; judicial activism new style was just around the corner.

For Chief Justice Warren, as for Jefferson, the Bill of Rights lay at the heart of any Constitution. Under his

---

[12] Judge Gibson's characterization in his classic attack on judicial review. *Eakin* v. *Raub,* 12 Sergeant and Rawle (Pa. Supreme Court, 1825), 330.

[13] *U.S.* v. *Butler,* 297 U.S. 1 (1936), 78–79.

[14] "A dependence on the people is, no doubt, the primary control on the government; but experience has taught mankind the necessity of auxiliary precautions." Edward G. Bourne, ed., *The Federalist* (New York, 1937), No. 51, 354–55. Judicial review is among the "auxiliary precautions."

leadership the Court assumed special guardianship of civil rights—a new brand of preferred freedom. Opposing the new trend were powerful and persistent dissenters, notably Justices Frankfurter and Harlan and, finally, erstwhile libertarian Justice Black. They deplored it as vehemently as had critics of the old activism prior to 1937. Rejecting any particular ranking of constitutional verities and calling for across-the-board judicial self-restraint, Justice Harlan repeatedly warned that "the Constitution does not confer on courts blanket authority to step into every situation where the political branch may be thought to have fallen short."[15] The dissenters argued that courts were not only ill-equipped but also unauthorized to do so.

Chief Justice Marshall articulated the patent myth that "Courts are mere instruments of the Law, and can will nothing."[16] Thus from the outset exponents and practitioners of judicial review have been confronted with an awkward dilemma, "a basic inconsistency," Justice Robert H. Jackson called it, "between popular government and judicial supremacy."[17]

The problem is a continuing one because Americans have not been willing to risk democracy without some judicial restraint. How can judges maintain the detached air, almost that of disembodied spirits, and at the same time wield real power over current and controversial political policy and practice? Alexander Hamilton and John Marshall in their day tried to answer this question. Despite disenchantment resulting from judicial decisions, includ-

[15] Dissenting in *Baker* v. *Carr,* 369 U.S. 186 (1962), and *Reynolds* v. *Sims,* 377 U.S. 533 (1964). Addresses of John M. Harlan at the American Bar Center, Chicago, August 13, 1963, and at the Dedication of the Bill of Rights Room, U.S. Subtreasury Building, New York City, August 9, 1964.

[16] *Osborn* v. *U.S. Bank,* 9 Wheaton 738, 866 (1824).

[17] Robert H. Jackson, *The Struggle for Judicial Supremacy: A Study of a Crisis in American Power Politics* (New York, 1941), vii.

ing many of our own time, the magic of what they said still has its abiding charm.

When the Federal Constitutional Convention met in 1787 the "injustice" of state laws had brought into question that "fundamental principle of Republican government—that the 'majority who rule are the safest Guardians both of public good and private rights.' " [18] The founding fathers, being skeptical of "popular government" and alert to the necessity of safeguarding individual rights against "interested and overbearing majorities," established "free government." "In all cases where a majority are united by a common interest or passion," Madison explained, "the rights of the minority are in danger." Experience had demonstrated "the necessity of providing more effectually for the security of private rights, and the steady dispensation of justice." The deliberate sense of the community should govern the conduct of those entrusted with the management of public affairs, but the framers opposed "unqualified complaisance to every sudden breeze of passion, or to every transient impulse which the people may receive from the arts of men, who flatter their prejudices and betray their interests." [19] "Popular government," majority rule, a system absolutely dependent on society, was objectionable as not providing adequate security for individual "liberties," "rights," and "privileges." Government must be dependent on the people, but the government itself should possess the independence necessary to guard the "liberties of a great community." [20]

There ought to be, Hamilton remarked on the floor of the Philadelphia Convention, "a principle in government

[18] *The Writings of James Madison*, edited by Gaillard Hunt (9 vols.; New York, 1901), II, 366.

[19] *The Federalist*, edited by Max Beloff (New York, 1948), No. 71, p. 366.

[20] *The Federalist*, No. 26, p. 128.

capable of resisting the popular current." [21] "When occasions present themselves in which the interests of the people are at variance with their inclinations," he wrote in *The Federalist*, No. 71, "it is the duty of the persons whom they have appointed to be the guardians of those interests to withstand the temporary delusion, in order to give them time and opportunity for more cool and sedate reflection."

A political system thus limited and controlled was called free government, a body politic where the majority is, for the sake of minority rights, bound by a constitution, where popular participation in government is basic, but where, in order to prevent sheer majority rule or democratic despotism, the popular participation principle is subordinate to the protection of individual rights.[22] "That government can scarcely be deemed to be free," Justice Story observed in 1829, "where the rights of property are left solely dependent upon the will of a legislative body, without any restraint. The fundamental maxims of a free government seem to require that the rights of personal liberty and private property should be held sacred."

The Constitution embodies a complexus of devices for implementing free government.[23] Power is divided between the federal government and the states. Three sep-

---

[21] Max Farrand (ed.), *The Records of the Federal Convention of 1787* (4 vols.; New Haven, 1937), I, 299; see also pp. 309, 310.

[22] Gottfried Dietze, "Hamilton's *Federalist*—Treatise for Free Government," *Cornell Law Quarterly*, XLII, No. 3 (Spring, 1957), 501–18.

[23] Burke underscored free government's complexity: "To make a government requires no great prudence. Settle the seat of power; teach obedience and the work is done. To give freedom is still more easy. It is not necessary to guide; it only requires to let go the rein. But to form a *free government;* that is to temper together these opposite elements of liberty and restraint in one consistent work, requires much thought; deep reflection; a sagacious, powerful and combining mind." Edmund Burke, *Reflections on the French Revolution* (Maynard's English Classic Series), 121.

arate organs of government share national power. The Supreme Court was thought of as an "intermediate body between the people and the legislature" to safeguard the "private rights of particular classes of citizens" against the "ill-humors in society" and especially against "unjust and partial laws." [24] The judiciary was envisaged as the guardian of free government.[25] Hamilton's famous essay in *The Federalist,* No. 78, is not only an apologia for judicial review, but also a demonstration of how the Court could be counted on to safeguard individual rights against the excesses of popular power. "In a monarchy," the New Yorker reasoned, the judiciary "is an excellent barrier to the despotism of the prince; in a republic, it is a no less excellent barrier to the encroachments and oppressions of the representative body." The judiciary is necessary "to guard the Constitution and rights of the individuals, from the effects of those ill-humours which the arts of designing men, or the influence of particular conjunctures, sometimes disseminate among the people themselves, and which, though they speedily give place to better information, and more deliberate reflection, have a tendency, in the meantime, to occasion dangerous innovations in the government and serious oppressions of the minor part in the community." [26] As Professor E. S. Corwin has put it, judicial review represented "an attempt by American democracy to cover its bet."

Hamilton was at special pains to square the Court's limiting and protective function with that other requisite of free government, the principle of participation—the notion that legitimate power is derived from the people

24 *The Federalist,* No. 78, pp. 398, 400–401.

25 "A fear of popular majorities . . . lies at the very basis of the whole system of judicial review, and indeed of our entire constitutional system." E. S. Corwin, "The Supreme Court and the Fourteenth Amendment," 7 *Michigan Law Review* 643 (1909), 669.

26 *The Federalist,* No. 78, pp. 396, 400.

and must ultimately reflect their will. Judicial review does not "suppose a superiority of the judicial to the legislative power. It only supposes that the power of the people is superior to both; and that where the will of the legislature declared in statutes stands in opposition to that of the people declared in the Constitution, the judges ought to be governed by the latter, rather than the former." [27] Since it is the "will of the people" which courts discover and declare, there was no possibility of placing the Court above Congress. "The judiciary," Hamilton asserted, "is beyond comparison the weakest of the three departments of power. . . . [It] has no influence over either the sword or the purse; no direction either of the strength or the wealth of the society; and can take no active resolution whatever. It may truly be said to have neither FORCE nor WILL, but merely judgment." [28]

It remained for Chief Justice Marshall to spell out Hamilton's ideas and give them official gloss. "It is emphatically the province and duty of the judicial department to say what the law is," [29] the Chief Justice commented in *Marbury* v. *Madison*. Marshall compared the section of the 1789 Judiciary Act in dispute with the relevant provisions of the Constitution and concluded that "the authority given to the Supreme Court by the act establishing the judicial courts of the United States, to issue writs of mandamus to public officers, appears not to be warranted by the Constitution." [30] The judicial process, as Marshall revealed it, is quite simple. The Chief Justice put the Constitution beside the law to determine whether or not they squared with each other. He "discovered" that they did not, so the act had to be disregarded.

Marbury v. *Madison* is notable not only because it es-

[27] *Ibid.*, 398.
[28] *Ibid.*, 396–97.
[29] *Marbury* v. *Madison*, 1 Cranch 137 (1803), 177.
[30] *Ibid.*, 176.

tablished the doctrine of judicial review but also because John Marshall, in asserting this power, set forth the notion that the judicial process is essentially an exercise in mechanics. Supreme Court Justices discover law; they do not make it. Two decades after the Marbury decision, the great Chief Justice avowed that "Judicial power, as contradistinguished from the power of the laws, has no existence. Courts are the mere instruments of the law, and can will nothing. When they are said to exercise a discretion, it is a mere legal discretion, a discretion to be exercised in discerning the course prescribed by law. . . . Judicial power is never exercised for the purpose of giving effect to the will of the Judge; always for the purpose of giving effect to the will of the Legislature; or, in other words, to the will of the law." [31] Constitutional interpretation consists in finding meanings which are clear only to judges. To judges the meaning of the Constitution is obvious. To others, whether legislators or executives, its meaning is hidden and obscure. These outsiders, as President Eisenhower's comment on the controversial 1957 decisions suggests, have not this transcendental wisdom. The only final and authoritative mouthpiece of the Constitution is the Supreme Court, and its every version gleaned from a sort of "brooding omnipresence in the sky" has the special virtue of never mangling or changing the original instrument.

But, surely, more is involved in the judicial process than Marshall would have one believe. "All would agree," Vincent Barnett observes, "that *when* a statute conflicts with the Constitution, the former must yield. The vital issue is *how* the Court decides *whether* such a conflict does in fact exist. The nature of this process is the point at which divergent opinions arise. Is it merely, as the pure mechanical theory must assume, the exposition and application of

[31] *Osborn* v. *U.S. Bank,* 9 Wheaton 738 (1824), 866.

a document of self-evident meaning? This can hardly suffice to explain legitimate differences of opinion among honest and able men—among the judges themselves. Obviously it is something more than this and less than the exercise of untrammeled will." [32]

"It will ever remain a mystery to me," Thomas Reed Powell wrote in 1956, "how intelligent jurists can make these professions of nonparticipation in the judicial process." Such judicial denials made Powell doubt "either the capacity or the candor of the men who made them." [33]

"Even when I became aware," Powell continues, "that in the long run judges make law as well as find it, I had the notion that they laid their conceptual bricks from a perfect design to achieve the beauty of harmony and the *summum bonum* of the highest possible wisdom." [34] The late Judge Jerome Frank saw all this as a manifestation of "Robe-ism"—the judicial robe serving to shield the Court from the "attack of critical reason."

These men are not the first, nor likely to be the last, to express skepticism as to the occult claims judges are in the habit of making. John Austin ridiculed Blackstone for crediting "the childish fiction employed by our judges, that judiciary or common law is not made by them, but is a miraculous something made by nobody, existing . . . from eternity, and merely *declared* from time to time by

[32] Vincent M. Barnett, Jr., "Constitutional Interpretation and Judicial Self-Restraint," 39 *Michigan Law Review* 213 (1940), 217.

"It is legitimate to reconcile the two sides of this centuries-old controversy," Zechariah Chafee writes, "by saying that the judges make law out of what they discover, and that law is the will of the justices trying to do what is right." See "So Judges Make or Discover Law," *American Philosophical Proceedings*, XCI, No. 5 (1947), 420.

[33] Thomas Reed Powell, *Vagaries and Varieties in Constitutional Interpretation* (New York, 1956), 28. See also Jerome Frank, "The Cult of the Robe," *Saturday Review*, XXVIII (Oct. 13, 1945), 12.

[34] *Ibid.*, 33.

the judges." [35] In a broader context, Jonathan Swift was most irreverent in discussing the ways of legalists:

It is a maxim among lawyers, that whatever hath been done before may legally be done again: and therefore they take special care to record all the decisions formerly made against common justice and the general reason of mankind. These, under the name of precedents, they produce as authorities, to justify the most iniquitous opinions; and the judges never fail of directing accordingly. In pleading they studiously avoid entering into the merits of the cause, but are loud, violent and tedious in dwelling upon all circumstances which are not to the purpose.

It is likewise to be observed, that this society hath a peculiar chant and jargon of their own, that no other mortal can understand, and wherein all their laws are written, which they take special care to multiply; whereby they have wholly confounded the very essence of truth and falsehood.[36]

Noting this tendency among lawyers to confound and confuse, Judge Frank suggested that it was motivated by the desire to "deepen the atmosphere of mystery" and thus make law a professional subject intelligible only to lawyers.

The language of the Constitution itself is ambiguous. This is perhaps the key to its enduring strength. The "words of the Constitution" are, Justice Frankfurter wrote in 1949, "so unrestricted by their intrinsic meaning or by their history or by tradition or by prior decisions that they leave the individual Justice free, if indeed they do not compel him, to gather meaning not from reading the Constitution but from reading life. . . . [M]embers of the Court are frequently admonished by their associates not to read their economic and social views into the neutral language of the Constitution. But the process of

[35] John Austin, *Lectures on Jurisprudence* (5th ed.; London, 1885), II, 634.

[36] Jonathan Swift, *Gulliver's Travels* (Modern Library; New York, 1931), 283–84.

constitutional interpretation compels the translation of policy into judgment. . . ." [37]

It is on the rocks of the Constitution's ambiguity, permitting, even compelling, the translation of judicial preference into law, that the mechanical theory[38] breaks down. "When one reflects upon the vague and general character of these many instruments," the economist Richard T. Ely commented in April, 1891, "and of the various interpretations which may be given . . . their provisions, one becomes aware that judges are our supreme rulers." [39]

The Justices themselves have made gratuitous contributions to the troubles growing out of the operation of the judicial process. In his book of 1928 Charles Evans Hughes cited three examples—*Scott* v. *Sandford, Hepburn* v. *Griswold,* and *Pollock* v. *Farmers' Loan and Trust Co.*—in which "the Court has suffered severely from self-inflicted wounds." [40] These cases were thus characterized because of their effect in destroying "public confidence" and popular respect for the Court.[41] Chief Justice Taney's ruling

[37] "The Supreme Court," 3 *Parliamentary Affairs* (1949), 68.

[38] This theory, Dean Pound observes, makes the court a "sort of judicial slot machine." The facts are put in the judicial hopper and the decision comes out automatically. The facts may not, as Pound suggests, "always fit the machinery, and, hence we may have to thump and joggle the machinery a bit in order to get anything out. But even in extreme cases of this departure from the purely automatic, the decision is attributed, not at all to the thumping and jogging process, but solely to the machine." Roscoe Pound, *The Spirit of the Common Law* (Boston, 1921), 170–71.

[39] "Report on Social Legislation in United States for 1889 and 1890," *Economic Review,* I (April, 1891), 236.

"I do not hesitate to declare that our form of government is the aristocracy of the robe, which I venture to regard as the best form of aristocracy in the world." Words of John W. Burgess, quoted in T. R. Powell, *Vagaries and Varieties in Constitutional Interpretation,* 15.

[40] Charles Evans Hughes, *The Supreme Court of the United States: Its Foundation, Methods, and Achievements—An Interpretation* (New York, 1928), 50.

[41] *Ibid.,* 50–53 *passim.*

in the Dred Scott case that a Negro, not being a citizen, could not sue in the federal courts and his holding that Congress could not prohibit slavery in the territories reduced Negroes to the lowest level.

Historian Von Holst denounced the decision as indicative of "the systematic and conscious aim of the South to make the Supreme Court the citadel of slaveocracy." Yet Taney declared, somewhat self-consciously, that no one could reasonably suppose that "any change in public opinion or feeling in relation to this unfortunate race," either in America or abroad, "should induce the Court to give to the words of the Constitution a more liberal construction in their favor than they were intended to bear when the instrument was framed and adopted." It was not, the Chief Justice pointed out, "the province of the Court to decide upon the justice or injustice, the polity or impolity of these laws." [42]

By this decision, the Court suffered a "grave injury." Hughes appraised its action as "a public calamity." "The widespread and bitter attacks upon the judges who joined in the decision undermined confidence in the Court. . . . It was many years before the Court, even under new judges, was able to retrieve its reputation." [43]

The Court dealt itself a second blow in *Hepburn* v. *Griswold*.[44] By vote of six to three it invalidated the wartime Legal Tender Act. Two vacancies existed on the Court when the decision came down, and that very day President Grant nominated William Strong and Joseph Bradley to fill them. Soon after their confirmation, reargument was ordered on the constitutional question. Rumor became current that the decision might be reversed. Such a reversal would, of course, pierce the façade of judicial

---

[42] *Scott* v. *Sandford,* 19 Howard 393 (1857), 405, 426.
[43] Hughes, *The Supreme Court of the United States,* 50.
[44] 8 Wallace 603 (1870).

automation—something the legal profession was anxious to prevent.

"The great objection to opening the Legal Tender decision," the *American Law Review* declared, "is that the Supreme Court cannot do it without degrading itself in the eyes of all intelligent men, and this fact, we should think the new members of the court should recognize quite as distinctly as the old. We believe we express the opinion of every unbiased lawyer throughout the United States when we say that the reopening of the legal tender case would be a terrible blow at the dignity and independence of the profession." [45]

Despite the warnings of the legal profession, President Grant's two appointees, joining with the dissenters, reversed the Court's decision of fifteen months earlier. The previous majority, now in dissent, complained that the Court ignored the clear mandate to defend the unchanging words of the Constitution—words as clear and binding as those of the Holy Writ. Said Justice Field:

Sitting as a judicial officer, and bound to compare every law enacted by Congress with the greater law enacted by the people, and being unable to reconcile the measure in question with that fundamental law, I cannot hesitate to pronounce it as being, in my judgment, unconstitutional and void. . . . The only loyalty which I can admit consists in obedience to the Constitution and the laws made in pursuance of it. It is only by obedience that affection and reverence can be shown to a superior having a right to command. So thought our great Master when he said to his disciples: "If ye love me, keep my commandments." [46]

Outvoted, the devout Justice's pleas went for naught.

In 1928, against a background of half a century, Mr. Hughes estimated the damage inflicted by this reversal and indicated what he himself would have done, and why,

---

[45] *American Law Review*, Vol. 5, No. 2 (1871), 367.
[46] *Legal Tender Cases*, 12 Wallace 457, pp. 680-81.

had he been in the position of the new appointees, Strong
and Bradley.

From the standpoint of the effect on public opinion, there
can be no doubt that the reopening of the case was a serious
mistake and the overruling in such a short time, and by one
vote of the previous decision shook popular respect for the
Court. . . . The Court alone was responsible for the unfortunate effect of its change of front and for its action in reopening the case which might well have been considered closed.
The argument for reopening was strongly presented in view
of the great importance of the question, but the effect of such
a sudden reversal of judgment might easily have been foreseen.[47]

Hughes did not deny that the Court's earlier decision
was in error, or that it should have been reversed. His
point was that the Justices should not have taken upon
themselves the responsibility of rectifying their own wrong
—especially one so recently committed. "Stability in
judicial opinion," the future Chief Justice commented,
"is of no little importance in maintaining respect for
the Court's work." [48]

The third "self-inflicted" wound mentioned in Hughes's
book was perhaps the most serious one, in that change of
mind on the part of a single judge after reargument resulted in the unconstitutionality of a federal income tax
by vote of 5 to 4.[49] As in the earlier cases, criticism of
the Court was bitter and widespread. Some critics advocated a drastic curb on the judiciary, while others suggested that Congress might simply pass an act reversing
the Court's reactionary decision. "I cannot conceive that
there can be any necessity of a constitutional amendment," Senator Hernando McLaurin observed. "I do not
see that the Congress of the United States should be called

47 Hughes, *The Supreme Court of the United States*, 52–53.
48 *Ibid.*, 53.
49 *Pollock* v. *Farmers' Loan and Trust Co.*, 158 U.S. 601 (1895).

upon to zigzag around inconsistent rulings of the Supreme Court." In considering corrective legislation, the Senator believed that the Congress should apply its own standards of constitutionality. Senator Anselm J. Money's irreverence went even further: "I am not one of those who regard the judgment of the Supreme Court as an African regards his particular deity. I respect such a decision just exactly to the extent that it is founded in common sense and argued out on reasonable logic, but when it violates the law of common sense, then I cease to so regard it, except that as a citizen I am bound by it." The Senator continued, "As a legislator, I have no more regard for it than I have for the decision of a magistrate in one of the counties of the State of Mississippi, especially when I know it runs counter to the decision of a hundred years and was decided by a vote of five to four and that one judge who voted in the affirmative changed his mind somewhat in the shadows between two different hearings." [50]

Discussion of McLaurin's proposal reached its height during the Presidency of William Howard Taft. The 1909 session of Congress debated the matter at length. A measure introduced by Senator Joseph Bailey of Texas, as an amendment to the tariff bill, was essentially the same as that the Supreme Court had invalidated in 1895. Said Senator Bailey:

The amendment is, in the main, the same as the law of 1894. . . . This far, and only this far, have I drawn this amendment for the purpose of meeting that decision. . . . In all other respects, instead of trying to conform the amendment to the decision of the court, the amendment distinctly challenges that decision. I do not believe that that opinion is a correct interpretation of the Constitution. . . . With this thought in mind, and remembering that the decision was by a bare majority, and that the decision itself overruled the decisions of a hundred years . . . I think that the court,

[50] *Congressional Record*, Vol. 44 (July 3, 1909), 4067, 4115.

upon a reconsideration of this question, will adjudge an income tax a constitutional exercise of power by Congress.[51]

The President himself agreed that the Court's decision outlawing the tax was wrong. He favored the income tax, and believed that an ordinary act of Congress was sufficient to reverse the disabling decision. Taft, nevertheless, advised against this course [52] and urged resort to the time-consuming amending procedures.

"Although I have not considered a constitutional amendment as necessary to the exercise of certain phases of this power," Taft explained, "a mature consideration has satisfied me that an amendment is the only proper course for the establishment to its full extent. . . . This course is much to be preferred to the one proposed of re-enacting a law once judicially declared to be unconstitutional. For the Congress to assume that the court will reverse itself, and to enact legislation on such an assumption, will not strengthen popular confidence in the stability of judicial construction of the Constitution. It is much wiser policy to accept the decision and remedy the defect by amendment in due and regular course." [53]

Senator Root of New York, eminent constitutional authority, spelled out Taft's views:

. . . what is it that we propose to do with the Supreme Court? . . . It is that the Congress of the United States shall deliberately pass, and the President of the United States shall sign, and that the legislative and executive departments thus conjointly shall place upon the statute books as a law a measure which the Supreme Court has declared to be unconstitutional and void. And then, . . . what are we to encounter? A campaign of oratory upon the stump, of editorials in the press, of denunciation and imputation designed to

[51] *Ibid.,* 1351. See also 4394, 4396, 4401.

[52] *Taft and Roosevelt: The Intimate Letters of Archie Butt* (2 vols.; New York, 1930), 134.

[53] Message from the President of the United States. *Senate Documents,* No. 98, 61st Congress, 1st Session, 2.

compel that great tribunal to yield to the force of the opinion of the executive and the legislative branches. If they yield, what then? Where then would be the confidence of our people in the justice of their judgment? If they refuse to yield, what then? A breach between the two parts of our Government, with popular acclaim behind the popular branch, all setting against the independence, the dignity, the respect, the sacredness of that great tribunal whose function in our system of government has made us unlike any republic that ever existed in the world, whose part in our Government is the greatest contribution that America has made to political science.[54]

President Taft and Senator Root placed high value on maintaining the fiction of an unchanging Constitution, even in the face of judicial action that did incalculable violence to it. Neither was under the illusion that the law either is or can be stationary and certain, but both were wary of encouraging the notion that Congress could reverse an objectionable decision by an ordinary act lest the popular image of identity between the judicial version of the Constitution and the Constitution itself [55] be fatally damaged.

[54] *Congressional Record,* Vol. 44 (July 1, 1909), 4003.
[55] New York lawyer Edward B. Whitney, like Taft, insisted that the error be corrected by constitutional amendment. Said Whitney: "If it be true that the confidence of the people in the judiciary was weakened in 1895 by an overruling of earlier decisions upon a point of political controversy in a time of political excitement, and that the logical and probable result of such a course would make the Constitution so plastic at all points in the hands of the contemporary judges that each new party in power would feel charged with the duty of providing a court that would sustain its own proposed legislation, then it would be urged that this loosening of the distinction between the legislature and the judiciary would become much more imminent if the Court, however unwise it may have been at the last occasion, should for a second time reopen a political controversy, even to restore the Constitution as originally defined. The problem is a difficult one, from whichever side it be viewed, one as to which a lawyer would hesitate either to express his own opinion or predict that of the court, and one with which lawyers hope that the court will never be faced." See "The Income Tax

Serious injury to this notion had already been inflicted by the Court itself. In the *American Law Review* of 1895, shortly after the income tax decision came down, Oregon's former governor, Sylvester Pennoyer, suggested:

The Supreme Court has not contented itself with its un-disputed judicial prerogative, of interpreting the laws of Congress, which may be ambiguous for the sole purpose of ascertaining its intent and enforcing it, but it has usurped the legislative prerogative of declaring what the laws shall not be. Our constitutional government has been supplanted by a judicial oligarchy. The time has now arrived when the government should be restored to its constitutional basis. The duty is plain and the road is clear. If Congress, at its next session, would impeach the nullifying judges for the usurpa-tion of legislative power, remove them from office, and in-struct the President to enforce the collection of the income tax, the Supreme Court of the United States would never hereafter presume to trench upon the exclusive power of Congress; and thus the government, as created by our fathers, would be restored with all its faultless outlines and harmoni-ous proportions.[56]

Later on the editor of the *American Law Review* charged that a narrow majority in cases such as *Pollock* v. *Farmers' Loan and Trust Co.* enforced not the Constitu-tion but the justices' own economic predilections:

Nay, we have reached the stage of constitutional develop-ment when acts of the legislature are set aside on economic and casuistic theories, and on the ground of being opposed to implied limitations upon the legislative power in every free government,—that is, upon limitations not found in any constitution, but found in the imaginations of the judges. It is said that, in the original argument in this income tax case,

and the Constitution," 20 *Harvard Law Review* 280 (1906–1907), 289–90.

[56] Sylvester Pennoyer, "The Income Tax Decision and the Power of the Supreme Court to Nullify Acts of Congress," 29 *American Law Review* 550 (1895), 558.

the court allowed itself to be harangued upon the economic features of the law,—questions with which the court had nothing to do. Nay, it appears, at least from one of the opinions which was rendered, that the Justice who rendered it proceeded with an imagination inflamed by the socialistic tendencies of the law, as involving an attack upon private property: considerations which lay totally outside the scope of his office as a judge interpreting the constitution. It is speaking truthfully, and therefore not disrespectfully, to say that some of the judges of that court seem to have no adequate idea of the dividing line between judicial and legislative power, and seem to be incapable of restraining themselves to the mere office of a judge.[57]

Justice Holmes reinforces this analysis: "When Socialism first began to be talked about, the comfortable classes of the community were a good deal frightened. I suspect that this fear has influenced judicial action both here and in England. . . . I think something similar has led people who no longer hope to control the legislatures to look to the courts as expounders of the Constitutions, and in some courts new principles have been discovered outside the bodies of those instruments, which may be generalized into acceptance of the economic doctrines which prevailed about fifty years ago, and a wholesale prohibition of what a tribunal of lawyers does not think about right." [58]

In the face of events immediately preceding the decision outlawing the income tax, the fiction of an inevitable correlation between the Constitution and the judicial version of it became increasingly difficult to maintain. For by 1870 "radical ideas," bequeathed by the Jacksonian revolution, began to be, as Thomas M. Cooley said, "characteristic of State constitutions, and the theory that officers of every department should be made as directly as possible responsible to the people after short terms of serv-

[57] 29 *American Law Review* (May–June, 1895), editor's notes, 427.
[58] O. W. Holmes, *Collected Legal Papers* (New York, 1920), 184.

ice was accepted as a political maxim." [59] An offshoot of
the Jacksonian concept of popular sovereignty was the
idea that the will of the people might be "discovered" at
the ballot box and in the legislative halls.

Falling in with this trend, the Supreme Court ruled
that aggrieved economic interests must look to the polls
rather than to courts for protection against regulatory
legislation. In 1878 the American Bar Association was
organized in opposition to this narrow conception of judicial authority. Soon thereafter a campaign of education
was under way designed to "constitute the Court a perpetual censor" of all legislation. The Bar Association's presidential addresses and the titles of papers read before it
clearly indicate agreement with Darwin's view of the inevitability of the human struggle and with Herbert Spencer's evolutionary theories of politics. One notes such
thoughts as these: "The great curse of the world is too
much government"; "if trusts are a defensive weapon
of property interests against the communist trend, they
are desirable"; "monopoly is often a necessity," and so
on.[60]

If these political dogmas were to be enforced as the law
of the land, however, lawyers and judges had to recapture
what the Jacksonian revolution had repudiated—their exclusive responsibility for interpreting and enforcing the
Constitution. Addressing the Bar Association in 1879,
President Edward J. Phelps deplored the spectacle of unhallowed hands on the Ark of the Covenant. The Constitution had become, he said, "more and more a subject to
be hawked about the country, debated in newspapers, discussed from the stump, elucidated by pothouse politi-

[59] Thomas M. Cooley, "Limits to State Control of Private Business," *Princeton Review,* March, 1878, p. 236.
[60] See Benjamin R. Twiss, *Lawyers and the Constitution: How
Laissez-faire Came to the Supreme Court* (Princeton, 1942), 153, 155.

cians, and dung-hill editors, scholars in the science of government who have never found leisure for the graces of English grammar, or the embellishments of correct spelling." [61]

Attempting in 1893 to recapture jurisprudence as the exclusive province of lawyers, Justice David J. Brewer addressed the New York Bar Association.[62] Various populist movements were then on the march. Brewer cited "the black flag of anarchism, flaunting destruction of property," and the "red flag of socialism, inviting a redistribution of property." "Power," the Justice commented soberly, "always chafes at but needs restraint." Individual liberty was endangered by "the mere weight of numbers," by the "so-called demand of the majority." This was the monster —"great beast," Hamilton called it—the founding fathers had been at such great pains to harness and control. Now the founders' worst fears were all but realized. The awful truth Edmund Burke voiced in 1790—"liberty, when men act in bodies, is *power*" [63]—was evident both in labor organizations and legislative bodies.

"Here there is no monarch threatening to trespass upon the individual," Brewer observed. "The danger is from the multitude—the majority, with whom is the power." Labor organizations were destroying "the freedom of the laborer" and controlling "the use of capital." Legislatures were regulating charges for the use of property, thus destroying its value. Taking into account the move afoot "to minimize the power of Courts" and block "judicial interference," the Justice asked, "What should be done?"

[61] American Bar Association, *Report of the Second Annual Meeting*, Saratoga Springs, N.Y., August, 1879 (Philadelphia, 1879), 190.
[62] "The Nation's Safeguard," *Report of N.Y. State Bar Association*, Vol. 16 (January, 1893), 37. All quoted material from Brewer in this chapter is in this address.
[63] Burke, *Reflections on the French Revolution*, 3.

"My reply," he retorted emphatically, "is strengthen the judiciary."

"The argument is," he went on, "that judges are not adapted by their education and training" to settle complex social and economic issues. Denying this, he said that "the great body of judges" are "well versed in the affairs of life." They must determine "what is right and wrong between employer and employees." They must decide whether "proposed rates of freight and fare are reasonable as between the public and the owners." "While as for speed," Brewer remarked, accurately foreshadowing a favorite judicial device for "settling" labor dispute, "is there anything quicker than a writ of injunction?" No untoward consequences could be expected to follow from the Court's assumption of the policy-determining function, Brewer suggested, since the people are unaware that Courts possess it. Courts are, in any event, relatively immune to popular pressure. "Somehow or other men always link the idea of justice with that of the judge." Other governmental agencies "more readily and more freely yield to the pressure of numbers, that so-called demand of the majority." Not so the judge. He, knowing that "nothing can disturb his position, does not hesitate promptly to 'lay judgment to the line and righteous to the plummet.' "

Unless majorities in the legislatures and at the ballot were thus restrained, Brewer foresaw "the departure from this western continent of government of the people, by the people and for the people." But even as he urged the Court to expand the range of its authority, Brewer insisted: "There is nothing in this power of the Judiciary detracting in the least from the idea of government of and by the people. The Courts hold neither purse nor sword; they cannot corrupt nor arbitrarily control. They make no laws, they establish no policy, they never enter into the domain of popular action. They do not govern. Their functions in relation to the State are limited to seeing that popular action does not trespass upon right and justice as it exists in written constitutions and natural law."

Brewer's double-talk, his plea that the judiciary be strengthened, coupled with the assertion that courts are powerless, coincided with a period when judges began to "deck themselves out in the atavistic robe." Conservative lawyers, Judge Frank suggests, were then hoping to utilize the courts as a bulwark against the rising populist movement. The property right constituted a "preferred freedom," and the Supreme Court was under an obligation, imposed by the Constitution itself, to uphold that preference. Elaborating this theme in 1908, President Arthur Twining Hadley of Yale noted that "private property in the United States, in spite of all the dangers of unintelligent legislation," is "constitutionally in a stronger position" than elsewhere. Said Hadley:

When it is said, as it commonly is, that the fundamental division of powers in the modern State is into legislative, executive and judicial, the student of American institutions may fairly note an exception. The fundamental division of powers in the Constitution of the United States is between voters on the one hand and property owners on the other. The forces of democracy on one side, divided between the executive and the legislature, are set over against the forces of property on the other side, with the judiciary as arbiter between them; the Constitution itself not only forbidding the legislature and executive to trench upon the rights of property, but compelling the judiciary to define and uphold those rights in a manner provided by the Constitution itself.

This theory of American politics has not often been stated. But it has been universally acted upon. . . . It has had the most fundamental and far-reaching effects upon the policy of the country. . . . The voter was omnipotent—within a limited area. He could make what laws he pleased, as long as those laws did not trench upon property right. He could elect what officers he pleased, as long as those officers did not try to do certain duties confided by the Constitution to the property holders. Democracy was complete as far as it went, but constitutionally it was bound to stop short of social democracy.[64]

By 1900 the twentieth-century idea that government must keep order not only physically but socially was being translated into legislation.[65] A significant shift from legal justice to social justice was in process. But judges of Brewer's persuasion often "discovered" unconstitutionality. The ruling, for example, that an hours-of-labor law for workers in a bakery was not "a fair, reasonable, and appropriate exercise of the police power of the state," but "an unreasonable, unnecessary and arbitrary interference with the right of the individual to his personal liberty" was not, the Justices said, a question of "substituting the judgment of the Court for that of the legislature." [66] The outlawing of an hours-of-labor statute represented not an evaluative judgment, but merely "discovery," a declaration of what law *is*.

This disingenuous attempt to screen judicial lawmaking stirred angry protest. Justice Holmes in dissent accused the majority of "discovering" the law in writings of Herbert Spencer rather than in the Constitution. Holmes's indictment stimulated judicial caution,[67] but it was not enduring. Shortly before his appointment to the Supreme

[64] A. T. Hadley, "The Constitutional Position of Property in America," *The Independent*, LXIV (April 7, 1908), 838.

[65] See L. D. Brandeis, "The Living Law," 10 *Illinois Law Review* (1916), 461.

[66] Justice Peckham, in *Lochner* v. *New York*, 198 U.S. 45 (1905), 56–57.

[67] See Charles Warren, "The Progressiveness of the United States Supreme Court," 13 *Columbia Law Review* 294 (1913), and "A Bulwark to the State Police Power—The United States Supreme Court," 13 *Columbia Law Review* 667 (1913).

Court in 1916, the Boston lawyer Louis D. Brandeis deplored the failure of lawyers and judges to "keep pace with the rapid development of the political, economic and social ideals." "Legal science," he charged, "the unwritten or judge-made laws as distinguished from legislation— was largely deaf and blind" to urgently needed social reform. Instead of applying the Constitution "they [the courts] applied complacently eighteenth-century conceptions of the liberty of the individual and of the sacredness of private property. . . . Where statutes giving expression to the new social spirit were clearly constitutional, judges, imbued with the relentless spirit of individualism, often construed them away." [68]

Among those who were disturbed by such outspoken protests against "government by judges" was Dean Harlan Fiske Stone of the Columbia Law School. Dean Stone was sorely troubled by the political aspiration then being promoted under the banner "social justice." He was especially concerned by commentators who linked "social justice" with the view that judges "should consciously endeavor to mould the rules of law to conform to their own personal notion of what is the correct theory of social organization and development." [69]

Dean Stone, approaching the problem from the opposite angle, registered an objection not unlike that voiced by Brandeis and Holmes. Believing with Holmes that the Constitution embodies no particular *economic* theory, Stone denied that the "desirability" of a social policy had any bearing on its constitutionality. In 1915 his attack was directed against those who seemed to think that a *desirable* social aspiration must be equated with constitutionality. As a Supreme Court Justice a decade later he opposed,

[68] Brandeis, "The Living Law," *loc. cit.*, 463–64.
[69] H. F. Stone, *Law and Its Administration* (New York, 1915), 3.

as we shall see, those who confused unconstitutionality with any policy they considered socially *undesirable*.

During the first two decades of this century bold measures were proposed to overcome the effects of judicial obtuseness to social and economic change. Recall of judges and of judicial decision was demanded. Radical amendment of the Constitution, even its abolition, was urged. Leading the attack was President Theodore Roosevelt. Inspired perhaps by the same thought that may have prompted his distant cousin's audacious court-packing proposal of 1937, T. R. commented: "I may not know much law but I do know that one can put the fear of God in judges." [70]

Brandeis, though not unmindful of the urgent need for reform, suggested a less drastic remedy. Closer judicial attention to the social sciences, he believed, might help judges resist the prevalent tendency to enforce uninformed personal preference as if it were the law of the land. "A lawyer," he commented in 1915, "who has not studied economics and sociology is very apt to become a public enemy." [71]

The Boston lawyer himself had introduced a new kind of brief in argument before the Supreme Court. In a case involving the constitutionality of an Oregon eight-hour law for women, he tried to prove by resort to social facts that long hours are in fact detrimental to the health of mothers of the race and hence the welfare of the entire community. The Court upheld the act, but Justice Brewer's endorsement of the use of nonlegal material in the judging process was not unqualified:

It may not be amiss, in the present case, before examining the constitutional question to notice the course of legislation

[70] Quoted in MacLeish and Pritchard (eds.), *Law and Politics*, 15.
[71] Quoting Charles R. Henderson in "The Living Law," *loc. cit.*, 470.

as well as expressions of opinion from other than judicial sources. In the brief filed by Mr. Louis D. Brandeis . . . is a very copious collection of all these matters. . . . The legislation and opinions referred to in the margin may not be technically speaking authorities, and in them is little or no discussion of the constitutional question presented to us for determination, yet they are significant of a widespread belief that woman's physical structure, and the functions she performs in consequence thereof, justify special legislation restricting or qualifying the conditions under which she should be permitted to toil. Constitutional questions, it is true, are not settled by even a consensus of present public opinion. . . . At the same time, when a question of fact is debated and debatable, and the extent to which a special constitutional limitation goes is affected by the truth in respect to that fact, a widespread and long continued belief concerning it is worthy of consideration.[72]

The Court's ambiguous approval of Brandeis' innovation encouraged other counsel to follow his lead. For the time being, however, all such efforts were doomed to failure. Under the orthodox theory of the judicial function factual demonstrations were of limited value, perhaps irrelevant. What possible use could extralegal knowledge be to a body whose business is merely to discover law and measure power in terms of an inflexible Constitution, a document whose meaning and intent are the same as when it came from the hands of its framers. The ineffectiveness of Brandeis' technique was demonstrated in 1916 when an enterprising lawyer, trying to prove the validity of a Washington state statute regulating private employment agencies, submitted to the high court a long list of agency wrongs against workers. Chief Justice White, quite unimpressed, picked up counsel's heavy brief and said: "Why, I could compile a brief twice as thick to prove that the legal profession ought to be abolished!"

In 1923 Mr. Justice Sutherland was quite cool toward

[72] *Muller* v. *Oregon*, 208 U.S. 412 (1908), 419–21.

the mass of reports, opinions of special observers, and so forth, which counsel laid before him to establish the existence of a cause-and-effect relationship between substandard wages and the health and morals of women. Declarations by experts and others favorable to minimum wage were "interesting" and "mildly persuasive," Sutherland conceded, "all proper enough for the consideration of the lawmaking bodies, since their tendency is to establish the desirability or undesirability of the legislation; but they reflect no legitimate light upon the question of its validity." "The elucidation of that question," the Justice commented summarily, "cannot be aided by counting heads." [73] But in this very case a count of five judicial heads had in fact turned the trick.

Sutherland's stand is quite consistent. If judges have no lawmaking function, social facts are indeed inappropriate to the judging process.

The theory that judges are helpless tools of constitutional imperatives ran into further difficulty in connection with judicial appointments. Under this theory shifts of judicial personnel do not and cannot alter the course of decision. The shocked reaction in 1916 to President Wilson's nomination of Louis D. Brandeis to be an Associate Justice of the Supreme Court subjected this idea to serious strain. A struggle within the Senate Judiciary Committee dragged on for months. Outstanding lawyers were vociferous in opposition. But why should there have been such an uproar? If Supreme Court Justices in deciding cases exert no discretion, no more will or power than a dry goods salesman measuring calico or a grocer weighing coffee, why should the appointee's social and economic views be relevant in considering his fitness as a judge? What difference does it make who holds the scales or applies the yardstick?

[73] *Adkins* v. *Children's Hospital,* 261 U.S. 525 (1923), 559–60.

Brandeis' critics did not allow themselves to be trapped. The opposition did not object openly to the Bostonian's "radical" views. Rather, they found him wanting on the vague scores of judicial temperament and professional ethics. The nub of the case against him was nevertheless self-evident. The opposition had come to look upon the Supreme Court as a stronghold protecting its vested interests. Brandeis' concept of legislative power was more spacious. As a lawyer he had expressed the conviction that "government must keep order not only physically but socially. . . . The law must protect a man from the things that rob him of his freedom, whether the oppressing force be physical or of a subtler kind." [74] Brandeis' confirmation would make every citizen feel insecure. This was the core of the case against him. In 1916, however, both sides chose to ignore the power aspect of the judging process. Both were under the spell of a magic chant: judges are mere instruments of the law and can will nothing.

In 1930 the shoe was on the other foot. Then a small contingent of insurgent senators were outspoken against confirmation of Wall Street lawyer Charles Evans Hughes to be Chief Justice of the United States. By this time, as we shall see, Chief Justice Taft's Court had made it clear that the Justices do, in fact, wield "the power of life and death over the political decisions of legislators and executives." [75] Brandeis' opponents had been careful not to explode the myth of judicial helplessness. Not so the opponents of Hughes. The insurgent lawmakers openly criticized the former Justice's "clouded" viewpoint. As a Wall Street lawyer, Hughes was accused of appearing "almost invariably" before the high Court in behalf of corporations of "untold wealth."

[74] Boston *Journal,* February 3, 1916.
[75] Frankfurter, "The Supreme Court and the Public," *Forum,* June, 1930, p. 334.

Why, the senators wanted to know, should discussion of the nominee's fitness be confined to the legal aspect? "Can it be true," Senator Tom Connally of Texas asked, "that in passing upon the competency of a man to sit upon this or any other court the mind of the Senate is to be closed to all questions except that of the character of the appointee and whether or not he is versed in the law." [76]

"The great questions that now confront us," the senator went on, "are economic questions, questions as to whether the powers of the Federal Government and of the State governments are adequate to control and regulate the great aggregated masses of wealth which are rapidly seizing upon and controlling many of the necessities of life of the people of the Nation." With remarkable perspicacity the senator predicted that this would be "the form of contest that is going to face us." [77]

The insurgents directed their fire against the Court itself, not at the man who had been nominated for the center chair. Under Chief Justice Taft the judiciary had become practically a third legislative chamber. Senator Norris put the matter bluntly: "We have a legislative body, called the House of Representatives, of over 400 men. We have another legislative body, called the Senate, of less than a hundred men. We have, in reality, another legislative body, called the Supreme Court, of 9 men; and they are more powerful than all the others put together." [78]

The senators' approach, though unorthodox, had been constructive rather than reckless in purpose.[79] By calling attention to the Court's discretionary power, the law-

[76] *Congressional Record,* Vol. 72 (1930), 3514.
[77] *Ibid.,* 3515.
[78] *Ibid.,* 3566.
[79] *Ibid.,* 3573.

makers hoped to destroy "the hush-hush and ah-ah atmosphere" shielding that political and very human institution. "There has not been a criticism of the Supreme
Court anywhere, even on the floor of the Senate, for several years," Norris went on, ". . . because we have set it
up on a pedestal beyond human criticism. . . . We have
made idols of them [the Justices]; . . . they have black
gowns over their persons. Then they become something
more than human beings. . . . [W]e have tried to make
plain that the power of the Supreme Court . . . has been
steadily growing; that, like human beings, they have been
reaching out for more and more power until it has become common knowledge that they legislate and fix policies." [80] Lest the Court under the new Chief Justice, as
under Taft, continue judicial aggrandizement, the senators used this opportunity to underscore the wisdom of
judicial self-restraint.

The debates on the nomination of Brandeis and of
Hughes indicate awareness that what "the law" is turns
primarily on the Court's personnel. More senators vetoed
Hughes's confirmation than had voted against Brandeis.
The public had begun to suspect that the contingencies
of judicial retirement and/or appointment are matters
of primary political importance.

It seems paradoxical that those Justices who freely confess their lawmaking power should be the ones most chary
in their use of it. "I recognize without hesitation," Justice
Holmes declared, "that judges do and must legislate." [81]
Brandeis frankly admitted that judges are called upon
to exercise a quasi-legislative function, to weigh "relative social values," to balance "public needs as against
private desires." [82] Stone and Cardozo made no secret

[80] *Ibid.*, 3645.
[81] *Southern Pacific Co.* v. *Jensen,* 244 U.S. 215, p. 221.
[82] *Truax* v. *Corrigan,* 257 U.S. 312 (1921), 357.

of the lawmaking power in their possession. Other Justices have disclaimed power even as they advocated its extension. On the eve of a long period (1890 to 1937) during which the Court broadened the scope of its authority over both state and national legislative policy, overturning precedents by narrow margins and against vigorous protest, Justice Brewer steadfastly maintained, as we have seen, that courts do not govern.

Holmes may have had judges such as Brewer in mind when he spoke of "naif, simple minded men," needing "education in the obvious." [83] They do not realize, as Holmes put it, that "behind the logical form lies a judgment," often inarticulate and unconscious, as to the "relative worth and importance of competing legislative grounds of social policy." [84] As an example, Holmes cited the extraordinary way in which judges, at the turn of the century, alarmed by that "vague terror" socialism, translated this fear into "doctrines that had no proper place in the Constitution or the common law." [85]

Holmes's recipe for judicial simple-mindedness was "education in the obvious," ability to "transcend our own convictions and to leave room for much that we hold dear to be done away with short of revolution by the orderly change of law." [86] Such tolerance would "lead judges habitually to consider more definitely and explicitly the social advantage on which the rule they lay down must be justified." The effect might be, Holmes suggested, to reveal to the Justices themselves that they were really "taking sides upon debatable and often burning questions." [87]

[83] Holmes, *Collected Legal Papers,* 295.
[84] *Ibid.,* 181.
[85] *Ibid.,* 295.
[86] *Ibid.*
[87] Holmes, *Collected Legal Papers,* 184.

In the transformed context of the 1950's and 1960's certain members of the Supreme Court recognize, as did Justice Holmes two generations ago, that the profession of judicial helplessness is a self-delusion, resulting perhaps in a grievous failure to discharge a judicial responsibility. Among the more significant aspects of the Warren Court decisions, especially in the civil rights orbit, is the unblushing way in which certain Justices take sides on burning issues. The activistic views long propounded by Justice Black *et al.* are now gaining the ascendancy. A note of fearlessness reminiscent of Holmes [88] rings in Justice Black's dissenting opinion in the case of the California communists.

Doubtlessly, dictators have to stamp out causes and beliefs which they deem subversive to their evil regimes. But governmental suppression of causes and beliefs seems to me the very antithesis of what our Constitution stands for. The choice expressed in the First Amendment in favor of free expression was made against a turbulent background by men such as Jefferson, Madison, and Mason—men who believed that loyalty to the provisions of this Amendment was the best way to assure a long life for this new nation and its Government. Unless there is complete freedom for expression of all ideas, whether we like them or not, concerning the way government should be run and who shall run it, I doubt if any views in the long run can be secured against the censor. The First Amendment provides the only kind of security system that can preserve a free government—one that leaves the way wide open for people to favor, discuss, advocate, or incite causes and doctrines, however obnoxious and antagonistic such views may be to the rest of us.[89]

[88] Dissenting in *Gitlow* v. *New York,* 268 U.S. 652 (1925), Holmes said: "If in the long run the beliefs expressed in proletarian dictatorship are destined to be accepted by the dominant forces of the community, the only meaning of free speech is that they should be given their chance and have their way" (p. 673).

[89] Dissenting in *Yates* v. *United States,* 354 U.S. 1356 (1957), 1389.

The judge inevitably takes sides and his predilection may well be the decisive factor. Nevertheless, the miraculous mechanical theory of the judicial process still has its defenders. The late Thomas Reed Powell went so far as to suggest that judicial impotence may be a cloak for the exercise of wide powers with relative freedom from restraint. Denials of power, Powell noted in 1956, are most categorical when its exercise is most patent. "It sometimes seems that these judicial professions of automatism are most insistent when it is most obvious that they are being honored in the breach rather than in the observance. They seem to appear less often when statutes are sustained than when they are condemned, less often when the Court is unanimous than when there is strong dissent." [90]

Plenty of recent examples can be cited in support of Powell's observation. The debate between a majority wielding great power while proclaiming its impotence and a vigorously dissenting minority accusing the Court of ruling by "judicial fiat," of "torturing" the Constitution under the guise of interpreting it, occurs in case after case. "Every Justice," Robert H. Jackson said in his lectures on the Supreme Court prepared shortly before his death, "has been accused of legislating and every one has joined in that accusation of others." [91] In the Dred Scott decision, perhaps the most conspicuous example of law-making prior to the outlawing of segregation in 1954, Chief Justice Taney insisted that the Constitution "speaks not only in the same words . . . but with the same meaning and intent with which it spoke when it came into the hands of its framers." [92] But if judicial interpretation is so narrowly circumscribed, why are contradictory results

[90] Powell, *Vagaries and Varieties in Constitutional Interpretation,* 43.

[91] Robert H. Jackson, *The Supreme Court in the American System of Government* (Cambridge, Mass., 1955), 80.

[92] *Scott* v. *Sandford,* 19 Howard 393 (1857), 426.

so often reached? One does not need to possess the perceptiveness of a Thomas Reed Powell to notice this; nor are examples of self-inflicted wounds confined to the nineteenth century. Instances of judicial mayhem, far from diminishing, have grown apace. Some of the most conspicuous additions to the list of self-inflicted damage occurred during the Chief Justiceship of Charles Evans Hughes. Yet judicial disclaimers of power then became more emphatic than ever. By that time, the heights whereon Chief Justice Taft had fortified judicial eminence had become the subject of outspoken criticism within the Court itself.

CHAPTER 2

TAFT:

The Court as Super-Legislature

WILLIAM HOWARD TAFT's term as Chief Justice spans the "fabulous" 1920's, an era of expansion, expense, and high finance. The gospel of goods —make the goods, sell the goods, get the goods—then dominated the American people. Industrial leaders inflamed by victory in war, encouraged by the political glory of Harding's triumphant election in 1920, were certain that under such a national administration progress must be unending. "God is still in His Heaven," John E. Edgerton, president of the National Association of Manufacturers, cheerfully assured his colleagues after Harding's death in 1923, "and there is in the White House a man [Calvin Coolidge] whose essential qualities of mind and soul, and whose unswerving attachment to the fundamentals of free government are going to be demanded by an awakening people in the next President of the United States." [1] Mr. Edgerton was an accurate forecaster. The Republican succession headed by Harding, Coolidge, and Hoover held the Presidency from March 4, 1921, to March 4, 1933, while businessmen strove mightily to remold the country nearer to their heart's desire. The Supreme Court could be counted on to save the busi-

[1] John E. Edgerton, Annual Address, *Proceedings of the 29th Annual Convention of the National Association of Manufacturers* (1924), 118.

nessmen from the folly of legislators, egged on by demagogues expounding human rights at the expense of property rights. The prospect for substantially unregulated enterprise had never been so bright.

Chief Justice Taft had often gloried in having appointed six Supreme Court judges during his four White House years, while President Wilson, in twice the time, appointed only three. This meant that the winning candidate in November, 1920, would reconstitute the Supreme Court. Alert to this certainty Taft addressed himself to the central issue, as he saw it, of the 1920 campaign.

Mr. Wilson is in favor of a latitudinarian construction of the Constitution of the United States to weaken the protection it should afford against socialistic raids upon property rights. . . . He has made three appointments to the Supreme Court. He is understood to be greatly disappointed in the attitude of the first of these [Mr. Justice McReynolds] upon such questions. The other two [Mr. Justice Brandeis and Mr. Justice Clarke] represent a new school of constitutional construction, which if allowed to prevail, will greatly impair our fundamental law. Four of the incumbent Justices are beyond the retiring age of seventy, and the next President will probably be called upon to appoint their successors. There is no greater domestic issue in this election than the maintenance of the Supreme Court as the bulwark to enforce the guaranty that no man shall be deprived of his property without due process of law. . . .[2]

In 1912, when campaigning for re-election, Taft deplored Theodore Roosevelt's brashness in dragging the Court into politics, but in 1920 he himself "made respectable what was heretofore tabooed. The door of the Holy of Holies had been opened." [3]

Harding entered the White House on a landslide vote,

[2] W. H. Taft, "Mr. Wilson and the Campaign," *Yale Review*, October, 1920, pp. 19–20.
[3] MacLeish and Pritchard (eds.), *Law and Politics*, 40.

a record seven-million majority, and within a year Taft himself was able to interpose the Constitution as a "bulwark" to protect property. A lifelong ambition had been fulfilled by his appointment as Chief Justice of the United States.

The biography of William Howard Taft is amazing both for length of public service (1880 to 1930) and for the variety of his activities: public prosecutor, solicitor-general, district and federal circuit judge, Cabinet member and administrator, President of the United States, law school dean, professor of law, and Chief Justice of the United States.

Taft's heart was long set on the Supreme Court. As early as 1889, at the age of thirty-two, he began to pull every available wire leading to President Benjamin Harrison and the seat then vacant on the supreme bench. Ohio governor Joseph Foraker pushed him for the place, but the appointment of an Associate Justice merely to please Ohio Republicans was not viewed with favor at the White House. Instead the President offered Taft the post of United States Solicitor-General. Taft's acceptance proved important for his entire political-judicial career. The office required thorough grounding in constitutional law and procedure; it brought him into close contact with the important Republicans, especially Theodore Roosevelt—a varied friendship of over twenty years.

But judging was Taft's primary interest. His judicial career had begun in 1887 when Governor Foraker appointed him, at the age of twenty-nine, to fill a vacancy on the Superior Court of Ohio. The next year he had been elected for a full term. In 1892 he resigned as solicitor-general to accept President Harrison's appointment as United States circuit court judge for the Sixth Judicial Circuit. After eight years on the federal bench, he was made head of a new commission for the Philippine Islands by President McKinley. The job was to be temporary. It was not, however, until February, 1904, that he could be persuaded to relinquish it. Not even President Roosevelt's repeated offers of a place on the Supreme Court could lure him away. Twice, while in the Philippines, he refused to accept his heart's desire.

The governorship of the Philippines seems to have been more satisfying to Taft than any other of the posts he held. "Taft was, to a marked degree," his biographer Henry F. Pringle writes, "a dictator in the archipelago of the far Pacific. No Senate Progressives plagued him there. No Gifford Pinchot quarreled about the forests. No Democrats abused and attacked him. No Theodore Roosevelt turned against him. The politicos of the Philippines disagreed with him in policies, of course, but in the last analysis Taft could impose his will. His voice was the law. He was, again, a judge." [4]

In 1903 President Roosevelt virtually ordered him to report to Washington and become Secretary of War. Taft was reluctant to go because "Politics when I am in it makes me sick." And, as he was soon to discover, Cabinet officers were "largely devoted to politics." [5] It seemed strange to him that despite every intention to keep out of politics, and despite his professed dislike of it, "I should thus be pitched into the middle of it." [6] "The fates," his biographer concluded, "were always pushing Taft higher and higher. Perhaps he was the only man in American political history who can, with complete accuracy, be described as a creature of destiny." [7]

But could this be strictly true of a man fifty years on the public payroll, who owned to keeping his "plate right-

[4] Henry F. Pringle, *The Life and Times of William Howard Taft* (2 vols.; New York, 1939), I, 165.

[5] *Ibid.*, 258.

[6] *Ibid.*, 236.

[7] *Ibid.*, 107.

side up" when appointive jobs were being passed round? It may be that Mrs. Taft, rather than "the fates," was "the spur to Will Taft throughout his life." [8] She long had her eye on the White House. When Theodore Roosevelt would have retired Taft to the Supreme Court— usually a safe haven from troublesome politics—Mrs. Taft more than once dissuaded him. She distrusted Roosevelt's sincerity when the President finally came out for Taft as the Republican nominee of 1908, and when the historic breach occurred four years later may have had doubtful pleasure in reminding her husband: "I told you so." [9]

Taft's lack of success as President and his rancorous quarrels with Roosevelt as to candidacy in 1910 and 1912 did not impede his public career. The Supreme Court still beckoned, but he had to wait until a conservative Republican President was solidly in the White House.

Taft's hopes soared May 19, 1921, when the news reached him that Chief Justice Edward Douglass White was dead. In post-election talks with Harding, Taft had mentioned the fact that "many times in the past the Chief Justice [White] had said he was holding the office for me and that he would give it back to a Republican administration." The President-elect had been almost reckless in his sympathetic understanding of the ex-President's ambition.

"I was nonplussed," Taft commented on December 26, 1920, "at the way in which he took me into his confidence and was nearly struck dumb when he asked me if I would go on the Supreme Court." [10]

But when the vacancy occurred, complications at once arose because Harding had made much the same sort of

[8] *Ibid.*, 70.
[9] *Ibid.*, 313, 318.
[10] Pringle, *The Life and Times of William Howard Taft*, II, 955.

offer to ex-Senator George Sutherland, his one-man brain
trust during the front-porch campaign for the White
House. The President suggested delay until both names
could be sent to the Senate at the same time, a suggestion
highly stimulating to Taft's impatience. He was nearly
sixty-four; as President he had made it a rule (honored in
the breach by his appointment of United States Circuit
Court Judge Horace H. Lurton) not to appoint any man
over sixty to the Supreme Court. At this point Gus
Karger, his publicity aide during the 1908 Presidential
campaign, became Taft's personal lobbyist. As ammunition for Karger's use, Taft listed his qualifications as a
fledgling lawyer might recommend himself for a junior
clerkship, and Attorney-General Harry M. Daugherty's
importunings hastened the appointment made on June
30, 1921.

Taft, while a professor of law at Yale, used to tell of a
Kentucky Republican, one Aleck Carter, who, in a rare
year when Republicans controlled the state house, came
down from the hills to apply for a job. It would be, Aleck
felt, his reward for faithful party service. He was told,
however, that the new administration believed in reform
and that under the new policy, the "office must seek the
man." Aleck waited patiently for an office to seek him,
but after a few weeks his money ran out and he started
home. As he was leaving, a friend called out: "Aleck,
where are you going?"

"I am going home," Carter replied. "I've heard tell,
since I've been here, a good mite about an office seeking a
man, but I hain't met any office of that kind. My money's
gin out, and I'm bound for the mountains."

Then a hopeful thought seemed to strike him, and he
continued, "But if any of you-uns see an office hunting a
man, tell 'em that you just seen Aleck Carter on his old

mare 'Jinny' going down the Versailles Pike and he was going damn slow." [11]

Did Taft seek the Chief Justiceship, or did he let the office seek him? Obviously he was going "damn slow."

History does not rule as to the best type of training for Supreme Court Justices.[12] Some have had backgrounds in practical politics, others in academic careers; still others came to the Court after service on lower courts. The record indicates that all these types of experience have value.[13] Taft, having done all three, had unique qualifications for the Chief Justiceship. He had, moreover, long

[11] W. H. Taft, *Popular Government: Its Essence, Its Permanence, Its Perils* (New Haven, 1913), 113–14.

[12] For a full discussion, see Cortez A. M. Ewing, *The Judges of the Supreme Court, 1789–1937: A Study of Their Qualifications* (Minneapolis, 1938).

[13] President Eisenhower, more than any other Chief Executive, with the possible exception of Taft, was convinced that prior judicial experience is an important qualification for service on the nation's highest bench. Justice Felix Frankfurter, an appointee of Franklin D. Roosevelt, takes strong exception to this view. "One is entitled to say without qualification," Frankfurter observes, "that the correlation between prior judicial experience and fitness for the function of the Supreme Court is zero."

Even Holmes and Cardozo—the examples most often cited in support of the Taft-Eisenhower policy—are invoked by Frankfurter to repudiate it. Prior judicial service for these stalwarts did not help. So different was the task of a Supreme Court Justice from that to which they had grown accustomed, the previous experience, Frankfurter suggests, may have hindered. "After having spent twenty years on the Supreme Judicial Court of Massachusetts, part of it as Chief Justice," Frankfurter writes, "Mr. Justice Holmes found himself not at all at home on coming to the Supreme Court." "After eighteen years on the New York Court of Appeals, five of them as Chief Judge," Cardozo did not "find that his transplantation from Albany to Washington was a natural step in judicial progression." Frankfurter, "The Supreme Court in the Mirror of Justice," *University of Pennsylvania Law Review* (April, 1957), 786.

Frankfurter may overstate his case, but one can sympathize with his concern lest rigid adherence to the Taft-Eisenhower pattern exclude creative judges such as Harlan Fiske Stone and Louis D. Brandeis—and Justice Frankfurter.

been a student of the Supreme Court, and held definite views on its place in American politics.

For Taft, as for Alexander Hamilton, judicial review was the hallmark of the American system of free government. "The greatest advantage of our plan of government over every other," Taft wrote, "is the character of the judicial power vested in the Supreme Court." European statesmen and historians, he noted, rightly looked upon it "as the chief instrument in the maintenance of that self-restraint which the people of the United States have placed upon themselves and which has made this Government the admiration of intelligent critics the world over." [14]

Symbolism pervades the judiciary and contributes to its practical effectiveness. "It is well that judges should be clothed in robes," Taft comments, "not only, that those who witness the administration of justice should be properly advised that the function performed is one different from, and higher, than that which a man discharges as a citizen in the ordinary walks of life; but also, in order to impress the judge himself with the constant consciousness that he is a high-priest in the temple of justice and is surrounded with obligations of a sacred character that he cannot escape and that require his utmost care, attention and self-suppression." [15]

Yet Taft was not under the illusion that the man who dons judicial robes thereby puts on superhuman ability. "Judges are men," he observed. "Courts are composed of judges and one would be foolish who would deny that courts and judges are affected by the times in which they live." [16]

[14] W. H. Taft, *Popular Government*, 184–85.
[15] W. H. Taft, *Present Day Problems: A Collection of Addresses Delivered on Various Occasions* (New York, 1908), 63–64.
[16] W. H. Taft, *The Anti-Trust Act and the Supreme Court* (New York, 1914), 33.

Far from blinking at its lawmaking role, Taft considered the shaping of law to meet new situations the Court's "highest and most useful function." The notion that "judges should interpret the exact intention of those who established the Constitution" was the "theory of one who does not understand the proper administration of justice." "Frequently," he wrote, "new conditions arise which those who were responsible for the written law could not have had in view, and to which existing common law principles have never before been applied, and it becomes necessary for the Court to make new applications of both." This "is not the exercise of legislative power. . . ." Rather, "it is the exercise of a sound judicial discretion in supplementing the provisions of constitutions and laws and custom, which are necessarily incomplete or lacking in detail essential to their proper application, especially to new facts and situations constantly arising. . . . Indeed it is one of the highest and most useful functions that courts have to perform in making a government of law practical and uniformly just." [17]

Judges should, Taft agreed, be independent of the populace, but they do not and ought not to live in a political vacuum. It is impossible to prevent "the influence of popular opinion from coloring judgments in the long run." The personal equation unavoidably plays a part. "There will be found a response to sober popular opinion as it changes to meet the exigency of social, political and economic changes," [18] he said.

Legal training alone could not prepare a judge for this creative task. Needed also was practical experience, especially in government. In Taft's opinion Justice Holmes was "a very poor constitutional lawyer . . ." for want of "experience of affairs in government that would keep him

17 W. H. Taft, *Popular Government*, 222–23.
18 *Ibid.*, 174.

straight on constitutional questions." [19] After working two years with Justice Harlan Fiske Stone, formerly dean of the Columbia Law School, Taft was not "always sure how experience as the head of a law school and supervising a law journal helps in making a first class judge." [20]

Taft's view that judges exercise political discretion is not inconsistent with his desire to keep the court beyond popular control and above criticism. The very role the court performs—its most important political function—is to soften the impact of popular passions, to restrain the impulsive desires of the majority. Individual liberty is the basis of our constitutional system—and liberty, to Taft, meant largely economic liberty. "Our Constitution rests on personal liberty and the right of property. In the last analysis, personal liberty includes the right of property, as it includes the right of contract and the right of labor. Our primary conception of a free man is one who can enjoy what he earns, who can spend it for his comfort or pleasure if he would. . . . This is the right of property . . . personal liberty and the right of property are indispensable to any possible useful progress of society." [21]

Even in the face of rising public clamor for government intervention in social and economic affairs, Taft looked to the future with confidence. Despite the expansion of the electorate from one twenty-fifth to one fourth of the people, the federal Constitution was "still substantially intact and works smoothly and effectively to accomplish the purpose of its framers and to defend us all against the danger of sudden gusts of popular passion and to secure for us the delay and deliberation in political changes es-

[19] Pringle, *The Life and Times of William Howard Taft*, II, 969.

[20] W. H. Taft to Robert A. Taft, April 10, 1927 (Taft Papers, Manuscripts Division of the Library of Congress).

[21] W. H. Taft, *Liberty Under Law: An Interpretation of the Principles of Our Constitutional Government* (New Haven, 1922), 25–26.

sential to secure considered action by the people. . . .."
"Ours is the oldest popular government in the world,"
he went on, "and is today the strongest and most conservative. . . . The people do rule and always have ruled
in the United States. They have their will, but they
have it after a wholesome delay and deliberation which
they have wisely forced themselves to take under the restrictions of a Constitution. . . . It is this voluntary restraint that has made their Government permanent and
strong. It is fundamental error to seek quick action in
making needed changes of policy or in redressing wrong.
. . . It is better to endure wrongs than to effect disastrous
changes in which the proposed remedy may be worse
than the evil. . . . Any reasonable suspension of popular
action until calm public consideration of reliable evidence
can be secured is in the interest of a wise decision." [22]

The ultimate guardians of America's basic rights are
courts. They have a positive task, a political function to
perform. They serve as a brake on popular demand and
public desire for quick change. "The judicial branch of
the Federal Government is vested with the final duty and
power of making effective this protection of the individual
in his right against the sovereign people." [23]

Stability in society and in judicial decisions was Taft's
primary goal. Unlike certain other conservative justices,
he did not try to gloss the Court's important policy-making function by pious invocation of the mechanical, slot
machine theory. He neither ignored the pleas of social
reformers nor pretended that the facts they introduced
were irrelevant. If "the militant social reformers and
lawyers . . . don't talk exactly the same language," he
observed, lawyers and judges must respond by "broaden-

[22] *Ibid.,* 20–21.
[23] *Ibid.,* 15.

ing the knowledge and studies of the members of the legal profession."

"We must be able to understand the attitude of the sociological reformer," he wrote. The education of the judge "ought to include a study of economics and a study of sociology," so that he can meet the reformer on "common ground." [24]

Louis D. Brandeis, as we have seen, urged training in economics and sociology for lawyers, but the reasons that lay back of Taft's recommendations differed from those of the Bostonian. Brandeis believed that awareness of the factual basis of social action would stimulate judicial self-restraint. Taft, on the other hand, advocated knowledge of sociology and economics so that the lawyer and judge could more effectively carry on their sacred mission of preserving those institutions without which America— or at least Taft's America—could not long survive. Judges who understood the social needs of the day could temper the demands of reformers by giving "proper weight" to the "valuable lessons of the past." It would then be possible to "avoid . . . radical and impractical changes in law and government by which we might easily lose what we have gained in the struggle of mankind for better things." [25] Brandeis' innovations were troublesome, because they "brought new strength to an old conflict— the conflict between the liberals and the hidebound." [26] Taft, therefore, urged lawyers and judges of his own persuasion to redress the balance.

As Taft had foreseen, reconstitution of the supreme bench quickly followed on the heels of Harding's election. By 1923 four of the nine Justices—George Sutherland,

[24] W. H. Taft, *Popular Government*, 235–38 *passim*.
[25] *Ibid.*, 238.
[26] Frankfurter, quoted in MacLeish and Pritchard (eds.), *Law and Politics*, 39.

Pierce Butler, Edward Sanford, and Taft himself as Chief Justice—had been appointed by the Republican President. With Willis Van Devanter, James McReynolds, and the infirm Joseph McKenna (succeeded in 1925 by Harlan Stone) these four judges—all staunchly conservative— heightened the rigidities of constitutional interpretation. The genial Chief Justice, described by his biographer as "conservative, if not reactionary," [27] had now realized his long-cherished ambition to preside over a court that could be counted on to quell any "socialistic raids on property rights." Soon after his appointment the Chief Justice (consistent with his view that the judge plays an active role in shaping the law) announced at a conference of the Justices that he "had been appointed to reverse a few decisions" and, with his famous chuckle, added, "I looked right at old man Holmes when I said it." [28]

Yet the Chief Justice found himself aligned with Holmes and against the conservative majority in one of the first major cases to come before his Court. In 1923 he wrote a dissenting opinion (one of only twenty written by him) objecting to Justice Sutherland's reactionary decision outlawing a minimum wage for women.[29] Sutherland, for the majority, started from the premise that freedom to contract about one's labor is "the general rule and restraint the exception." Legislative authority to abridge it can be justified only by "exceptional circumstances." "It cannot be shown," Sutherland observed, "that well paid women safeguard their morals more carefully than those who are poorly paid. Morality rests upon other considerations than wages; and there is, certainly, no such prevalent connection between the two as to justify a broad

[27] Pringle, *The Life and Times of William Howard Taft*, II, 967.
[28] Quoted by Judge George M. Bourguin, in *Investor's Syndicate v. Porter*, 52 F. 2d 189 (1931), 196.
[29] *Adkins* v. *Children's Hospital*, 261 U.S. 525 (1923), 556.

attempt to adjust the latter with reference to the former." [30]

The Chief Justice was less certain. During World War I he had served fourteen months as chairman of the National War Labor Board. After having personally conducted hearings in the munitions and textile mills, he remarked to Secretary of Labor W. Jett Lauck: "Why I had no idea. How can people live on such wages?" [31] This experience may have led to the belief that the Court had gone too far in limiting the power of the legislature to set a minimum wage for women.

"I agree," he wrote in dissent, "that it is a disputable question in the field of political economy how far a statutory requirement of maximum hours or minimum wages may be a useful remedy for these evils [the sweating system], and whether it may not make the case of the oppressed employee worse than it was before. But it is not the function of this Court to hold congressional acts invalid simply because they are passed to carry out economic views which the Court believes to be unwise or unsound." [32]

A long series of cases led Taft to believe that the regulation of wages provided in the District of Columbia law had "become a well-formulated rule." *Lochner* v. *New York,* invoked by Sutherland as controlling, had been "overruled *sub silentio*" [33] in *Bunting* v. *Oregon.*[34] In upholding the minimum wage, Taft adhered to his conviction that sanctity of the judicial process is best preserved by maintenance of a line of judicial precedents against challenge by both court and legislature.

[30] *Ibid.*
[31] Pringle, *The Life and Times of William Howard Taft,* II, 916.
[32] 261 U.S. 525, p. 562.
[33] *Ibid.,* 564.
[34] 243 U.S. 426 (1917).

Taft's objection to Sutherland's majority opinion was based not only upon the belief that the Court should uphold social regulations the legislature might have considered not unreasonable—a view he would later ignore —but also because it violated the Chief Justice's basic rule of stability, the sanctity of precedents. The limits of the guarantee of liberty in the Fifth and Fourteenth amendments, Taft admitted, "is not easy to mark." But the Court, he declared, had been "engaged in pricking out a line in successive cases." "We must be careful," he told his fellow Justices, "to follow that line as well as we can and not to depart from it by suggesting a distinction that is formal rather than real." [35]

The mote of economic predilection which Taft detected in the eyes of his brethren in the minimum wage case seems to have blurred his own vision in his opinion setting aside the restriction Arizona placed on the use of injunctions in labor disputes. His early judicial record as a lower federal court judge had featured Justice Brewer's "quick" remedy for the solution of the labor problem. In 1908 Taft himself had declared that the writ of injunction "is one of the most beneficial remedies known to the law. . . ." [36] But on November 20, 1919, perhaps because of knowledge gained while on the War Labor Board, he stated that "Government of the relations of capital and labor by injunction is a solecism." He then denounced the injunction as an "absurdity," and expressed the opinion that "frequent application of them would shake to pieces the whole machine." [37] As Chief Justice, however, he destroyed the statutory limitations Arizona put on this very "solecism."

Under a "latitudinarian construction" of the Constitu-

[35] 261 U.S. 525, p. 562.
[36] W. H. Taft, *Present Day Problems,* 266.
[37] *Public Ledger,* November 20, 1919.

tion, which Taft deplored, the statute restricting the use of injunctions in labor disputes (unless necessary to protect property from violence) might have been sustained. This was not possible, however, since the effect in Taft's eyes would be "to weaken" the constitutional safeguards of property. There is a minimum of protection, the Chief Justice reasoned, to which property is entitled and of which it may not be deprived without exceeding the constitutional bounds of the Fourteenth Amendment. The due process clause guaranteed this minimum, and the equal protection guarantee spelled it out. He could see no good social or economic reason why employers should be singled out and denied the extraordinary protection which equity affords property rights. "The framers and adopters of this Amendment were not content to depend on a mere minimum secured by the due process clause, or upon the spirit of equality which might not be insisted on by local public opinion. They, therefore, embodied that spirit in a specific guaranty. . . . It [the Amendment] sought an equality of treatment of all persons, even though all enjoyed the protection of due process." [38]

Justices Holmes, Brandeis, John H. Clarke, and Mahlon Pitney dissented. Brandeis and Holmes, echoing Taft's own charge against the majority in the minimum wage decision, suggested that the Court enforced not the Constitution, but its economic predilections.

"The real motive in seeking the [labor] injunction," Brandeis remarked, "was not ordinarily to prevent property from being injured nor to protect the owner in its use, but to endow property with active, militant power which would make it dominant over men." The law of property was not, he suggested, "appropriate for dealing with the forces beneath social unrest; . . . in this vast struggle it was unwise to throw the power of the State on

[38] *Truax* v. *Corrigan*, 257 U.S. 312 (1921), 332–33.

one side or the other according to the principles deduced
from that law." [39] In contrast to Taft's view that the Constitution was designed to stop experimentation, Brandeis
asserted that the "rights of property and the liberty of the
individual must be remolded from time to time, to meet
the changing needs of society." Since government is not
an "exact science," courts should not declare a particular
law unreasonable "merely because we are convinced that
it is fraught with danger to the public weal, and thus . . .
close the door to experiment within the law."

Holmes was repelled by the "delusive exactness" implicit in the Chief Justice's ruling. "By calling a business
property," the dissenter commented, "you make it seem
like land, and lead up to the conclusion that a statute
cannot substantially cut down the advantages of ownership
existing before the statute was passed. . . . Legislation
may begin where an evil begins. If, as many intelligent
people believe, there is more danger that the injunction
will be abused in labor cases than elsewhere, I can feel no
doubt of the power of the legislature to deny it in such
cases." [40]

Justice Pitney, himself a conservative of the Taft stripe,
commented: "I cannot believe that the use of the injunction in such cases—however important—is so essential to
the right of acquiring, possessing and enjoying property
that its restriction or elimination amounts to a deprivation of liberty or property without due process of law,
within the meaning of the Fourteenth Amendment." [41]

In no other case decided during Taft's Chief Justiceship was the broad review he sometimes espoused more
sharply contrasted with the dissenters' dedication to judicial self-restraint, and their deference to legislative ex-

[39] *Ibid.*, 368.
[40] *Ibid.*, 342–43.
[41] *Ibid.*, 349.

perimentation. "The Constitution was intended, its very purpose was, to prevent experimentation with the fundamental rights of the individual," [42] Taft insisted. Rather than discuss the real question whether or not the employers' right to injunctive relief in a labor dispute is "fundamental," the Chief Justice chose merely to assert the affirmative answer. For him the limit Arizona placed on the use of injunctions in labor disputes constituted a denial of "a fundamental principle of liberty and justice which inheres in the very idea of free government and is the inalienable right of a citizen of such government." Yet this "unmistakable principle of liberty and justice"— the labor injunction—had emerged as recently as 1888.[43]

Taft's construction of the commerce clauses was more realistic, more statesmanlike. Beginning with a circuit court decision of 1898,[44] his record was a long and generally consistent one on the side of broad construction of the national commerce power. As Chief Justice, he followed Holmes's landmark opinion in *Swift* v. *U.S.*,[45] completely ignoring Chief Justice Melville Fuller's crippling decision in the old Sugar Trust case of 1895.[46] With

[42] *Ibid.*, 338.

[43] Frankfurter, quoted in MacLeish and Pritchard (eds.), *Law and Politics*, 47.

[44] See Pringle, *The Life and Times of William Howard Taft*, I, 143.

[45] 196 U.S. 375 (1905).

[46] *U.S.* v. *E. C. Knight*, 156 U.S. 1 (1895).

Fuller held that commerce is primarily transportation. Goods do not become a part of it until they start their movement from one state to another. He conceded that combinations in manufacture might affect sales and price, but they do so only "incidentally" and "indirectly." The object was "private gain in the manufacture of the commodity" and manfacturing was purely "local." Fuller expressed his position sharply: "Contracts, combinations, or conspiracies to control enterprise in manufacture, agriculture, mining production in all its forms, or to raise or lower prices or wages, might unquestionably tend to restrain external as well as domestic trade, but the

Holmes, Taft held that the commerce clause must be applied "to the real and practical essence of modern business growth." "Whatever amounts to more or less constant practice," he declared, "and threatens to obstruct or unduly to burden the freedom of interstate commerce is within the regulatory power of Congress under the commerce clause, and it is primarily for Congress to consider and decide the fact of the danger and meet it. This Court will certainly not substitute its judgment for that of Congress in such a matter unless the relation of the subject to interstate commerce and its effect upon it are clearly non-existent." [47] On the basis of this doctrine the Court, under Taft's leadership, sustained the Packers and Stockyards Act,[48] the Grain Futures Act,[49] and the Motor Vehicle Theft Act.[50]

Chief Justice Taft did not, however, always support broad interpretation of congressional power. In *Bailey* v. *Drexel Furniture Co.,*[51] he struck down the child labor tax of 1919. This was not a tax but an attempt by Congress to regulate a subject matter not within its power. "A Court must be blind," he wrote, "not to see that the so-called tax is imposed to stop the employment of children within the age limits prescribed." [52] Instead of upholding, as in the commerce cases, the right of Congress to define

---

restraint would be an indirect result, *however inevitable and whatever its extent,* and such result would not necessarily determine the object of the contract, combination or conspiracy." (Italics added.)

Under this reasoning the American Sugar Refinery Company, despite the Sherman Anti-Trust Act, was allowed to get and keep 98 per cent control of the manufacture of sugar in the United States. (156 U.S. 1 [1895], 16.)

47 *Stafford* v. *Wallace,* 258 U.S. 495 (1922), 521.
48 *Ibid.*
49 *Board of Trade* v. *Olsen,* 262 U.S. 1 (1923).
50 *Brooks* v. *U.S.,* 267 U.S. 432 (1925).
51 259 U.S. 20 (1922).
52 *Ibid.,* 37.

the scope of its own power and to choose the means of carrying out its express powers into execution, he invoked the Tenth Amendment as a limit on national power.

It is the high duty and function of this court in cases regularly brought to its bar to decline to recognize or enforce seeming laws of Congress, dealing with subjects not entrusted to Congress but left or committed by the supreme law of the land to the control of the States. . . . Grant the validity of this law, and all that Congress would need to do, hereafter, in seeking to take over to its control any one of the great number of subjects of public interest, jurisdiction of which the States have never parted with, and which are reserved to them by the Tenth Amendment, would be to enact a detailed measure of complete regulation of the subject and enforce it by a so-called tax upon departures from it. To give such magic to the word "tax" would be to break down all constitutional limitation of the powers of Congress and completely wipe out the sovereignty of the States.[53]

Taft's objection, as President, to reversing the income tax decision by act of Congress clearly foreshadowed his stand on the child labor tax. Earlier, as now, he held that if a judicial decision on a constitutional issue is to be changed, it must be done by constitutional amendment, and by no other means. The child labor tax law was, in his opinion, but an attempt by Congress to do by other means what the Court had previously decided it could not do in *Hammer* v. *Dagenhart*.[54] Lashing out at the presumptuous attempt on the part of Congress to circumvent an established precedent, he argued that "The case before us cannot be distinguished from Hammer v. Dagenhart." In that case the Court had declared that Congress did not have power under the commerce clause to regulate "the hours of labor of children in factories and mines within the States." "In the case at the

[53] *Ibid.*, 37–38.
[54] 247 U.S. 251 (1918).

bar, Congress in the name of a tax which on the face of the act is a penalty seeks to do the same thing, and the effort must be equally futile." [55] In other words, the modern need for national power recognized in his commerce clause cases had to yield before the even greater need of preserving the sanctity and inviolability of judicial decisions.

Taft's absorbing ambition was, in his own phrase, to "mass" the Court. And, during his first years as Chief Justice, he demonstrated unusual capacity for keeping the brethren in line. But contrary to confident expectations when he was appointed Chief Justice, all was not sweetness and light on the bench he headed.

"Mr. Taft has such tact and good humor," the New York *Tribune* had editorialized on the Chief Justice's appointment in 1921, "and has so unconquerable a spirit of fair play, that he is greatly beloved of his fellow citizens. . . . With Justice Taft as a moderator . . . it is probable that not a few asperities that mar the harmony of the celestial chamber . . . will be softened and that not quite so often in the future will the Court divide 5 and 4." [56]

For a while it looked as if the divisions so common during Chief Justice White's incumbency might be smiled away. In 1925 Justice Holmes assured the Chief Justice "that never before in the Court have we gotten along with so little jangling and dissension." [57] We haven't had many dissents," Taft reported in 1925, "and we have been pretty nearly solid in all cases." [58] "Things go hap-

[55] 259 U.S. 20 (1922), 39.

[56] Quoted in Frankfurter, "Chief Justices I Have Known," *Virginia Law Review*, November, 1953, pp. 899–900. Reprinted in Frankfurter, *Of Law and Men* (New York, 1956), 111–38.

[57] W. H. Taft to Robert A. Taft, May 3, 1925 (Taft Papers).

[58] W. H. Taft to Charles D. Hilles, June 9, 1925 (Taft Papers).

pily in the conference room with Taft," Brandeis commented. "The judges go home less tired emotionally and
less weary physically than in White's day. . . . When
we differ we agree to differ, without any ill-feeling. It's all
very friendly." [59]

The Chief Justice pressed hard for unanimity. Deep
rifts were screened by his colleagues' natural desire to
assist his effort. Sometimes as many as three Justices
would reluctantly go along with the majority because no
one of them felt strongly enough about the issue to raise
his voice in protest. During the early years of Taft's
Chief Justiceship, it was not unusual for Justices to write
on the back of circulated slip opinions: "I shall acquiesce
in silence unless someone else dissents"; or, "I do not
agree, but shall submit." For the sake of harmony staunch
individualists such as Holmes, Brandeis, and Stone,
though disagreeing, would sometimes go along with the
majority. It seems probable that such considerations help
in accounting for the unanimity achieved in the reactionary child labor tax decision.

The peace which prognosticators foresaw in 1921 proved
to be short-lived. By 1925 the bench was entangled in the
complexities of state social and economic policy, and
before long dissents outnumbered those of Taft's predecessor. Almost a year to the day after Stone's appointment, in 1925, the phrase "Holmes, Brandeis, and Stone
dissenting" resounded for the first time on the genial
Chief Justice's ears.

Controversy centered on the requirement that a business, to be within the purview of government control,
must be "affected with a public interest." Chief Justice
Morrison R. Waite had used this concept to validate government regulation of business. In the leading case of

[59] Quoted in A. M. Bickel, *The Unpublished Opinions of Mr. Justice Brandeis* (Cambridge, 1957), 203.

Munn v. *Illinois* [60] of 1876 the Court held that a state legislature could fix the prices charged for storage in grain elevators without violating the due process clause. On the basis of this principle the Court began to take judicial cognizance of the untoward social effects of private economic power. But long before Taft headed the Court, slow strangulation had begun to beset Chief Justice Waite's liberal doctrines. It remained for Taft's Court to deal the well-nigh fatal blow. By sharply defining the categories of business which the Court considered "affected with a public interest," the applicability of this standard was greatly limited. [61]

The restrictive implications of this formula became clear in the ticket scalper's decision of 1927. [62] Justice Sutherland then enforced the differentiation, insisted upon by dissenting Justice Stephen Field in the Munn case, between price-fixing and other aspects of the contractual relation. Prices and wages, Sutherland contended, are the very "heart of the contract," and therefore, relatively free from government control and regulation. When Sutherland used a similar argument in 1923 to outlaw the minimum wage for women, the Chief Justice suggested that the decision was prompted by judicial predilection. Now he was solidly joined with the conservative majority.

The New York statute limiting the markup on theater tickets to fifty cents above the price printed on the ticket was wanting because price-fixing, a drastic inroad on the property right, could be justified only by unusual circumstances. The theater, not being a business "affected with a public interest," could not be subjected to such a regula-

[60] 94 U.S. 113 (1876).

[61] See *Wolff Packing Co.* v. *Court of Industrial Relations,* 262 U.S. 522 (1923).

[62] *Tyson* v. *Banton,* 273 U.S. 418 (1927).

tion. Taft himself had once denounced the notion that "judges should interpret the exact intention" of those who framed the Constitution "as a theory of one who does not understand the proper administration of justice." Now he joined Sutherland in holding that "constitutional principles" must be "applied as they are written. . . . They may not be remoulded by lawmakers or judges, to save exceptional cases of inconvenience, hardship, or injustice." [63]

Meanwhile, other power-crippling formulas against state legislative power were discovered or rediscovered in the commerce clause. When Pennsylvania attempted to protect immigrants from the frauds of unscrupulous steamship agents, the Supreme Court struck down the licensing statute as a "direct" state interference with foreign commerce forbidden by the Constitution. In a forceful dissent Justice Stone queried this judicially created "test of the limit of state action." For him the criterion "whether the interference with commerce is direct or indirect," like the measure "business affected with a public interest," was "too mechanical, too uncertain in its application, and too remote from actualities, to be of value." "We are," he declared, "doing little more than using labels to describe a result rather than any trustworthy formula by which it is reached." Instead of the "direct" and "indirect" abstraction, Stone urged pragmatic inquiry—recourse to reality. To determine whether the challenged statute infringes the "national interest" or "concerns interests peculiarly local" requires "a consideration of all the facts and circumstances, such as the nature of the regulation, its function, the character of the business involved, and the actual effect on the flow of commerce." [64]

[63] *Ibid.*, 445.
[64] *Di Santo* v. *Pennsylvania*, 273 U.S. 34 (1927), 44.

The line drawn between the conservative Right, led by the Chief Justice, and the liberal Left, consisting of Holmes, Brandeis, and Stone, became increasingly sharp. By the fall of 1926 the Chief Justice began to fear that he would not be able to complete the full decade. He foresaw, with grave misgivings, "some questions coming before our Court for decision that I should like to take part in deciding." [65] The bias he attributed to Holmes, Brandeis, and Stone, especially in labor cases, sorely troubled him. A case decided in 1927 clearly indicated which way the judicial winds were blowing.

In 1921 the Bedford Cut Stone Company, producers of Indiana limestone, refused to renew contracts with their employees' union, the Journeymen Stone Cutters' Association. A strike by the union failed and was followed by a lockout. Intent on driving organized labor out of the industry, the producers formed "independent" unions. Against this move, the national union invoked that provision of its constitution which pledged members to refuse to "cut, carve, or fit any material that has been cut by men working in opposition to this Association." The producers immediately sought an injunction against the union on the ground that the directive to its members was a restraint of interstate commerce prohibited by the Sherman Act. The district court refused to issue an injunction, and its decree dismissed the suit. On appeal, the circuit court agreed. Soon the case was before the high court in Washington.

At conference, the Justices voted 5 to 4 to uphold the injunction. Taft, Sutherland, McReynolds, Butler, and Van Devanter comprised the majority. The prospect of a 5 to 4 decision distressed the Chief Justice. Added to his aversion to dissents was his wish that the full prestige of the bench might meet this serious threat from organized

[65] W. H. Taft to Elihu Root, August 14, 1926 (Taft Papers).

labor. "The only class which is distinctly arrayed against
the Court," he had told his brother Horace in 1922, "is a
class that does not like the Courts at any rate, and that
is organized labor. That faction we have to hit every little
while, because they are continually violating the law and
depending on threats and violence to accomplish their
purpose." [66]

Holmes and Brandeis were intransigent against what
must have impressed them as a deliberate blow at labor.
In conference the Chief Justice detected uncertainty in
the votes of Sanford and Stone, and their wavering
prompted him to center his persuasive power on them.
Resorting to an argument that reflected his overall attitude on the sanctity of precedents, the Chief Justice
wrote Stone:

"I am quite anxious, as I am sure we all are, that the
continuity and weight of our opinions on important questions of law should not be broken any more than we can
help by dissents. Of course there are some [presumably
Holmes and Brandeis] who have deep convictions on the
subject of the law governing the relations between employer and employee, whether it involves interstate commerce or not. It is to be expected that in their attitude of
protest in the past they should find distinctions enabling
them to continue their attitude in cases presenting what
are substantially the same issues." [67]

Justice McReynolds, perhaps at Taft's suggestion,
joined in the campaign of conversion by appealing to
Stone's innate conservatism. "Please don't think me presumptuous," McReynolds wrote. "Certainly I do not mean
to be. All of us get into a fog now and then, as I know so
well from my own experience. Won't you 'Stop, Look, and
Listen'? In my view, we have one member [presumably

[66] Pringle, *The Life and Times of William Howard Taft,* II, 967.
[67] W. H. Taft to H. F. Stone, January 26, 1927 (Stone Papers,
Manuscripts Division, Library of Congress).

Brandeis] who is consciously boring from within. Of course, you have no such purpose, but you may unconsciously aid his purpose. At least do think twice on a subject—three times indeed. If the Court is broken down, then there will be rejoicing in certain quarters." [68]

In the end Stone succumbed to the majority's stress on "stability," on the importance of "continuity" in judicial decisions. "As an original proposition," he commented in a concurrence, "I should have doubted whether the Sherman Act prohibited a labor union from peaceably refusing to work upon material produced by non-union labor or by a rival union, even though interstate commerce were affected. . . . These views, which I should not have hesitated to apply here, have now been rejected again largely on the authority of the Duplex case. For that reason alone, I concur with the majority." [69]

The Chief Justice's failure to keep Stone and Sanford in line left him extremely bitter. The day before the decision came down, he commented: "We have an important labor opinion to deliver which Sutherland wrote, and in which Brandeis has written one of his meanest opinions. Holmes sides with him, and while Sanford and Stone concur in our opinion, they do it grudgingly, Stone with a kind of kickback that will make nobody happy." [70]

Before taking over the Court's center chair, Taft had expressed the view that courts must look beyond the law. He had considered it both proper and necessary for the judge to adapt the law to new social conditions. As his regime neared its end, he grew firm in the belief that the Court must hold the line; it must protect the sacred institutions of property and contract from troublemakers

[68] James C. McReynolds to H. F. Stone, undated, handwritten note (Stone Papers).

[69] *Bedford Cut Stone Co.* v. *Journeymen Stone Cutters' Association,* 274 U.S. 37 (1927), 56.

[70] W. H. Taft to Robert A. Taft, April 10, 1927 (Taft Papers).

who stimulate popular passion and threaten encroachment. Outsiders, even though they be lawyers, who opposed the "sound," "legal" way or suggested new lines of development—experimentation—were "a lot of sentimentalists," "socialists," "progressives," "bolshevists." [71] The Chief Justice was alarmed by Dean Roscoe Pound and his sociological jurisprudence.[72] Charles A. Beard, known for his economic interpretation of the Constitution, was brushed off as outstanding among "all the fools I have run across." [73] Brandeis was denounced as "a muckraker, an emotionalist for his own purposes, a Socialist . . . a man of much power for evil." [74] President Wilson's "domestic program was far too radical." [75] Even Charles Evans Hughes was suspected of entertaining "a few progressive notions." [76] In contrast, Andrew Mellon was praised as "a long-headed financier," [77] and President Harding extolled for having, "on the whole . . . done remarkably well." [78]

Under Taft's leadership, the majority envisioned itself in the van of national progress. The laissez-faire dogma, glorified in the writings of Adam Smith and Herbert Spencer, was the principal avenue to wealth and power. A minimum of lawmaking was raised to the level of an ideal. "To sustain the individual freedom of action contemplated by the Constitution," Mr. Justice Sutherland proclaimed in 1923, "is not to strike down the common good but to exalt it; for surely the good of society as a whole cannot be better served than by the preservation against arbitrary restraint of the liberties of its constituent

[71] Pringle, *The Life and Times of William Howard Taft,* I, 129.
[72] *Ibid.,* II, 860.
[73] *Ibid.*
[74] *Ibid.,* 952.
[75] *Ibid.,* 880.
[76] *Ibid.,* 886.
[77] *Ibid.,* 967.
[78] *Ibid.*

members." [79] Without the judicial check, popular reform
would likely be hasty and ill considered. It was doomed
to failure in any case if it did "not conform to human nature."

"We can waste money," Taft wrote, "in helping individuals to a habit of dependence that will weaken our
citizenship. . . . We must stop attempting to reform people by wholesale. It is the individual upon whom our
whole future progress depends. In giving and securing
scope for his ambition, energy, and free action our constitutional system has its chief merit, whatever would-be
reformers say." [80]

Judicial pre-eminence (assuming the Justices were of
the "correct" persuasion) was society's best assurance that
the sober second thought of the community would prevail. "The leviathan, the People, cannot thus be given a
momentum that will carry them in their earnestness and
just indignation beyond the median and wise line." [81]

Despite his own unshakable belief to the contrary,
Taft's mind was not of a judicial cast. "Taft worshipped
the law," Pringle writes in his final appraisal. "No understanding of him is possible without appreciation of that
fact. The fallacy in his philosophy lies, of course, in the
fact that there is no such thing as 'the law.' . . . What
Taft really did was to revere the law, as he understood it,
himself, or as judges with whom he agreed had interpreted it." [82]

[79] *Adkins* v. *Children's Hospital,* 261 U.S. 525, p. 561.
[80] W. H. Taft, *Liberty Under Law,* 42.
[81] W. H. Taft, *The Anti-Trust Act and the Supreme Court,* 34.
[82] Pringle, *The Life and Times of William Howard Taft,* I, 129.

Taft's major contribution as Chief Justice was administrative reform. Outstanding among his achievements was the Judges Act of
1925, restricting the right of appeal, and leaving to the Court's discretion what cases it would receive from the federal circuit courts.
"The sound theory of the new Act," Taft explained, "is that litigants
have their rights sufficiently protected by the courts of first instance,

More than is usually supposed, Taft disliked the give and take of free discussion. He distrusted dissenters, and was prone to attribute improper, even evil motives to those who differed with him on constitutional issues. When Brandeis dissented in the famous postmaster's case he promptly listed him among that "class of people that have no loyalty to the Court and sacrifice almost everything to the gratification of their own publicity and wish to stir up dissatisfaction with the decision of the Court,[83] if they don't happen to agree with it." [84] He had been enthusiastic about Stone's elevation to the supreme bench, but he turned sour as soon as his Republican colleague began aligning himself with Holmes and Brandeis. Shortly before his retirement he began to suspect that "if a number of us died, Hoover would put in some rather extreme

---

and by one review in an immediate appellate federal court. The function of the Supreme Court is conceived to be, not the remedying of a particular litigant's wrong, but the consideration of those cases whose decision involves principles, the application of which are of wide public and governmental interest." See "The Jurisdiction of the Supreme Court Under the Act of February 13, 1925," *Yale Law Journal,* November, 1925, p. 2.

By means of this legislation, enacted under Taft's sponsorship, our most august tribunal lost some of the attributes of a small claims court, enabling it to devote its energies to matters worthy of its attention. Without such reform the Court in 1957 would have been bogged down completely. Taft's administrative facility was also manifest in his management of the court's work. "As Chief Justice," Justice Stone recalled, Taft "was extremely generous in the assignment of cases, often keeping himself some of the least desirable ones in order to treat his brethren fairly." H. F. Stone to Marshall and Lauson Stone, November 24, 1939 (Stone Papers). For detailed consideration of Taft as judicial reformer and administrator, see my *William Howard Taft: Chief Justice* (New York, 1965).

[83] This appraisal conflicts with another of Taft's judgments on Brandeis: "He thinks much of the Court and is anxious to have it consistent and strong, and he pulls his weight in the boat." Quoted in Bickel, *The Unpublished Opinions of Mr. Justice Brandeis,* 203.

[84] Quoted in Pringle, *The Life and Times of William Howard Taft,* I, 1025.

destroyers of the Constitution." When rumors reached him that the President planned to appoint Stone his successor, he objected, saying that this would be "a great mistake." In a flash of perspicacity Taft declared that "Stone is not a leader," and predicted that he "would have a good deal of difficulty in massing the Court." [85]

Meanwhile, to frustrate dissent among the "unpatriotic" and "disloyal," Taft invited the Justices in his own camp to his home "for a Sunday afternoon," described by his biographer as "extra-curricular conferences at which . . . plans were made to block the liberal machinations." [86]

"When I first went on the Court in Taft's time," Stone recalled in 1932, "the discussion was very free, although sometimes discursive. During the last of his service there was much more inclination to rush things through especially if he thought he had the support of certain members of the Court." [87]

Under Taft's leadership the judiciary wielded the authority of a "super-legislature." To protect the property interests he indulged in what Dean Pound spoke of as a "carnival of unconstitutionality." Up to 1925 only fifty-three congressional acts were set aside. In the 1920's twelve, or nearly one fourth as many, of these adverse rulings were handed down. Between 1890 and 1937, 228 state statutes were nullified.

"Since 1920," Professor Frankfurter wrote in 1930, "the Court has invalidated more legislation than in fifty years preceding. Views that were antiquated twenty-five years ago have been resurrected in decisions nullifying minimum wage laws for women in industry, a standard-weight bread law to protect buyers from short weights and honest

[85] W. H. Taft to Charles P. Taft, May 12, 1929 (Taft Papers).

[86] Pringle, *The Life and Times of William Howard Taft,* II, 1043–44.

[87] H. F. Stone to John Bassett Moore, May 17, 1943 (Stone Papers).

bakers from unfair competition, a law fixing the resale price of theater tickets by ticket scalpers in New York, laws controlling exploitation of the unemployed by employment agencies and many tax laws. . . . Merely as a matter of arithmetic," Frankfurter continues, "this is an impressive mortality rate. But a numerical tally of the cases does not tell the tale. In the first place, all laws are not of the same importance. Secondly, a single decision may decide the fate of a great body of legislation. . . . Moreover, the discouragement of legislative efforts through a particular adverse decision and the general weakening of the sense of legislative responsibility are destructive influences not measurable by statistics." [88]

The Chief Justice carried his court to such dizzy heights in our politics that Holmes was prompted to say that he saw "hardly any limit but the sky" against the veto of state laws under the Fourteenth Amendment.[89] Brandeis, in an effort to stem the rising tide of judicial aggrandizement, spoke out firmly: "This Court has the power to prevent an experiment. . . . But in the exercise of this high power, we must be ever on our guard, lest we erect our prejudices into legal principles. If we would guide by the light of reason we must let our minds be bold." [90]

The labels "liberal" and "conservative" mistake the underlying basis of the cleavage. They were all conservatives. The division among them was rooted in fundamental differences as to the nature of the judicial function. Taft and his majority of six believed that there are certain rights beyond the reach of experimentation, and it was the business of the Court to stay all such effort. The mi-

[88] Frankfurter, "The United States Supreme Court Molding the Constitution," *Current History*, May, 1930, p. 239.

[89] *Baldwin* v. *Missouri*, 281 U.S. 586 (1930), 595.

[90] *New State Ice Company* v. *Liebman*, 285 U.S. 262 (1932), 311. Brandeis had used much the same language in *Jay Burns Baking Co.* v. *Bryan*, 264 U.S. 504 (1924), 520.

nority, on the other hand, held that experimentation is essential to a changing society. When the Court interrupts this vital process it is, Brandeis noted, "an exercise of the powers of a super-legislature—not the performance of the Constitutional function of judicial review." [91] "It is our judges who formulate our public policies and our basic law," a North Dakota judge commented in 1924. "We are governed by our judges and not by our legislatures." [92]

Taft's triumphant march continued to the end, but the future was, he realized, quite unpredictable. "Safety and the preservation of a conservative majority in the court," the Chief Justice's biographer tells us, "became an obsession with Taft as the final days approached." [93] To him the world seemed engulfed in a whirlpool of radicalism. In 1928 even the Republican party had picked a man for the Presidency who needed to "remember the warnings of the Scriptures about removing landmarks." In a senile rage the ex-President lumped his tormentors together. "The truth is that Hoover is a Progressive, just as Stone is, and just as Brandeis is and just as Holmes is." [94]

Though he came to it at the age of sixty-four, Taft's Chief Justiceship might have been constructive, but for his haunting fear of progressivism. Had he maintained the powerful position he assumed in his commerce cases and minimum wage dissent of 1923, he might have, with the backing of Holmes, Brandeis, Stone, and possibly Sanford, swung the Court along the line the great triumvirate was so eloquently staking out.

Taft loathed politics and usually bungled it. Yet his

[91] *Jay Burns Baking Co.* v. *Bryan,* 264 U.S. 504, p. 534.

[92] Andrew A. Bruce, *The American Judge* (New York, 1924), 6, 8.

[93] Pringle, *The Life and Times of William Howard Taft,* II, 1044.

[94] W. H. Taft to Horace Taft, November 14, 1929. Quoted in *ibid.,* 967.

relish for power was great. He took no stock in the refinements judges are accustomed to make. The attraction of the Chief Justiceship was, as he said, "the comfort and dignity and power without worry I like." [95] This power, relieved of the responsibilities of the democratic process, he wielded on behalf of laissez faire and in an America which had long since rendered the dogma obsolete.

[95] W. H. Taft to Horace D. Taft, January 28, 1900. Quoted in Pringle, *The Life and Times of William Howard Taft*, I, 148.

CHAPTER 3

HUGHES:

The Court in Retreat

WHEN Chief Justice Taft retired in 1930 the Court was sharply divided into two camps: Taft, Butler, McReynolds, Van Devanter, Sutherland, and Sanford construed the powers of government narrowly, thus disabling in advance any effort to deal with social and economic complexities. Holmes, Brandeis, and Stone deplored judicial review of such dimensions as discouraging experiment and change. Judge Cardozo referred to this cleavage as representing "a problem in the choice of methods."

On the one hand the right of property, as it was known to the fathers of the republic, was posited as permanent and absolute. Impairment was not to be suffered except within narrow limits of history and precedent. No experiment was to be made along new lines of social betterment. The image was a perfect sphere. The least dent or abrasion was a subtraction from its essence. Given such premises, the conclusion is inevitable. The statute becomes an illegitimate assault upon rights assured to the individual against the encroachments of society. The method of logic or philosophy is at work in all its plenitude. The opposing view, if it is to be accepted, must be reached through other avenues of approach. The right which the assailants of the statute posit as absolute or permanent is conceived of by the supporters of the statute as conditioned by varying circumstances of time and space and environment and degree. The limitations appropriate to one stage of development may be inadequate for another. Not logic alone, but logic supplemented by the social sciences becomes the instrument of advance.[1]

By 1930 the divergence was clearly marked. Yet the margin of safety for conservatism remained perilously narrow. Chief Justice Taft had horrid premonitions of what might happen when he died. Though failing in health, he was determined to stick it out.

The most that could be hoped for, he wrote Justice Butler on September 14, 1929, "is continued life of enough of the present membership . . . to prevent disastrous reversals of our present attitude. With Van and Mac and Sutherland and you and Sanford, there will be five to steady the boat. . . . We must not give up at once."[2]

As in 1920, Taft realized that the recruitment of Supreme Court Justices was a matter of major political importance. He knew, as did North Carolina Chief Justice Clark in 1906, that "if five lawyers can negative the will of 100,000,000 men, then the art of government is reduced to the selection of those five lawyers."[3]

What would President Hoover do? We have seen that Taft distrusted Hoover as a progressive, and in the Senate recent Supreme Court decisions had reinflamed the "radical spirit." A decision bearing the name "O'Fallon" had become a rallying point. This embattled litigation had arisen under the Transportation Act of 1920. In Section 15A thereof Congress had directed that the Interstate Commerce Commission give "due consideration to all the elements of value recognized by the law of the land for rate-making purposes." A minority of the Commission ob-

[1] B. N. Cardozo, *The Growth of the Law* (New Haven, 1924), 72–73.

[2] Quoted in Pringle, *The Life and Times of William Howard Taft*, II, 1044.

[3] Quoted in Charles A. Beard, *The Supreme Court and the Constitution* (New York, 1912), 6.

jected to the valuation of the railroad's property in the case because preponderant weight had not been given the "reproduction-cost" theory. Chief Justice Taft disliked the whole problem and candidly confessed his incompetence but, he commented, "We have some experts on our court. One is Pierce Butler, the other is Brandeis." [4] The "experts," however, were in complete disagreement. Butler, a former railroad attorney, upheld "reproduction cost" and, with the aid of like-minded colleagues, the Court elevated this theory to the status of a constitutional directive. Billions were thus construed into the total railroad valuation. Increased rates and profits became inevitable.

In the backlash of public resentment against the O'Fallon case and similar cases,[5] and within a year after Taft had penned his neurotic words as to the Court's future, death claimed the Chief Justice and his colleague Sanford—both veterans of the Court's conservative wing. To fill the center chair President Hoover nominated New York's most eminent lawyer, Charles Evans Hughes, who along with John W. Davis had been counsel for the O'Fallon railroad, upholding the dubious theory of reproduction cost.

Superficially the President's choice seemed admirable. "The chorus of approval is as emphatic as it is unanimous," the *Literary Digest* announced, February 15, 1930. The Troy *Times* suggested that if there had been a nationwide straw vote to determine popular choice for the vacancy, "at least a plurality and probably a large majority would have voted for the man President Hoover has nominated."

A man of unquestioned integrity, Hughes had been

[4] W. H. Taft to Robert A. Taft, October 21, 1928. Quoted in Pringle, *The Life and Times of William Howard Taft*, II, 1066.

[5] *St. Louis and O'Fallon Railroad Co.* v. *U.S.*, 279 U.S. 461 (1929) and *United Railways* v. *West*, 280 U.S. 234 (1930).

named to the Court in 1910 by President Taft. As an Associate Justice until 1916, he had demonstrated qualities of judicial statesmanship. But in 1930 the nominee was strangely apprehensive when President Hoover broached his appointment: "I don't want a fight over the nomination. . . . If you are convinced that the nomination will be confirmed by the Senate without a scrap, I will accept it. But I don't want any trouble about it." [6] The President was confident there would be no trouble, and it looked at first as though he was right. Senator George Norris, insurgent Nebraska Republican, and chairman of the Senate Judiciary Committee, told reporters "that favorable action would be taken at the regular meeting of the committee." [7] But a few days later the committee recommended confirmation by a split vote of ten to two, with Norris himself in opposition. What was to be a cut-and-dried formality of acquiescence was destined to become "a flaming controversy," "one of the most significant developments in the political life of this Nation in many years." [8]

The Nebraska senator questioned the propriety of Hughes's resignation from the Court in 1916 to enter the race for the Presidency. Norris believed that "we have reached a time in our history when the power and influence of monopoly and organized wealth are reaching into every governmental activity." "Perhaps," the senator explained, "it is not far amiss to say that no man in public life so exemplifies the influence of powerful combinations in the political and financial world as does Mr. Hughes." [9]

Other senators voiced the same objection. "If the system

[6] Merlo J. Pusey, *Charles Evans Hughes* (2 vols., New York, 1951), II, 652.

[7] *New York Times,* February 5, 1930.

[8] *Philadelphia Record,* Feb. 13, 1930. Quoted by Senator Norris, *Congressional Record,* Vol. 72 (1930), 3566.

[9] *Congressional Record,* Vol. 72 (1930), 3373.

of judicial law that is being written in defiance of state legislation and of congressional legislation is continued," Senator Dill of Washington observed prophetically, "there is no human power in America that can keep the Supreme Court from becoming a political issue, nation-wide, in the not far distant future." [10] The very struggle which the senator foresaw in 1930 became conspicuous, as we shall see, in 1937.

Hughes's confirmation, fifty-two to twenty-six, seemed almost an anticlimax. The very next day, however, Senate insurgents launched an attack on "judge-made law," "government by injunction," and "federal judicial interference in the internal concerns of the states." Constitutional amendments stripping the Court of its power to declare acts of Congress unconstitutional and popular elections of judges were suggested. The crusade against the Court was resumed a few weeks later when, to fill the Sanford vacancy, President Hoover nominated John J. Parker, a Federal Circuit Court judge, Fourth Circuit. North Carolina Republican Parker's nomination had been successfully urged on Hoover as a "master political stroke." But that politically inept President bungled it again. Parker was not confirmed. Hoover at once nominated Owen J. Roberts, well known as the prosecutor in the Teapot Dome scandal, and confirmation quickly followed.

The campaign against Hughes and Parker had been both exploratory and educational. Accepting Hughes's confirmation as a foregone conclusion, the insurgents merely wished, as Senator Dill said, "to place in the Record . . . a warning." The senators wanted to call the attention of the people of this country to the fact that if they "would free themselves and have justice at the hands of their Government they must reach the Supreme Court of the United States by putting men on that bench who

[10] *Ibid.*, 3642.

hold economic theories which are fair and just to all, and not in the interest of the privileged few." [11]

"We all realized from the very beginning," Senator Norris commented, "that we had no hope of victory." The insurgents had been motivated by the "conscientious belief that . . . profit will come perhaps even to the Supreme Court if they will read the debates of the Senate, and if the majority members of that Court will even read the dissenting opinions of their brethren, Brandeis, Holmes, and Stone." [12] Implicit in the Senate debates was stern admonition that the Justices take to heart their own oft-professed principle of judicial self-restraint. A flippant commentator suggested that Hughes might be "a better Chief Justice for the experience." [13]

"He has lost practically all his tail feathers," Frank R. Kent wrote, "and reaches this highest and most secure of all perches in our governmental tree a badly battered and bedraggled bird. . . . To have permitted without protest such a man, graciously accepting as merely his due the almost unanimous chorus of journalistic eulogy to become Chief Justice, would have been a pity. . . . It was extremely salutary to have the liberal point of view in connection with the Supreme Court presented. . . . The debate can hardly fail to be enlightening to the members of the Supreme Court."

Justice Stone, noting the harsh things said about the Supreme Court, yet accepting the debates as evidence of "wholesome interest in what the Court was doing," felt disappointed. "What troubles me most," he wrote Professor Frankfurter, April 4, 1930, "is that some of the people who ought to be quickest to see this and most prompt

[11] *Ibid.*, 3501.
[12] *Ibid.*, 3573.
[13] Frank R. Kent, quoted in Alfred Leif, *Democracy's Norris* (New York, 1939), 344.

to give present tendencies a different trend, seem not to appreciate the situation. I think one aspect of the matter which is not adequately understood is that it is not a contest between conservatism and radicalism, nearly so much as it is a difference arising from an inadequate understanding of the relation of law to the social and economic forces which control society."

The senators had left untouched a matter which, if explored, might have afforded a clue to Hughes's constitutional jurisprudence. In his book on the Supreme Court, published in 1928, the new Chief Justice had made clear, as we have seen, that he considered the public's favorable opinion of the Court as an institution, especially the "stability" manifest in the continuity of decisions, of more importance than judicial statesmanship on crucial questions of constitutional power.

"It is more than a mere matter of curiosity," Louis B. Boudin commented in 1932, "that with all the fuss raised about Mr. Hughes' views when he was nominated for the Chief Justiceship, it never occurred to anyone to inquire into the views held by him." One who made such an investigation, Boudin suggested, might have anticipated that in any situation where the Chief Justice was bound to choose between recognizing the power to govern, even in matters of major importance to the country, and the maintenance of "stability in judicial opinions," Hughes would take the latter course.[14]

Any reader of the book Hughes wrote in 1928 might have anticipated that the Chief Justice would consider "dual federalism" vital to the maintenance of our system. Hughes wrote:

The dual system of government implies the maintenance of the constitutional restrictions of the powers of Congress as

[14] Louis B. Boudin, *Government by Judiciary* (2 vols.; New York, 1932), II, 542–43, 44n.

well as of those of the States. The existence of the function of the Supreme Court is a constant monition to Congress. A judicial, as distinguished from a mere political, solution of the questions arising from time to time has its advantages in a more philosophical and uniform exposition of constitutional principles than would otherwise be probable. Moreover, the expansion of the country has vastly increased the volume of legislative measures and there is severe pressure toward an undue centralization. In Congress, theories of State autonomy, strongly held so far as profession goes, may easily yield to the demands of interests seeking Federal support. Many of our citizens in their zeal for particular measures have little regard for any of the limitations of Federal authority. We have entered upon an era of regulation with a great variety of legislative proposals, constantly multiplying governmental contacts with the activities of industry and trade. These proposals raise more frequently than in the past questions of national, as opposed to State, power. If our dual system with its recognition of local authority in local concerns is worth maintaining, judicial review is likely to be of increasing value.[15]

The Senate debates on Hughes's confirmation raised a warning flag. The power to govern was needed as never before. Yet the effectiveness of that power—even its existence—turned absolutely on the votes of nine men appointed for life and politically responsible to no one. By the spring of 1933 the outlines of Franklin D. Roosevelt's national policy and program were rapidly taking shape, but its validity was by no means assured. "A political revolution in the United States," a perceptive student of the Court has observed, "is not a *fait accompli* until the incoming party secures sufficient judicial appointments, and especially upon the Supreme Court, to protect its program from the limbo of unconstitutional statutes." [16] Whether the federal government could meet the exploding problems of an industrialized community came to turn, prac-

15 Hughes, *The Supreme Court of the United States*, 95–96.
16 Ewing, *The Judges of the Supreme Court, 1789–1937*, p. 3.

tically and primarily, on the leadership of Chief Justice Charles Evans Hughes.

Hughes, an "only child," his father an orthodox Baptist clergyman, was born on April 11, 1862. His parents plied their son with attentions designed to develop "pious submission to their counsel." There was endless prodding, preaching, cajoling. Even play had to be saturated with moral uplift. His hobbyhorse galloped him to the holy lands he learned of from the Bible, or in approved travel stories. Juvenile games, children's books, and other trivialities were not favored. There were so many more important things to do. When he was five his mother got him a New Testament and Psalms so he "could take his turn in reading the verses at family prayers." [17] On the lad's eighth birthday, his father gave him a Greek New Testament with lexicon. "Be thorough, Be thorough, BE THOROUGH," was their educational slogan. His parents once thought of an adoption to give him companionship. But hearing of it, the son "marched into the room and said he thought it would be a mistake." [18] Education, he declared, was more important than companionship.

Even after he had entered Brown University in the class of 1881 no detail was overlooked. "I try to follow your injunctions in regard to everything," [19] he wrote his parents reassuringly. But there were worldly attractions hard to resist. He liked fraternity life and wanted a roommate. "Pa" turned thumbs down on the latter as making it impossible to "throw yourself on your knees frequently and whenever you were inclined to do so. . . ." [20]

That this upbringing was effective there can be no doubt. Hughes said: "Whatever I may do, or become,

17 Pusey, *Charles Evans Hughes*, I, 6.
18 *Ibid.*, 12.
19 *Ibid.*, 36.
20 *Ibid.*, 33.

there is no danger that I will ever be able to rid myself of the truth implanted in early childhood." But naturally the son's views differed at times from those of his parents. He yielded once to a worldly ambition to own a pair of skates. For the requisite three dollars, he wrote essays for fellow students gauging quality to the customer's usual performance in such work. For a fair essay the rate was one dollar, for a fine one, two dollars. "I shouldn't wonder," he wrote his father proudly, "if I had more such jobs." When his parents vetoed this not unusual enterprise there was no penitence.

"I think my conduct proper," he argued in a sort of brief; skating was "very healthy exercise," and "earning money a fine thing"; writing for money was a "perfectly legitimate business." There were also "advantages accruing to myself from much writing." "No blame could attach itself to me in any case. . . . And the other fellows must settle the moral point with themselves." Nor was he persuaded when his parents tried to fix their verdict on him.[21] "You know the proverbial rashness of youth," he explained. "You also know my fondness for skating." As his clincher the youthful ghost writer insisted on the law of custom. He knew "perfectly well [as his needy customers obviously did not] that my course is not reprehensible before the faculty or before justice." [22] He was pleading his case in his own way, and years later explained: "As I look back upon that training at home, in the light of subsequent views and experiences, I realize that what interested me most was the dialectic rather than the premises." [23]

Charles Evans Hughes is, by any standard, one of the most important and truly national public figures of this century. His life represents not one but at least eight

21 *Ibid.,* 49.
22 *Ibid.,* 50.
23 *Ibid.,* 25.

careers: law teacher and eminent lawyer, feared and fearless investigator, crusading governor, Associate Justice of
the Supreme Court, Republican Presidential candidate—
and near winner—in the 1916 race for the Presidency (of
which a shrewd observer said "he seemed not to really
want to be elected"), Secretary of State, World Court
judge, and Chief Justice of the United States. Hughes, as
counsel for the Armstrong Insurance Committee of 1905,
set the highest standard of skill and energy for public in-
vestigators. He could not be deceived, dodged, or shaken
off. As governor of New York his courageous and powerful
leadership established a record in social reform. In the
same pattern was his eloquent defense in 1920 of five
duly elected Socialist members expelled from the New
York State Assembly because of their political views. All
this stamped him as a liberal. As Secretary of State in
Harding's shoddy administration, however, he fell easily
into the conservative groove and became known for his
"narrow and uncomprehending insistence at all cost on
the most extreme interpretation of American property
rights, notably in our oil diplomacy and our relations with
Mexico and Russia." [24] This record, marked by an extraordinary mixture of liberal and conservative ingredi-
ents, is not the one by which Hughes's place in history
is likely to be judged.

His larger fame is as Chief Justice of the United States.
Even his prior work as an Associate Justice, "six stun-
ningly liberal years," [25] is slighted. The explanation may
be that he presided over the most serious crisis in the
Court's history. Three questions suggest themselves: What
is his responsibility for the critical impasse between Court

[24] *The Nation,* February 12, 1930, p. 165. Quoted in Samuel Hendel, "The 'Liberalism' of Chief Justice Hughes," 10 *Vanderbilt Law
Review* 259 (1957), 262.
[25] Fred Rodell, *Nine Men* (New York, 1955), 223.

and Congress? What did he do or undo in the heat of
that fierce battle? After the storm receded, what contribution did he make to an understanding of the Court's role
in American politics?

Legislation having a New Deal tinge fell under the
microscope of the judiciary in 1934, when the Justices
passed on the constitutionality of a Minnesota law giving
courts the power to postpone mortgage foreclosures.[26]
Debtors brought their holdings under its protection,
while creditors challenged the act's validity. The Minnesota act seemed to fly in the face of the Constitution's
categorical imperative—that no state shall pass any law
"impairing the obligation of contract." The Chief Justice,
speaking for a majority of five, upheld the act by distinguishing between the "obligation" of contract and the
"remedy." He tried to demonstrate that the moratorium
statute did not really impair the obligation of Minnesota
mortgages; it only modified the remedy. He also went out
of his way to relate emergency to power. "While emergency
does not create power," he said, "emergency may furnish
the occasion for the exercise of power." [27]

Cardozo and Stone read the Chief Justice's first draft
with misgivings; each considered writing a concurring
opinion. Cardozo actually prepared a draft, and Stone submitted a long memorandum. Their approach, in the tradition of Marshall and Holmes, contrasted sharply with
that of the Chief Justice. "We must never forget that it is
a constitution we are expounding," Marshall had observed. "The constitution was intended to endure for
ages to come, and, consequently, to be adapted to the
various crises of human affairs." Cardozo referred to the
bold note Holmes had struck in 1920: "The case before

[26] *Home Building and Loan Association* v. *Blaisdell,* 290 U.S. 398
(1934).
[27] *Ibid.,* 426.

us must be considered in the light of our whole experience and not merely in that of what was said a hundred years ago." The Minnesota statute, Cardozo admitted, "may be inconsistent with things" which the men of 1787 believed or took for granted, but "their beliefs to be significant must be adjusted to the world they knew. It is not . . . inconsistent with what they would say today." For them as for us, Cardozo suggested, "the search was for a broader base, for a division that would separate the lawful and forbidden lines more closely in correspondence with the necessities of government." [28]

Stone threatened to speak out independently if certain of his points were rejected. "I have taken more than the usual time to study your opinion," he wrote the Chief Justice, "because of the great importance to the public and to the Court of the questions involved." Stone, like Cardozo, wished to elevate the tone of the opinion and eliminate its unrealistic refinements.

"I am not inclined to join in so much of the [opinion] . . . as states that the relief afforded could only be of a temporary character. . . . I think we should be meticulous in not making pronouncements with respect to cases other than that before us. . . . We may yet have to deal with cases where the moratorium is for longer periods than those involved in this case; whether they could be regarded as temporary or not is, of course, a relative matter, and other and controlling considerations might come in. Therefore, it seems to me that we should leave ourselves absolutely unhampered by pronouncements which might be taken to affect situations not presented to us in this case." [29]

[28] Quoted from Justice Cardozo's unpublished concurrence (Stone Papers).

[29] Stone's undated memorandum to Hughes on the Blaisdell case (Stone Papers).

As finally announced, the Chief Justice's opinion included passages from the Cardozo draft opinion and from Stone's memorandum. But Hughes kept intact his logomachy about "emergency" and "power," "obligation" and "remedy," thus exposing himself to Justice Sutherland's devastating broadside:

The opinion concedes that emergency does not create power, or increase granted power, or remove or diminish restrictions upon power granted or reserved. It then proceeds to say, however, that while emergency does not create power, it may furnish the occasion for the exercise of power. I can only interpret what it said . . . as meaning that while an emergency does not diminish a restriction upon power it furnishes an occasion for diminishing it; and this, as it seems to me, is merely to say the same thing by the use of another set of words, with the effect of affirming that which has just been denied.[30]

Sutherland conceded that war constituted an emergency, justifying legislative modification of rent leases. Ruinous economic depression was not, however, a comparable holocaust. This was no occasion for slackening the stubborn "strength of the fabric" woven by the founding fathers. The aging justice had seen "economic emergencies" before. "The present exigency is nothing new. From the beginning of our existence as a nation, periods of depression, of industrial failure, of financial distress, of unpaid and unpayable indebtedness, have alternated with years of plenty . . . and the attempt by legislative devices to shift the misfortune of the debtor to the shoulders of the creditor without coming into conflict with the contract impairment clause has been persistent and oft-repeated." Experience and observation led to only one conclusion: "If the provisions of the Constitution be not

[30] *Home Building and Loan Association* v. *Blaisdell,* 472.

upheld when they pinch as well as when they comfort, they may as well be abandoned." [31]

The same pressure that led to moratorium legislation in Minnesota moved the New York state assembly to approve a milk-control law, setting up a board to establish minimum retail prices. Acting promptly, this board pegged the price at nine cents a quart. In the face of this statute Leo Nebbia, an obscure Rochester grocer, sold two quarts of milk and a five-cent loaf of bread for eighteen cents. The state courts upheld his conviction under the milk-control act, and he appealed to Washington.[32]

As in the moratorium case, the verdict was five to four. The Chief Justice and Justice Roberts, aligning themselves with Stone, Brandeis, and Cardozo, voted to sustain the statute. A definable cleavage within the Court now seemed established. "With the wisdom of the policy adopted," Justice Roberts said for the majority, "with the adequacy or practicability of the law enacted to forward it, the courts are both incompetent and unauthorized to deal." [33] Justice McReynolds disagreed. "I think," he said for the dissenters, "this Court must have regard to the wisdom of the enactment." [34] That is, the Supreme Court, under the Fourteenth Amendment, must act as a super-legislature.

Justice Roberts' opinion, especially his blanket statement that "the power to promote the general welfare is inherent in government," [35] raised high hopes. These were soon dampened, however, by his opinion in *R.R. Retirement Board* v. *Alton R.R.*[36] This case involved an act re-

[31] *Ibid.*, 471, 483.
[32] *Nebbia* v. New York, 291 U.S. 502 (1934).
[33] *Ibid.*, 537.
[34] *Ibid.*, 556.
[35] *Ibid.*, 524.
[36] 295 U.S. 330 (1935).

quiring railroad carriers to contribute to a pension fund for superannuated employees. The Court, speaking through Justice Roberts, set the statute aside as not falling within the commerce power. The act, the Justice said, "has and can have no relation to the promotion of efficiency, economy or safety by separating the unfit from the industry. If these ends demand the elimination of aged employees, their retirement from the service would suffice to accomplish the object." [37] That is, the railroads might fire superannuated employees, but Congress could not require the roads to contribute to a pension fund for them.

Chief Justice Hughes, joined by Brandeis, Stone, and Cardozo, dissented. The commerce power, the minority said, authorized Congress to secure essential justice to interstate employees. Congress has the same power as any civilized legislature. Its authority to promote the general welfare under the commerce clause equaled that of the state under the police power. The majority had raised "a barrier against all legislative action of this nature by declaring that the subject matter itself lies beyond the reach of the congressional authority to regulate interstate commerce." If that view prevails, the Chief Justice suggested, "no matter how suitably limited . . . or how appropriate the measure of retirement allowances, or how sound actuarially the plan, or how well adjusted the burden, still under this decision Congress would not be at liberty to enact such a measure." [38]

Justice Roberts was in opposition. The crucial question now was whether the Chief Justice himself would hold fast.

The answer came May 27, 1935, when the sloppily drafted National Industrial Recovery Act was unanimously

[37] *Ibid.*, 367.
[38] *Ibid.*, 375.

set aside in the Schechter Brothers case.[39] The statute was found wanting as an unconstitutional delegation of legislative power as well as transcending the national commerce authority. Two major precedents bolstered the Chief Justice's argument under the commerce clause. One was Justice Joseph Bradley's opinion in *Brown* v. *Houston.*[40] Hughes mentioned this case by name. Just as the coal involved in *Brown* v. *Houston,* having been brought in from another state, came to rest in Louisiana, so the chickens shipped into New York from another state had come to rest in Brooklyn. The poultry, like the coal, had lost their distinctive character as articles of interstate commerce. But Hughes ignored an important qualification in reading Justice Bradley's opinion. Local taxation of the coal shipped from another state was valid, Bradley said, "in the absence of Congressional action." [41] In a short opinion, Bradley repeated this qualification five times, yet the Chief Justice overlooked it. But for this oversight, and aside from objections based on delegation of legislative powers, *Brown* v. *Houston* might have been a precedent for upholding NIRA, not authority for setting it aside. Congress had acted.

As a precedent for his decision the Chief Justice also invoked, though not by name, that old judicial landmark of evil memory, *U.S.* v. *E. C. Knight,*[42] known as the Sugar Trust case. To paralyze national power under the commerce clause Chief Justice Fuller had applied the formula of direct and indirect effects. The distinction was one of kind rather than of degree. Indirect effects on interstate commerce, Fuller argued, "however inevitable and to whatever extent" are beyond the power of Congress. Hughes accepted this view:

[39] *Schechter Brothers* v. *U.S.,* 295 U.S. 495 (1935).
[40] 114 U.S. 622 (1885).
[41] *Ibid.,* 630.
[42] 156 U.S. 1 (1895).

In determining how far the federal government may go in controlling intrastate transactions upon the ground that they "affect" interstate commerce, there is a necessary and well-established distinction between direct and indirect effects. The precise line can be drawn only as individual cases arise, but the distinction is clear in principle. . . . [W]here the effect of intrastate transactions upon interstate commerce is merely indirect, such transactions remain within the domain of State power. If the commerce clause were construed to reach all enterprises and transactions which could be said to have an indirect effect upon interstate commerce, the federal authority would embrace practically all the activities of the people and the authority of the state over its domestic concerns would exist only by the sufferance of the federal government. . . . [T]he distinction between direct and indirect effects of intrastate transactions upon interstate commerce must be recognized as a fundamental one, essential to the maintenance of our constitutional system. Otherwise . . . there would be virtually no limit to the Federal power, and for all practical purposes we should have a completely centralized government.[43]

Stone and Cardozo wrote a separate opinion stressing unconstitutional delegation of Congress' power to the President—"delegation running riot," they called it. At the same time they seemed wary of accepting Chief Justice Hughes's view that the distinction between direct and indirect effects is one of kind rather than of degree. "The law is not indifferent to considerations of degree," their concurrence suggested.[44]

The revolt of Stone and Cardozo, though mild, indicated a breach among the Justices which cracked wide open a year later in *Carter* v. *Carter Coal Company*,[45] known as the Guffey Coal case. In dispute was the Bituminous Coal Conservation Act, legislation designed to bring order into one of the most chaotic industries in the

[43] *Schechter Brothers* v. *U.S.*, 546, 548.
[44] *Ibid.*, 554.
[45] 298 U.S. 238 (1936).

United States. The act included two sets of provisions, one regulating labor conditions, the other fixing prices. The framers of the act took pains to say that these provisions were separable; one could stand if the other fell.

Sutherland, speaking for a majority of five, held that the legislation constituted one connected scheme of regulation. He did not deny that Congress might have regulated the price of soft coal by a single act, but the price regulation was so dependent on the wages and hours provisions that it would have to be considered as one inseparable whole. The magic formula, "direct" and "indirect" effects, was still considered necessary to preserve the federal system. In support of his reasoning Sutherland, like Hughes in setting aside NIRA, went back to *U.S.* v. *E. C. Knight.* But Sutherland, unlike Hughes, mentioned that old reactionary precedent by name.

"It is of vital moment," Justice Sutherland explained, "that in order to preserve the *fixed balance* intended by the Constitution, the powers of the general government be not so extended as to embrace any not within the express terms of the several grants or the implications necessarily to be drawn therefrom." [46]

For Sutherland power over certain subject matter—agriculture, production, and the employer-employee relation —is reserved exclusively to the states. State power to regulate these is for all practical purposes enumerated, beyond the reach of Congress, even under its implied powers. "The local character of mining, of manufacturing and of crop growing is a fact, and remains a fact, whatever may be done with the products." [47] Under this reasoning the second dimension of national power—Congress' choice of means for carrying its enumerated powers into

[46] *Ibid.,* 294. Italics added.
[47] *Ibid.,* 304.

execution, along with the fact of national supremacy—
was seriously qualified if not eliminated.

In a concurrence, Chief Justice Hughes charged that
Sutherland had been mistaken in denying the separability
of the act's price-fixing and labor provisions. But there was
no doubt as to where the Chief Justice stood on the distinction between direct and indirect effects. Like Sutherland, he held that the difference was one of kind:

I agree . . . that production—in this case mining—which
precedes commerce, is not itself commerce; and that the
power to regulate commerce among the several States is not
a power to regulate industry within the State.
The power to regulate interstate commerce embraces the
power to protect that commerce from injury, whatever may be
the source of the dangers which threaten it. . . . But Congress may not use this protective authority as a pretext for the
exertion of power to regulate activities and relations within
the states which affect interstate commerce only indirectly.
Otherwise, in view of the multitude of indirect effects, Congress in its discretion could assume control of virtually all
the activities of the people to the subversion of the fundamental principle of the Constitution. If the people desire to
give Congress the power to regulate industries within the
State, and the relations of employers and employees in those
industries, they are at liberty to declare their will in the appropriate manner [that is by Constitutional Amendment], but
it is not for the Court to amend the Constitution by judicial
decision.[48]

Agreeing with Sutherland, Hughes declared that the act's
labor provisions went "beyond any proper measure of
protection of interstate commerce and attempts a broad
regulation of industry within the State." The Chief Justice's approach was the same as in his Schechter opinion
in which he had said: "The question of chief importance
relates to the provisions of the code as to the hours and

[48] *Ibid.,* 317–18.

wages of those employed in defendants' slaughterhouse markets. . . . Their hours and wages have no *direct* relation to interstate commerce." [49]

Justice Cardozo, joined by Stone and Brandeis, dissented. They also clarified their position on the meaning of the "direct and indirect effects" formula. Rejecting the sharpness of the Sutherland-Hughes distinction, Cardozo declared that "a great principle of constitutional law is not susceptible of comprehensive statement in an adjective." [50]

The fundamental basis of divergence within the Court was now clear. Six of the Justices, including Roberts and Hughes, believed that the states limited national power. Six Justices had come to believe that those who framed the Tenth Amendment had inadvertently omitted the word "expressly." Instead of reading the words of the amendment "All power not delegated," they read it, "all powers not *expressly* delegated to the United States by the Constitution, nor prohibited by it to the States, are reserved to the States respectively, or to the people."

The six to three line-up had occurred previously in *United States* v. *Butler*,[51] setting aside the Agricultural Adjustment Act. Following Chief Justice Taft's line in the child labor tax case, Justice Roberts ruled that the AAA was not really a tax; rather, it was part of a plan to control agricultural production, a subject matter clearly within the state's domain. The Justice agreed that Congress could lay and collect taxes, and spend money for the general welfare, but Congress could not spend money for the purpose of curtailing agricultural production.

Justice Stone, joined by Brandeis and Cardozo, dissented. The AAA could be set aside, they contended, only by a "tortured construction of the Constitution."

[49] *Schechter Brothers* v. *U.S.*, 548. Italics added.
[50] *Carter* v. *Carter Coal Company*, 327.
[51] 297 U.S. 1 (1936).

Chief Justice Hughes might have been prepared to go either way on the validity of the AAA, but finally decided to join the majority. "The Chief Justice does not like 5 to 4 opinions," Attorney-General Homer Cummings told fellow Cabinet members, "and if Justice Roberts had been in favor of sustaining AAA, the Chief Justice would have cast his vote that way also." [52] In terms of the value Hughes customarily placed on "stability," a 6 to 3 vote in a major case was obviously preferable to a 5 to 4.

If this was the Chief Justice's reasoning, he gravely misjudged the outcome. *United States* v. *Butler* was destined to become a "self-inflicted wound" of the first dimension. Its tendency was to stabilize chaos and depression rather than lend certainty to judicial decisions and thus stimulate "public confidence" in the Court and the Constitution. In the face of this narrow construction of the national taxing power and within less than a year, the Chief Justice himself joined in sustaining the constitutionality of the Social Security Act,[53] leaving *United States* v. *But-*

[52] Harold L. Ickes, *The Secret Diary of Harold L. Ickes* (3 vols.; New York, 1953), I, 535–36.

[53] *Steward Machine Co.* v. *Davis,* 301 U.S. 548 (1937). The prevailing doctrine was stated by Justice Cardozo. "The line must still be drawn between one welfare and another, between particular and general. Where this shall be placed cannot be known through a formula in advance of the event. There is a middle ground or certainly a penumbra in which discretion is at large. The discretion, however, is not confided to the courts. The discretion belongs to Congress, unless the choice is clearly wrong, a display of arbitrary power, not an exercise of judgment." *Helvering* v. *Davis,* 301 U.S. 619 (1937), 640. See also *Mulford* v. *Smith,* 307 U.S. 38 (1939); *Sonzinsky* v. *U.S.,* 300 U.S. 506 (1937); *United States* v. *Sanchez,* 340 U.S. 42 (1950).

In flat rejection of the decision in the AAA case, the Court in 1950 (*United States* v. *Sanchez,* 340 U.S. 42) held that a tax is not invalidated because it reaches activities which Congress may not otherwise regulate. The same broad doctrine was sustained in *United States* v. *Kahriger,* 345 U.S. 22 (1953), evoking Justice Frankfurter to protest: "To allow what otherwise is excluded from con-

ler without a leg to stand on. Few today would deny that the decision upsetting the AAA was a far greater threat to stability and effective government than the legislative experiment it halted.

As a sort of last straw, at the very end of what Justice Stone called the "most disastrous term in its history," the Court set aside the New York state minimum wage law for women.[54] New York had tried to correct the error Justice Sutherland found in the District of Columbia statute declared invalid in 1923, but the effort proved vain. Hughes, more generous in his estimate of New York's effort to avoid the pitfall of unconstitutionality, dissented from the majority opinion, but only because there were "material differences" in the District of Columbia and New York cases.[55] Justice Sutherland's 1923 decision thus remained a viable precedent; all judicial bridges were still intact. The continuity of decisions, "stability," as Hughes interpreted it (stability in words only), was achieved. Stability in the broader sense of social order had been seriously imperiled. Overlooked was the wisdom implicit in

---

gressional authority to be brought within it by casting legislation in the form of a revenue measure could . . . offer an easy way for the legislative imagination to control 'any one of the great number of subjects of public interest, jurisdiction of which the States have never parted with . . .' " (p. 38).

In 1954 a lower federal court (*Waialua Agricultural Co.* v. *Maneja*, 216 F. 2d 466, 9th circuit, 1954) held that since "agriculture is not commerce," federal regulation of it "invades the reserved rights of the States." This apparent return to Justice Roberts and *U.S.* v. *Butler*, 297 U.S. 1 (1936), was repudiated the next year in *Maneja* v. *Waialua Agricultural Co.*, 349 U.S. 254, 259 (1955).

54 *Morehead* v. *Tipaldo*, 298 U.S. 587 (1936). Stone put this characterization of *Morehead* v. *Tipaldo* in a letter to his sister, Helen Stone Willard, June 2, 1936 (Stone Papers).

55 For a detailed discussion of the contrasting views of Hughes and Stone, see my *Harlan Fiske Stone: Pillar of the Law* (New York, 1956), 423–24.

Attorney-General Robert H. Jackson's words of 1941: "The measure of success of a democratic system is found in the degree to which its elections really reflect rising discontent before it becomes unmanageable, by which government responds to it with timely redress and by which losing groups are self-disciplined to accept election results." [56] As we shall see, the President's Court-packing plan (well-nigh inevitable after the Guffey Coal and minimum wage decisions) was just around the corner.

The judicial opinions handed down during the 1935–1936 term carried overtones of decisive finality. From January through June, 1936, the Court wove a constitutional fabric so tight as to bind political power at all levels. Looking back in 1941 on the judicial wreckage of 1936, President Roosevelt spoke of his program as "fairly completely undermined." [57] In one term the tally of "self-inflicted wounds" reached an all-time high. Hughes joined Roberts in upsetting the AAA. The Chief Justice's concurring opinion in the Guffey Coal case indicated judicial determination to maintain the Tenth Amendment as an impassable wall against national power. Despite the Chief Justice's dissenting opinion in the second minimum wage case, Sutherland's reactionary 1923 decision remained a paralyzing precedent. This same year Hughes joined the majority in a vehement attack on the Securities and Exchange Commission for refusing to permit a registrant to withdraw an allegedly false statement.[58] He supported the majority's revival of the "privileges and immunities" clause as a bar against state power.[59] The Justices' wide-

[56] Robert H. Jackson, *The Struggle for Judicial Supremacy: A Study of a Crisis in American Power Politics* (New York, 1941), 316.

[57] Franklin D. Roosevelt, *Public Papers and Addresses* (13 vols.; New York, 1938–50), VI, lviii.

[58] *Jones v. Securities and Exchange Commission,* 298 U.S. 1 (1936).

[59] *Colgate v. Harvey,* 296 U.S. 404 (1935).

spread use of "opportunistic" formula "to enforce their will" [60] evoked strong minority protest. Stone, in particular, was disturbed by "the shortage of time left for unshackling the government's legislative power before disaster ensued." Troubled by the Chief Justice's apparent effort to defeat the New Deal at all cost, he left two carefully prepared memoranda criticizing the cavalier way in which Hughes disposed of the cases in conference.[61]

All by narrow margins, these 1935–1936 decisions were obviously born of the travail of economic and political conflict. Justice Stone discerned in them the deliberate purpose of upsetting F.D.R.'s legislative program.[62]

We finished the term of Court yesterday, [Stone wrote his sister, June 2, 1936] I think in many ways one of the most disastrous in its history. At any rate it seems to me that the Court has been needlessly narrow and obscurantic in its outlook. I suppose no intelligent person likes very well the way the New Deal does things, but that ought not to make us forget that ours is a nation which should have the powers ordinarily possessed by governments, and that the framers of the Constitution intended that it should have. Our latest exploit was a holding by a divided vote that there was no

[60] Language of Learned Hand, "Chief Justice Stone's Conception of the Judicial Function," 46 *Columbia Law Review* 696 (1946), 698–99. Quoted in S. J. Konefsky, *The Legacy of Holmes and Brandeis: A Study in the Influence of Ideas* (New York, 1956), 234.

[61] See my *Harlan Fiske Stone,* 401–402, 414–16.

[62] Beginning with the October term 1933 through 1936, the Court held twelve acts of Congress unconstitutional, all but nullifying the New Deal. See Jackson, *The Struggle for Judicial Supremacy,* 86. The resulting disaster must be measured not only by the number of acts set aside but also in terms of the sweeping language of the opinions.

"All in all," Bernard Schwartz observes, "government by lawsuit during 1934–36 did much to render ineffective government by the elected representatives of the people. . . . In striking at the New Deal legislation, the Court allowed its language to run riot. It sought to engraft its own nineteenth-century laissez-faire philosophy into the Constitution. . . ." *The Supreme Court: Constitutional Revolution in Retrospect* (New York, 1957), 11–12.

power in a state to regulate minimum wages for women. Since the Court last week [in the Guffey Coal case] said that this could not be done by the national government, as the matter was local, and now it is said that it cannot be done by local governments even though it is local, we seem to have tied Uncle Sam up in a hard knot.

Dictated by political-economic dogma rather than by the Constitution, the commerce clause decisions marked a shrinking departure from Chief Justice Marshall's bold concept of the commerce power, a gratuitous betrayal of the grand design of the Constitution he extolled and enforced. The Justices made it apparent, Robert H. Jackson (later Justice) told the Judiciary Committee in 1937, that "the greatest objectives of this administration and this Congress offend their deep convictions." Recession from the Marshall conception, Bernard Schwartz writes,

fitted in perfectly with the laissez-faire theory of governmental function that dominated political and economic thinking for almost a century after the death of the great Chief Justice. To bar federal intervention, as the Supreme Court did in these cases [especially Guffey Coal] was all but to exclude the possibility of any effective regulation in them. This was, of course, exactly what was demanded by the advocates of laissez faire; for, to them, the economic system could function efficiently only if it was permitted to operate free from governmental interference. The Supreme Court's narrow notion of the commerce power was a necessary complement of laissez faire.[63]

Conservatives greeted the stalemate between Court and Congress with loud cheers. The vice president of the American Liberty League, Raoul E. Desvernine, applauded the Court as "the bulwark of defense against the subtle and skilful manipulation of democratic processes to achieve unsanctioned theories." [64] Former President

[63] *Ibid.*, 34.
[64] Raoul E. Desvernine, *Democratic Despotism* (New York, 1936), 182.

Fred O. Seibel in the Richmond Times-Dispatch, *January 8, 1937*

Hoover thanked "almighty God for the Constitution and the Supreme Court." [65] Hughes encouraged the acclaim. "I am happy to report," the Chief Justice told the American Law Institute, "that the Supreme Court is still func-

[65] Herbert Hoover, *Crisis of Free Men: A Series of Ten Addresses upon Pressing National Problems* (New York, 1936), 3.

tioning." His audience applauded so vigorously that the speaker had "to pause for more than two minutes." [66]

The President and his Cabinet referred to Hughes's speech as "political" and considered the desirability of a radio reply "demonstrating that the Supreme Court is in politics, with particular reference to the political activities of the Chief Justice himself." [67] The Chicago *Daily Tribune,* apparently of the same opinion, headed its account of the Law Institute speech: "CHIEF JUSTICE HUGHES APPEALS: PROTECT COURTS FROM TYRANNY." [68]

"Judicial usurpation" had again become a political warcry. Soon to be vindicated were precisely the forebodings Senate insurgents had voiced in 1930—that no human power could prevent the Court from becoming a "political issue."

Various correctives were open. As five or six recalcitrant Supreme Court Justices were chiefly responsible for the crisis, the simplest remedy lay within the power of the Court itself. But this was precisely the solution Chief Justice Hughes was most anxious to avoid. Reversal of decisions might mar the public image of judicial stability. Nevertheless, it was quite clear that the trouble lay not with the Constitution but with men, the nine Justices of the Supreme Court. "In law also," Felix Frankfurter commented in an essay of 1938, "men make a difference. . . . There is no inevitability in history except as men make it." [69] Armed with this brand of realism, F.D.R. girded for battle. Rather than resort to the long-drawn-out process of amending suggested by Chief Justice Hughes in his Guffey Coal concurrence, the President chose to effect a show-

[66] *New York Times,* May 8, 1936, p. 2, col. 2.

[67] Ickes, *The Secret Diary of Harold L. Ickes,* II, 136.

[68] *Ibid.*

[69] Frankfurter, *Mr. Justice Holmes and the Supreme Court* (Cambridge, Mass., 1938), 9.

down by drawing on existing constitutional resources—
congressional control over the size of the Court and the
President's appointing power. Soon after the 1936 election the President told George Creel that if the Supreme
Court set aside the Wagner Labor Disputes Act, the Social
Security Act, and other measures designed to promote the
general welfare, "Congress can enlarge the Supreme
Court, increasing the number of Justices from nine to
twelve or fifteen." [70]

In January, 1937, President Roosevelt told advisers of
his dominant preoccupation: "The time for action with
respect to the Supreme Court really cannot be postponed,
and unpleasant as it is, I think we have to face it." [71] "I
think," Interior Secretary Harold Ickes commented at
the first Cabinet meeting following the electoral landslide,
"that the President is getting ready to move in on that issue." [72]

Though seemingly favored by the gods, his proposal of
February 5, 1937, to reorganize the judiciary (dubbed
"Court-packing") immediately ran into strong opposition.
Overnight Supreme Court Justices were once more pic-
tured as demigods far above the sweaty crowd, abstractly
weighing public policy in the delicate scales of law. Con-

[70] George Creel, "Roosevelt's Plans and Purposes," *Collier's*,
December 26, 1936.

[71] Samuel I. Rosenman, *Working with Roosevelt* (New York,
1952), 153.

As to the President's action, Attorney General Jackson wrote:
"The Court Reorganization Message of President Roosevelt was the
political manifestation of a long smouldering intellectual revolt
against the philosophy of many of the Supreme Court's decisions
on constitutional questions. This protest was led by outspoken
and respected members of the Court itself. Among its most influen-
tial spokesmen were those in our universities distinguished for dis-
interested legal scholarship. It counted among its followers many
thoughtful conservatives and practically all liberal and labor leadership." Jackson, *The Struggle for Judicial Supremacy*, v.

[72] Ickes, *The Secret Diary of Harold L. Ickes*, I, 705.

stitutionality was discussed as if it were undeviating and precise, rather than a majority of the Justices' "current theory of what ought and what ought not to be done under the Constitution." [73] The same congressmen who, prior to Roosevelt's proposal, had demanded the scalps of reactionary Justices now turned angrily against the President. Closing ranks with the bar associations, the newspapers lined up heavily against Court-packing. There were big headlines and lots of them. Staunchly upholding the shattered myth that in constitutional cases judges discover *the* law, merely place the controverted statute beside the relevant clause of the Constitution, American Bar Association President Frederick H. Stinchfield wrote:

He [F.D.R.] derisively uses the word veto as applied to the Supreme Court. Now, each of us is aware that the Supreme Court, in no sense, exercises a veto. What the Court does is to examine the legislation in the light of the Constitution, to ascertain whether or not any of the liberties retained by the people or by the individual states are invaded by the legislation. If they find that to be true, the Court declares the legislation invalid because of the invasion of retained rights. With the legislation, as such, or with its present significance, the Court has no dealing.[74]

Every segment of society was soon joined in the struggle. Only the Justices themselves kept evasively silent. Few doubted where they stood, or that they held the trump card in the game. The problem was to enlist them in the squabble without impairing their professional assumptions of dignity, or showing up the fiction as to their remoteness from politics. Senator Burton K. Wheeler, leader of the opposition to Roosevelt's plan, hesitated to consult members of the Court on a purely political matter. The senator knew personally only one Justice, and as the hour

[73] Rexford G. Tugwell, *Battle for Democracy* (New York, 1935), 12.
[74] *American Bar Association Journal*, Vol. 23 (April 1937), 235.

approached for his appointment with Justice Brandeis, known to be a stickler for the proprieties, Wheeler became quite apprehensive. As the interview began, he realized that this anxiety was groundless.

"Why don't you confer with the Chief Justice?" Brandeis suggested. The senator demurred, explaining that he did not know Mr. Hughes. "Well," Brandeis said reassuringly, "the Chief Justice knows you and knows what you are doing." [75]

Events moved swiftly. The senator did not reach him until Saturday, March 20, but the Chief Justice prepared a long and closely reasoned document to present to the Judiciary Committee on the following Monday, March 22. "The baby is born," Hughes said "with a broad smile as he put the letter into Wheeler's hand" late Sunday afternoon.[76]

The Chief Justice's cold statistical analysis scotched the President's allegation that the Justices had fallen behind their docket. "The Supreme Court is fully abreast of its work," Hughes wrote. "There is no congestion of cases upon our calendar. This gratifying condition has obtained for several years." "An increase in the number of Justices would not," he said, "promote the efficiency of the Court." Repressing the doubts he had voiced in his book of 1928 on the propriety of advisory judgments, the Chief Justice ventured the opinion that the proposal of an enlarged Court to hear cases in divisions might run afoul of the constitutional provision for "one Supreme Court." "The Constitution does not appear to authorize two or more Supreme Courts or two or more parts of a Supreme Court functioning in effect as separate courts," he said.

[75] For the full story see my *Brandeis: A Free Man's Life* (New York, 1946), 625–26. Wheeler has since elaborated the incident in his *Yankee from the West: The Crowded Turbulent Life Story of the Yankee-born U.S. Senator from Montana* (New York, 1962).

[76] Pusey, *Charles Evans Hughes,* II, 755.

"On account of the shortness of time," Hughes explained, "I have not been able to consult with members of the Court generally," but he was "confident that it is in accord with the views of the justices." [77] Ignoring the customary disavowal of authority to speak for those not consulted, the Chief Justice thus conveyed the impression that the entire Court endorsed his letter.

Hughes's biographer suggests that "considering the delicacy of the issue, Hughes' action with the approval of only two (Brandeis and Van Devanter) of his eight colleagues was certainly a tactical error." [78] But was it? If the Chief Justice had consulted all his colleagues, they would have been divided. In that case, there might have been no letter, or at least a very different one.

Wheeler and others immediately drew the inference that whatever the Court's differences on other matters, they were unanimous on the Chief Justice's letter. It was not until 1939 that the matter was clarified. "I should perhaps have put the matter in its proper light at the time," Justice Stone wrote Felix Frankfurter, December 29, 1939, "but it did not occur to me that such an expression of opinion would, in the circumstances, be attributed to members of the Court who were not consulted. . . ."

I first learned of the Chief Justice's letter, [Stone's letter continues] when a copy of it was printed in the newspapers shortly after its date. I was not consulted in connection with its preparation. Justice Cardozo told me that he was not. I have never formed any opinion on the constitutional point in question or discussed it with any members of the Court.

There was no reason of which I am aware why all the members of the Court should not have been consulted in connection with the preparation of a document which purported to

[77] For full text of the Hughes letter, see "Reorganization of Federal Judiciary," *Hearings before the Senate Judiciary Committee,* 75th Congress, 1st Session, Part III, 488–92.

[78] Pusey, *Charles Evans Hughes,* II, 756.

state "the views of the Justices," or for expressing the views of Justices who for any reason could not be consulted. Although the Court was then in recess, all its members were in the city. They could have been brought together for a conference on an hour's telephone notice, or less. Throughout the recess Justices Sutherland, Cardozo, and myself were in our homes, which are five minutes' walk of the residence of the Chief Justice.[79]

The Chief Justice's letter put a crimp on President Roosevelt's plan for overhauling the Court. But it did not rebut the fact that many leading citizens considered reform as necessary now as in the days of Jackson and Grant. While the fight raged around them, the Court itself, as if to confess its guilt, went on playing fast and loose with the Chief Justice's primary values—stability and continuity of judicial decisions. The first redoubt to fall was that most recent, *Morehead* v. *Tipaldo*, the decision of less than a year before, which set aside the New York minimum wage law. Misled by the Chief Justice's dialectic, Robert H. Jackson commented later on: "The Chief Justice read the opinion confessing error. But his voice was of triumph. He was reversing his Court, but not himself. He was declaring in March the law as he would have declared it the previous June, had his dissent been heeded." [80]

But in fact it was not quite that way. Taking specific exception to the narrow basis of Hughes's dissent in the Tipaldo case, Stone had said:

While I agree with all the Chief Justice has said, I would not make the differences between the present statute and that involved in the Adkins case the sole basis of decision. I attach little importance to the fact that the earlier statute was aimed only at a starvation wage and that the present one does

[79] H. F. Stone to Felix Frankfurter, Dec. 29, 1939 (Stone Papers).
[80] Jackson, *The Struggle for Judicial Supremacy*, 208. The overruling case was *West Coast Hotel* v. *Parrish*, 300 U.S. 379 (1937).

not prohibit such a wage unless it is also less than the reasonable value of the service. Since neither statute compels employment at any wage, I do not assume that employers in one case, more than in the other, would pay the minimum wage if the service were worth less.

In words directed to Hughes's dissent quite as much as to the majority, Stone continued: "The vague and general pronouncement of the Fourteenth Amendment against deprivation of liberty without due process of law is a limitation of legislative power, not a formula for its exercise. It does not purport to say in what particular manner that power shall be exerted. It makes no fine-spun distinctions between methods which the legislature may and which it may not choose to resolve a pressing problem of government."

With specific reference to the claims of "stability" and continuity of judicial decisions to which the Chief Justice had paid lip service, Stone concluded: "Unless we are now to construe and apply the Fourteenth Amendment without regard to our decisions since the Adkins case, we could not rightly avoid its reconsideration even if it were not asked. We should follow our decision in the Nebbia case and leave the selection and the method of solution of the problems to which the statute is addressed where it seems to me the Constitution has left them, to the legislative branch of the government." [81]

On April 1, 1937, Justice Stone elaborated the distinction between his own position and that of Hughes. "The Chief Justice wrote an opinion that the New York statute was distinguishable in some of its features from that one before the Court in the Adkins case, and that the Adkins consequently was not controlling. I wrote an opinion stating that while I agreed that there were the distinctions pointed out by the Chief Justice, I, nevertheless, thought

[81] *Morehead* v. *Tipaldo,* 631–32, 636.

that it should be placed on broader grounds, namely that due process had nothing to do with wage regulation wherever at least there was a serious legislative problem presented. . . . Monday the Chief Justice wrote the opinion, overruling the Adkins case and *adopting the views expressed in my opinion of last June.*"

Applying the standards Hughes set up in 1928 for self-inflicted wounds, *Morehead* v. *Tipaldo* must be added to the judiciary's arsenal along with Dred Scott, Hepburn and Pollock, and so forth.

Hughes's opinion for the Court in *West Coast Hotel* v. *Parrish* (1937), upholding the minimum wage on the broad ground insisted on by Stone, indicates that an important change had occurred in his thinking about the best way to achieve stability. Within a year after the New York minimum wage law was thrown out, during a period in which the Presidential election[82] and the Court-packing threat intervened, Chief Justice Hughes appraised stability precisely in the terms Brandeis, Holmes, and Stone had long advocated. For now he saw with Edmund Burke that "a state without the means of some change is without the means of its own conservation." Now he realized that "without the means of such change it might even risque the loss of that part of the Constitution which it wished most religiously to preserve." [83]

On the same day that the Hughes-Roberts switch won judicial sanction for minimum wages, a chastened Court unanimously approved broad extensions of national power. "What a day!" Robert H. Jackson gloated. "To labor, minimum-wage laws and collective bargaining; to farmers,

[82] This factor should not be minimized. Roosevelt's victory was 523 to 8 electoral votes—the most overwhelming electoral endorsement since the 1820 re-election of President James Monroe.

[83] Burke, *Reflections on the French Revolution*, 10.

relief in bankruptcy; to law enforcement, the fire arms control. The Court was on the march!" [84]

But the central and vital issue remained unresolved. What was to be the fate of the Wagner Labor Relations Act? The answer came on April 12, 1937, when in a series of cases led by that of *NLRB* v. *Jones and Laughlin Steel Corp.*,[85] Chief Justice Hughes put forward a broad and encompassing definition of interstate commerce, conceding to Congress power to protect the lifelines of national economy from private industrial warfare. Arguments that had proved effective in the Schechter Brothers and Guffey Coal cases were now unavailing.

"These cases," the Chief Justice commented summarily, "are not controlling here." They were not controlling because he now chose to stress that fundamental distinction between direct and indirect effects as one of degree rather than of kind. They were not binding because he now minimized the point emphasized in the Schechter case, namely, that the fundamental nature of the distinction between direct and indirect effects of intrastate transactions upon interstate commerce arises from the fact that it is "essential to the maintenance of our constitutional system." Interstate commerce was now seen as a practical conception. Interference with it "must be appraised by a judgment that does not ignore actual experience." Somewhat disdainfully the Chief Justice now declared that, in the light of the industry's farflung activities, it was idle to say that interference by strikes or other labor disturbances "would be indirect or remote. It is obvious that it would be immediate and might be catastrophic." [86]

Even after these dramatic shifts took place, Hughes, in keeping with the high value he placed on continuity of

[84] Jackson, *The Struggle for Judicial Supremacy*, 213.
[85] *NLRB* v. *Jones and Laughlin Steel Corp.*, 301 U.S. 1 (1937).
[86] *Ibid.*, 41–42 *passim*.

judicial decisions, tried to make it seem as if the Court had stood firm all along. Since the facts were not exactly the same, he would have us believe that these reversals of recently established precedents must be excluded from the ignominious category of self-inflicted wounds. The

"Spring Practice"; Hungerford in the Pittsburgh Post Gazette, *April 1, 1937*

Chief Justice's colleagues and others thought they knew better and said so quite irreverently. "Every consideration brought forward to uphold the Act before us was applicable to support the Acts held unconstitutional in causes decided within two years," [87] Justice McReynolds bellowed in his Jones and Laughlin dissent. Justice Sutherland reminded the new majority now supporting minimum wages of a point the Chief Justice himself had made in his Guffey Coal concurrence, that the judicial function "does not include the power of amendment under the guise of interpretation." [88] Justice Stone, now in the majority, sent off a report in substantial agreement with the complaint of the dissenters. "The Wagner Labor decisions" (Jones and Laughlin, etc.), he wrote, "seem popularly to be regarded as very revolutionary, and perhaps they are in view of the decision of the Court in the Guffey Coal case." [89] President Roosevelt was unfeignedly incredulous. "It would be a little naive," the President commented on Hughes's insistence that no judicial shift had occurred, "to refuse to recognize some connection between these 1937 decisions and the Supreme Court fight." [90] Congress had improved the draftsmanship of legislation, it is true, but it is hard to believe, as apologists for Hughes insist, that the "revolution" was legislative rather than judicial.

To Professor Corwin the conclusion seemed inescapable that the Chief Justice had seen a new light.[91] If the Con-

[87] *Ibid.*, 77.

[88] *West Coast Hotel* v. *Parrish*, 300 U.S. 379 (1937), 404.

[89] H. F. Stone to his sons, April 15, 1937 (Stone Papers).

[90] Roosevelt, *Public Papers and Addresses*, VI, lxix.
Starting in March, 1937, only a few weeks after the President submitted his court-packing proposal, Bernard Schwartz writes, the Court "upheld every New Deal law presented to it, including some that were basically similar to earlier statutes which it had nullified. It is, in fact, hardly too far-fetched to assert that, in 1937, there took place a veritable revolution in the jurisprudence of the Supreme Court." *The Supreme Court*, 16.

[91] E. S. Corwin, "The Court Sees New Light," *New Republic*, August 4, 1937, p. 354. See also Corwin's penetrating review of

stitution on May 18, 1936, when the Guffey Coal case was decided, prevented Congress, without resort to constitutional amendment, from regulating employer-employee relationship in industry, then the Constitution was in that respect amended on April 12, 1937, when the Wagner Labor Relations Act was upheld. These 1937 decisions "marked the beginning of a significant return to the commerce-clause jurisprudence of John Marshall." [92] "A retreat to the Constitution," [93] Robert H. Jackson called it.

Those who had watched the Court's disingenuous strategy from afar ridiculed the Chief Justice's avowal of consistency. "We are told," a paragrapher for the *New Yorker* noted, "that the Supreme Court's about-face was not due to outside clamor. It seems that the new building has a sound-proof room, to which the Justices retire to change their minds." [94]

The secret was out. "Americans learned," in the words of Max Lerner, "that judges are human, and that the judicial power need be no more sacred in our scheme than any other power. . . . They dared look upon the judicial Medusa-head, and lo! they were not turned to stone. . . . It was then that the symbol of divine right began to crumble." [95]

The law, however, had not been clarified. Indeed, Chief Justice Hughes's customary dialectics had left the situation more clouded than ever.

What are the facts? Did Hughes shift? The answer must be, like the Jones and Laughlin opinion itself, equivocal.

Hughes's views on the scope of the commerce power do

Pusey's biography in *American Political Science Review* (1952), 1171–72.

[92] Schwartz, *The Supreme Court*, 34.

[93] Jackson, *The Struggle for Judicial Supremacy*, 197.

[94] Howard Brubaker, "Of All Things," *New Yorker*, April 10, 1937, p. 34.

[95] Max Lerner, *Ideas for the Ice Age* (New York, 1941), 259–60.

seem to have undergone change. His concurrence in the Guffey Coal case subscribed to Sutherland's distinction between indirect and direct effects on commerce, and to the principle that labor relations are, by their very nature, beyond the realm of federal control. In the Jones and Laughlin case he tried hard to distinguish the earlier ruling, but the two decisions still seem quite inconsistent. Professor Corwin detects "a revolutionary shift" in Hughes's conception of the relation of the commerce power to the states. But the Chief Justice did retain a tie with the past. For though the Jones and Laughlin opinion is the high-water mark of his liberal interpretation of the commerce clause, he still held on to the distinction "between what is national and what is local in the activities of commerce" and cited the Tenth Amendment as an explicit bar against national authority. "He could," Thomas Reed Powell commented, "pose polar opposites without confessing that they were opposites, but he would leave it clear what the Court was deciding." [96]

[96] Thomas Reed Powell, "Charles Evans Hughes," 67 *Political Science Quarterly* 161 (1952), 172.

Others noted this quality, especially in the Chief Justice's gold clause opinions. In reply to Frankfurter's request for comment on an article ("Chief Justices I Have Known," *loc. cit.*) in which he rated Hughes considerably above Chief Justice White, John W. Davis observed:

"I think the main difference is that I put White ahead of Hughes. Hughes had a better-trained mind, a more scholarly mind, than White, but from the point of view of personal character I would put White ahead of Hughes. . . . He (Hughes) was too apt to reach his conclusion and then reason to it, instead of reasoning to it and reaching his conclusion. For instance, in the gold cases, if you marched right down the line you'd say, 'He's going to declare that void.' Then all at once, without any warning, he turned at right angles and declared it good. I don't think anybody can ever read that opinion and find out where the mental processes were."

For similar reactions of Justice Stone, Judge Learned Hand, and others to Hughes's opinions in the gold clause cases, see my *Harlan Fiske Stone*, 388–92. Burton C. Bernard ("Avoidance of Constitu-

Powell's diagnosis penetrates only one aspect of the Hughes enigma. The usual effect of the Chief Justice's opinions was not to clarify what the Court was doing but to becloud and confuse. "On questions involving social issues," the *New Republic* editorialized June 9, 1941, "it was almost always more difficult to predict where Hughes would stand than where other members of the Court would be found."

It was this aspect of the Chief Justice's jurisprudence that notably aroused Justice Stone. "I can hardly see the use of writing judicial opinions," Stone savagely exploded shortly after the six-three decision setting aside AAA, "unless they are to embody methods of analysis and of exposition which will serve the profession as a guide to the decision of future cases. If they are not better than an excursion ticket, good for this day and trip only, they do not serve even as protective coloration for the writer of the opinions and would much better be left unsaid." [97]

Frankfurter and other close students of the Court's work were puzzled and critical. A week before Stone's acid comment was made, the Justice had responded to Professor Frankfurter's persistent request for explanation of the meandering course of judicial decisions under Hughes's leadership:

It seems that you have been trying to find an answer to a question which continually recurs to you, as it does to me. I don't know that I shall ever reach a satisfactory answer, but perhaps it can be summed up in two phrases which you have doubtless heard me repeat before: lack of vision and the unwillingness of certain gentlemen to trust their own intellectual processes.

tional Issues in the United States Supreme Court: Liberties of the First Amendment," 50 *Michigan Law Review* 261 [1951], 274–76) notes the same trait in cases involving First Amendment freedoms.

[97] H. F. Stone to Felix Frankfurter, February 25, 1936 (Stone Papers).

Just why we should be afflicted as we are just at present is another question, but I think there has never been a time in the history of the Court when there has been so little intelligible, recognizable pattern in its judicial performance as in the last few years. Take, for example, as simple a matter as the presumption to which we occasionally pay lip service in favor of the constitutionality of a statute. It would be interesting to have some of your bright young men discover how often in recent years it has been relied upon and repudiated by the same judge. . . . It just seems as though, in some of these cases, the writer and those who united with him didn't care what was said, as long as the opinion seemed plausible on its face, if not compared with any other. The worst of it is that the one [Hughes] that you find it most difficult to understand is the one chiefly responsible.[98]

In 1940 it was no longer possible for the Chief Justice to follow his usual strategy of "posing polar opposites." For in that year the Court upheld the far-reaching Fair Labor Standards Act. Speaking for a unanimous bench, Justice Stone stated flatly that the Tenth Amendment was a "truism." "Our conclusion is unaffected by the Tenth Amendment," he observed. "There is nothing in the history of its adoption to suggest that it was more than declaratory of the relationship between the national and state governments as it had been established by the Constitution before the amendment or that its purpose was other than to allay fears that the new national government might seek to exercise powers not granted. . . ." [99]

In the face of this unequivocal ruling it could no longer be maintained that the Tenth Amendment reserves to the

[98] H. F. Stone to Felix Frankfurter, February 17, 1936 (Stone Papers).

[99] *United States* v. *Darby*, 312 U.S. 100 (1941), 123–24. Compare the words of Chief Justice Marshall (*McCulloch* v. *Maryland*, 4 Wheaton 316 [1819], 406). Marshall says that the purpose of those who framed the Tenth Amendment was that of "quieting the excessive jealousies which had been excited."

states any inviolable sovereignty whatsoever.[100] The Chief
Justice's constitutional dialectics were at long last frustrated. The next year he quit the Court.

"What happened in the 30's," Judge Charles E. Clark
asked in 1952, "that affairs could so suddenly develop to
a crisis without careful planning and forethought of the
judiciary's role?" [101] The answer may be put in terms of
the value Hughes placed on stability, interpreted at first
as requiring merely continuity of judicial decisions. This
value prevailed even after the Court surrendered under
Presidential pressure. Determination to hold fast the
appearance of stability even while shifting decisions is the
key to Charles Evans Hughes's constitutional jurisprudence. "The whole tone of the Chief Justice's elaborate
opinion" (in the Jones and Laughlin case), Samuel Konefsky has written, "carried the implication that he was not
saying anything new." [102]

The Chief Justice, Judge Clark suggests, seemed to think
of his function as "a holding operation, to keep the Court
as it was, to 'save' it from the attack of the democratic
leader elected by the people. . . . To attempt to control
or shape the future of the Court, or to direct it in strange
waters would have been foreign to his nature." [103]

---

[100] As to the Court's decision, former Justice Roberts commented:
"Of course, the effect of sustaining the act was to place the whole
matter of wages and hours of persons employed throughout the
United States, with slight exceptions, under a single federal regulatory scheme and in this way completely to supersede state exercise
of the police power in this field." See *The Court and the Constitution* (Cambridge, Mass., 1951), 56; see also 38. It was this entering
wedge that Hughes fought off to the bitter end.

[101] Review of Pusey's *Charles Evans Hughes,* 27 *Notre Dame
Lawyer* (Spring, 1952), 481.

[102] Review of Pusey's *Charles Evans Hughes,* 61 *Yale Law Journal*
765 (1952), 774

[103] Lerner, *Ideas for the Ice Age,* 259–60.

"When," Samuel Hendel declares, "the pressure for innovation became great, and the risks to the nation and to the Court itself apparent, reluctantly at first, but increasingly he went along with change. Having sedulously sought to protect the precedents of the Court, sometimes at the risk of offending logic, he witnessed and often participated in the shattering of one precedent after another. He stood thus as a kind of heroic and, in a sense, tragic figure, torn between the old and the new, seeking at first to stem the tide but then relentlessly caught up and moving with it." [104]

Hendel's observation heightens the irony and may perhaps deepen the mystery. At stake was Hughes's own prestige as well as that of the institution he headed. So completely did he identify himself with the Court as an institution, that observers became quite confused. "The Chief Justice," the *New Republic* commented on the Court fight, "could hardly have been concerned with prudential considerations concerning himself or his prestige. . . . But he may well have been governed by the prestige of the Court and its influence on the life of the nation. . . ." [105]

The outcome does not support this hypothesis. Judge Clark refers to the Chief Justice going "to rather extreme lengths to distinguish away rather than overrule, out-worn cases." Another commentator notes Hughes's "consummate skill in distinguishing adverse or apparently adverse cases." [106] Another close student of the Chief Justice's jurisprudence holds that "few judges were more adept in clinging to precedents in the very process of their emascula-

[104] Samuel Hendel, *Charles Evans Hughes and the Supreme Court* (New York, 1951), 279. See also Irving Brant, "How Liberal Is Justice Hughes?" *New Republic*, 1937, pp. 295–98, 329–32.

[105] *New Republic,* June 9, 1941, p. 777.

[106] F. D. G. Ribble, "The Constitutional Doctrines of Charles Evans Hughes," 41 *Columbia Law Review* 1190 (1941), 1210.

tion or repudiation than Hughes." [107] So far as the Court was concerned this effort was fruitless. Observers are practically unanimous in believing that the somersault of 1937 revolutionized judicial decisions, but they are about equally certain that Hughes never reversed himself. By laying down a constitutional smokescreen, he came through the battle with his reputation unscathed, indeed enhanced. The Court, however, suffered from a host of self-inflicted wounds.

So successfully did the Chief Justice camouflage his own activities that commentators were misled. Attorney-General Jackson mistakenly declared, as we have seen, that in the triumphant minimum wage decision of 1937, "the Chief Justice . . . was reversing his Court, but not himself." [108] Attorney-General Francis Biddle, also misinformed, said that in sustaining the Washington statute the Chief Justice "reiterated [?] the views stated shortly before in his dissent in the case from New York." [109] Professor Noel T. Dowling believed that "West Coast Hotel is a natural consequence of Hughes' earlier exposition of due process of law, particularly in the Tipaldo case. . . ." [110] Each of these commentators overlooked the narrow bases of Hughes's New York minimum wage dissent, and Stone's fruitless effort to get him to lay solid foundations for a reversal.

The Chief Justice kept his judicial skirts clear with equal success in the commerce clause cases. By comparing his position in the Jones and Laughlin case with his earlier views as an Associate Justice, and by ignoring the intervening Guffey Coal concurrence, it was concluded that

[107] Hendel, "The 'Liberalism' of Chief Justice Hughes," *loc. cit.,* 268.
[108] Jackson, *The Struggle for Judicial Supremacy,* 208.
[109] 41 *Columbia Law Review* 1157 (1941), 1158.
[110] Review of Pusey's *Charles Evans Hughes,* 38 *Virginia Law Review* 271 (1952), 273.

"Jones and Laughlin Steel is a direct descendant of the Shreveport Rate Case, where the opinion on the commerce clause was by none other than Associate Justice Hughes in 1914." [111] Hughes's judicial smokescreen was so thick that the most discerning could not tell a dissent from a concurrence. "On the crucial issue of federal power," Attorney-General Biddle observed, "Chief Justice Hughes' dissents in the *Alton Railroad* case and again in the case of the *Carter Coal Company* [sic] advanced the views which ultimately prevailed when he spoke for a majority of the Court, sustaining the National Labor Relations Act under the commerce clause. . . ." [112] "Hughes was generally on the 'liberal side,'" F. B. Weiner wrote, "as his powerful and eloquent dissents in *Retirement Board* v. *Alton Railroad, Morehead* v. *New York ex rel Tipaldo* [?] and *Carter* v. *Carter Coal* [sic] amply demonstrate." [113]

Whether full awareness of Hughes's subtleties would have affected the estimate of him as "a great Chief Justice," one cannot say. But one thing is certain—the circumlocution exhibited in formulating this estimate rivals that of Hughes himself: "One can find apparent inconsistencies in his legal reasoning from one decision to another," the *New Republic* observed on June 9, 1941. "Mr. Chief Justice Hughes will probably be remembered not as a great jurist in the technical sense, but rather as a great judicial statesman." "To seek the equal of Hughes among the Chief Justices," Francis Biddle suggested, "the mind turns back to Marshall and Taney, and dwells longer on Marshall as his true predecessor. . . ." "He was a great man, and a great Chief Justice,"

[111] *Ibid.*
[112] Francis Biddle in 41 *Columbia Law Review* 1157 (1941).
[113] Review of Pusey's *Charles Evans Hughes*, 20 *George Washington Law Review* 359 (1952), 361.

Weiner commented. "His constitutional views were sound, he had precious little backtracking to do. . . ."[114]

On June 2, 1937, after the dust of Court-packing battle had settled, Felix Frankfurter, later Justice, began to suspect that a deliberate effort was under way to fix the Chief Justice's place in history. "A synthetic halo," he wrote Justice Stone, "is being fitted upon the head of the most politically calculating of men." Samuel Konefsky's appraisal is more charitable:

Hughes was profoundly convinced that what was at stake in the crisis precipitated by the Court Plan was nothing less than the fate of the Supreme Court's historic role as "guardian" of the Constitution. . . . The decision to retreat in the immediate skirmish in order to insure victory in the larger "struggle for judicial supremacy" need not have come as the result of active intrigue or cajoling of colleagues. . . . Neither the Chief Justice nor Mr. Justice Roberts—the two key participants in the judicial "about face"—was so fixed in his basic constitutional philosophy that the "switch" in their application of essentially flexible doctrines demanded sacrifice of "soul." [115]

Hughes's biographer, Merlo J. Pusey, promptly took exception to the shadows Konefsky cast upon the Chief Justice's statesmanship. Quoting from Hughes's so-called biographical notes, Pusey pointed out that the Chief Justice himself had said "there was not the slightest change in my viewpoint as a result of the President's action as to the Supreme Court." Standing firm, reinforcing his position and broadening his attack, Konefsky suggested that biography based on the subject's "notes" may not be the most effective way to write history: "In the history of social forces, even as in the life of an individual, there are times when conduct speaks for itself, particularly when

114 *Ibid.*, 362.
115 S. J. Konefsky, review of Pusey's *Charles Evans Hughes*, 61 *Yale Law Journal* 765 (1952), 774.

the course that is pursued represents a crucial choice in the presence of reasonable alternatives. Just as hindsight is no substitute for insight, so the backward glance even by an honest man may turn out to be a kind of ex post facto rationalization. . . . [I]t is conceivable that Hughes' lofty conception of the judicial function may have made it difficult to admit even to himself that the Court played strategy." [116]

An explanation of Hughes's strategy involves practical considerations. After February, 1937, both he and Justice Roberts had fresh insights as to how the judiciary might contribute to stability. These Justices on the flying trapeze finally learned what Brandeis, Stone, and Cardozo had tried so long and hard to teach—that the majority's obscurantist assumption of power in the face of unprecedented public pressure on Congress and in support of the President, had in fact aided the forces of radicalism, made for uncertainty rather than stability, and placed in jeopardy both Court and Constitution. It became clear that guardianship of the Constitution did not mean unswerving adherence to a highy conceptualized view of the federal system, much less the enforcement of any particular economic dogmas. It meant an elevated sense of responsibility to the "undefined and expanding future" envisaged by the framers conscious of what this nation might become. This, in essence, was the constitutional jurisprudence of Marshall, Holmes, Stone, Brandeis, and Cardozo. It marked a return to the wisdom Hughes himself had expressed in 1928—that proper discharge of the judicial function depends less on formulas and more "on a correct appreciation of social conditions and a true appraisal of the actual effect of conduct." [117]

At first he had sought, in line with views expressed in

[116] *Yale Law Journal* 62 (1953), 313–14.
[117] Hughes, *The Supreme Court of the United States,* 166.

his book of 1928, to maintain public confidence by continuity of judicial decision. He adhered, more or less consistently, to this narrow view during the early years of his Chief Justiceship. In 1937, however, he was destined to lead his Court in reversals that made the "serious mistake" committed in "overruling" *Hepburn* v. *Griswold*, "in such a short time," [118] pale by comparison. Stability still ranked high in his hierarchy of values, but he had now discovered other ways of achieving it. "Hughes had the acumen," the *Nation* commented June 14, 1941, "to recognize the inevitable." As Robert H. Jackson, later Associate Justice, put it: "He evidently came in a decade to the belief that to be right is a better way of maintaining respect than to be stable in the wrong." [119]

That same light broke in on Justice Roberts. In 1951, he said:

Looking back, it is difficult to see how the Court could have resisted the popular urge for uniform standards throughout the country—for what in effect was a unified economy. . . . An insistence by the Court on holding federal power to what seemed its appropriate orbit when the Constitution was adopted might have resulted in even more radical changes in our dual structure than those which have been gradually accomplished through the extension of the limited jurisdiction conferred on the federal government.[120]

The popular urge of which Justice Roberts speaks, and which he and Chief Justice Hughes had for a time ignored,

[118] *Ibid.*, 52.
[119] Jackson, *The Struggle for Judicial Supremacy*, 44.
[120] Roberts, *The Court and the Constitution*, 61–62.

"The earnestness and extent of popular demand," Professor F. D. G. Ribble has observed, "may well have been a factor in determining this adjustment. Those who believe that judges legislate . . . will have no difficulty with the idea that in legislating they may take into some account the scale of values of the people for whom their task is performed." See "The Constitutional Doctrines of Charles Evans Hughes," *loc. cit.*, 1199–1200.

found effective expression in Roosevelt's plan to pack the Supreme Court. Responding to it in 1937, Hughes and Roberts felt the same pressure and were perhaps motivated by the same conservative impulses that prompted the President's audacious proposal.

After 1937 the Justices were somewhat less concerned than formerly to avoid any action that might remove the protective coloration disguising their power. President Taft feared, as we have seen, that reversal of the income tax decision by an ordinary act of Congress might impair the Court's prestige and jeopardize judicial magic. Taft successfully advocated the amending process as the appropriate way out, thus delaying the income tax for nearly twenty years. In 1937, however, without resort to the formal amending process, without a single change in judicial personnel, the Justices had suddenly amended the Constitution. "In politics," Jackson commented, "the blackrobed reactionary Justices had won over the master liberal politician of our day. In law the President defeated the recalcitrant Justices in their own Court." [121] Thus Roosevelt's major premise, that the judicial function in the constitutional field is inevitably political, was confirmed by the Court itself.

The decision to retreat in the immediate skirmish in order to win in the more crucial battle for judicial supremacy must be credited primarily to Chief Justice Hughes. His was, to say the least, a skillfully executed campaign. For political-judicial maneuvers of equal cunning one must revert to 1803, and to that struggle of the giants in *Marbury* v. *Madison.* Just as arch-Federalist Chief Justice Marshall scored in his encounter with President Jefferson, resourceful leader of Democratic Republicanism, so Chief Justice Hughes handily outdid Roosevelt, the most astute politician of modern times. Albert

[121] Jackson, *The Struggle for Judicial Supremacy,* 196.

J. Beveridge applauds John Marshall's epoch-making decision as "a coup as bold in design and as daring in execution as that by which the Constitution was framed." Cubits
were thereby added to Marshall's judicial stature. Though
Hughes's political victory in the Court-packing struggle is
comparable to that of Marshall in the Marbury case, no
such accolade has been accorded him. It seems odd that
Hughes's admirers and apologists should be at such great
pains to note other similarities between the two Chief
Justices, yet be notably reluctant to portray their hero
in the role that most closely resembles Marshall—that of
political strategist. This failure or oversight is significant.
Under John Marshall's leadership, the Court exerted a
political influence freely recognized by his contemporaries
and fully credited in the long perspective of history. Lat-
ter-day judicial politics, on the other hand, must be disguised as theology.

For those bent on scuttling the President's plan the
Hughes and Roberts switch came in the nick of time. But
the victory was not unmixed. To defeat the President's
plan, the Justices had to backtrack, and Roosevelt never
doubted that his own "clear-cut victory on the bench did
more than anything else to bring about the defeat of the
plan in the halls of Congress." Before a single judge retired, before any appointment was made "the Court began
to interpret the Constitution instead of torturing it." [122]
Out of this historic struggle a new-old Constitution was
destined to emerge.

The idea of Chief Justice Hughes heading a revolution[123] staggers the imagination. It is irony beyond belief

[122] Roosevelt, *Public Papers and Addresses,* 1937 volume, lxvii,
passim.

[123] What took place in the councils of the Supreme Court in the
spring of 1937 has usually been characterized as a "revolution." A
more accurate description of what happened, especially in the light
of subsequent developments, is Professor Corwin's expression—
Constitutional Revolution, Ltd.

that he, a jurist whose primary value was stability, should have sanctioned a constitutional transformation which, in terms of scope and speed of execution, is unprecedented in the annals of the Supreme Court. To accomplish it, he and Justice Roberts had to beat a retreat. Among the first casualties was the ancient myth that judges can will nothing. Yet the two Justices especially responsible for its destruction tried to keep the fiction alive.[124] In the decision that upset AAA, Justice Roberts solemnly avowed that the 6 to 3 majority merely performed a squaring operation.

It is sometimes said that the Court assumes a power to overrule or control the action of the people's representatives. This is a misconception. . . . When an act of Congress is appropriately challenged in the Courts as not conforming to the constitutional mandate the judicial branch of the Government has only one duty—to lay the article of the Constitution which is invoked beside the statute which is challenged and to decide whether the latter squares with the former. All the Court does, or can do, is to announce its considered judgment upon the question. The only power it has, if such it may be called, is the power of judgment. This Court neither approves nor condemns any legislative policy.[125]

Chief Justice Hughes also kept the judicial helplessness pose. When Court-packing supporters quoted his aphorism

[124] "It was the conversion of 'odd men' Roberts and Hughes that made the constitutional revolution of 1937 possible." Schwartz, *The Supreme Court,* 20.

[125] *United States* v. *Butler,* 62–63.

Roberts' statement is the more remarkable in the light of his own record. Professor Fred Rodell calls him "the perfect personification of the chanciness of government by judges. It was he who, during a court career from 1930 to 1945, changed his mind and his major votes three separate times—from liberal to conservative to liberal to conservative—on the bedrock issue of government power to regulate business; it was he who, by holding the decisive Court vote in the first three stages of his switch act, was for years the most powerful person in the United States." Rodell, *Nine Men,* 221.

of 1907, "The Constitution is what the judges say it is,"
he became greatly annoyed. These words made it appear
that the Chief Justice himself had long ago given the lie
to official theory. Of course, nothing could have been
further from his purpose than to shake public confidence
by revealing the Court as a lawmaker.[126] Stability, or the
appearance of it, must be maintained—even to the point
of preserving erroneous precedents and denying power
granted by the Constitution. The irony of Hughes's Chief
Justiceship is that he should have demonstrated what his
own smug assertions were at such pains to deny, even by
inference. By 1937 his own opinions supplied a context
so apt for his words of 1907 that any attempt thereafter to
make them mean anything but what they said seemed like
Pandora's attempt to lock the box she had idly opened.[127]

"The fundamental transformations in constitutional
theory," Samuel J. Konefsky cautiously observes, "although
not always candidly acknowledged as such by the Justices
—suggest . . . that the 'wound' sustained by the Court
was, in Hughes' own phrase of an earlier day, at least in

[126] The context of Hughes's 1907 statement reads: "I have the
highest regard for the courts. My whole life has been spent in work
conditioned upon respect for the courts. I reckon him one of the
worst enemies of the community who will talk lightly of the dignity
of the bench. We are under a Constitution, but the Constitution is
what the judges say it is, and *the judiciary is the safeguard of our
liberty and of our property under the Constitution*" (italics added).
In the chapters he wrote for the guidance of his biographer,
Hughes explained: "The inference that I was picturing constitutional interpretation by the courts as a matter of judicial caprice
. . . was farthest from my thought. I was not talking flippantly
or in disrespect of the courts, but on the contrary with the most
profound respect. I was speaking of the essential function of the
courts under our system in interpreting and applying constitutional safeguards and I was emphasizing the importance of maintaining the courts in the highest public esteem as our final judicial
arbiters. . . ." Quoted in Pusey, *Charles Evans Hughes*, I, 204.
[127] Pusey, *Charles Evans Hughes*, I, 205.

part 'self-inflicted.' And while the Chief Justice cannot be assumed to have exerted the decisive influence on the Court's deliberations, neither can he be absolved of all blame." [128]

The nature of our political system makes it almost inevitable that "the type-figure of a great revolution in political thinking" will occur in the judiciary. For in no other country are "the permissible directions of self-development of the living body politic so largely determined by the courts." Elsewhere a member of the judiciary can, at most, become a great judge. In America he has the opportunity also of becoming "a great exponent of statecraft." [129] The Constitution being, as Woodrow Wilson said, "a vehicle of the nation's life," rather than a strait jacket, the Chief Justice may influence whether the forces of inevitable change will be stymied or allowed to express themselves in orderly and timely fashion. It is within his power to establish roadblocks in the way of change or build bridges facilitating it. Such tests are not easily applied to Hughes. He held strong convictions as to civil rights and, as we shall see, made notable contributions in their defense. Prior to 1930, his sensitivity to popular aspirations, both off and on the Court, had been frequently demonstrated. In the 1930's, however, the Chief Justice became hard of hearing. An inclination to resist irresistible change and then to move along with solutions one has had no conspicuous role in shaping are not the marks of statesmanship. At the expense of both the form and substance of the law, he seemed unduly interested in preserving the Court's symbolic function.

[128] S. J. Konefsky, review of Pusey's *Charles Evans Hughes,* 61 *Yale Law Journal* 765 (1952), 771.
[129] The words in quotation are those of B. K. Sandwell, Canadian journalist and Rector of Queens University, *American Bar Association Journal,* Vol. 18 (1932), 805.

It took an agonizing rumpus to force Charles Evans Hughes to realize that "statesmanship in a democratic community consists in the use of public authority to make the necessary adaptations to a changing political and social environment and to the demands of the time." [130]

[130] Dexter Perkins, *Charles Evans Hughes* (Boston, 1956), xxiv.

CHAPTER 4

STONE:

The Court in Search of Its Role

ARLAN FISKE STONE often said that he attained high judicial position not by definitely planning it but "as the dog went to Dover, leg by leg." He had no set goal. Writing in 1941, the Chief Justice recalled:

> I was twenty-one in October, 1893. As near as I can remember I was then just setting out in the third year of my college course and beginning to look forward to securing something to do after graduation which would enable me to earn enough to go on to law school. I was also realizing that in those days college and law school education did not grow on every bush for students in my position in life, and I was doing the best I could to get the full advantage of my college courses in the belief that diligence and loyalty to my immediate job would best serve to fit me for some useful achievement in the years ahead.
>
> I cannot say I had any thought of being a member of the Supreme Court or any other court, for I believed then, as I do now, that the best insurance of a happy life and reasonable success in it is devotion to one's immediate job and happiness in doing it.[1]

For twenty-five years Stone divided his time between law teaching and law practice in New York City. After thirteen years as dean of the Columbia Law School, President Coolidge appointed him, in 1924, Attorney-General

[1] H. F. Stone to Justin Miller, April 25, 1941 (Stone Papers).

of the United States. Less than a year later he became an Associate Justice of the Supreme Court. In 1941 President Roosevelt, ignoring partisan politics, appointed him Chief Justice of the United States. Senior Associate at the time of his promotion to the center chair, Stone thus became the only man in American history to occupy consecutively every seat on the supreme bench. All this happened, he explained, "because someone who had authority to invite me to occupy the position asked me to do so." This explanation, while explanatory, does not explain.

Stone had judicial temperament to a degree that attracted his teachers in precollege years. It was as an Amherst undergraduate that he wrote his first judicial opinion, overruling a faculty decision to dismiss a fellow undergraduate without having the approval of the student senate which the faculty had joined in establishing.[2] Fellow students at Columbia Law School predicted he would in time sit on the supreme bench. When these predictions came true Stone, unlike his admiring friends, was content with his lot. For nearly two decades correspondents and politicians prodded him to get into line for the Presidency. Later on, devoted friends urged him to resign from the Court so as to take a Cabinet post they thought of as a stepping stone to the White House. Though flattered by these promptings the Justice showed no interest in a political promotion.

"I have a conscience, right or wrong," he kept telling his boosters, "that I am fitted for the job which I am doing and am supremely interested in it, and when a man is in that situation, it is well for him to stick to his last."

The judicial role was highly congenial to Stone's cast of mind. For him there was nothing more binding and satis-

[2] For the full text of this opinion, see my *Harlan Fiske Stone*, 51–52.

fying than service as a judge. It just seemed "to exclude everything else." His method was to proceed slowly, deliberately, and to render judgment only after full inquiry and careful weighing of evidence. This was his way whether the issue fell within the formal context of a law case or required informal judgments on personal and public affairs. Popular passion for causes and scapegoats did not engulf him. When, in 1924, the press shouted loudly that Harry M. Daugherty, his predecessor in the Department of Justice, had left him "a legacy of chaos," Stone denied it. He did not minimize Daugherty's deficiencies, but such unqualified indictment was unjust to the faithful veterans in the attorney-general's office. "After all," he commented, "we're all human and we must take an interest in one another's work."

A line from Stone's favorite short story, Stephen Benet's "The Devil and Daniel Webster," suggests his judicial approach: "One could admit all the wrong that has ever been done and yet recognize that out of the wrong and the right, something new had come, and everybody had played a part, even the traitors."

Whether judicial temperament is natural or acquired one cannot say. But one thing is certain: it was reinforced at Amherst. Stone came to intellectual maturity during the philosophic movement known as pragmatism. A science major in college, he was imbued with the scientific method. But the most enduring influence he met there was a course he took in philosophy under Charles Edward Garman. Of Garman's impact, Stone wrote: "The student's critical faculties were stimulated; he was required to *weigh evidence,* to draw his conclusions and defend them. This method was the ultimate secret of Garman's profound influence on his students. For the first time in their daily lives, they were made to realize that they possessed a thinking apparatus of their own, and that only by use of it could they become masters of their own moral and intellectual destiny." [3]

Experience gained at the Columbia Law School contributed directly to his preparation for a judicial career. His lifework of teaching and judging was completely integrated. At the university he had time and opportunity for study and reflection, time to develop ideas as to the nature of law and the function of courts. The methods learned from Professor Garman and the teaching technique employed in his own chemistry laboratory at Newburyport High School and in the law school classroom were carried over into his work on the Supreme Court. His transition from scientific research to judicial recognition of the right of legislative experiment was easy and natural.

Stone's part-time law practice, though helpful, was not closely related to issues of the kind that absorbed him as a judge. Constitutional law had not been his field of special interest either in teaching or in practice. Before putting on judicial robes he had argued only one case[4] before the high court. In 1920, as counsel for J. P. Morgan, he presented oral argument in defense of a judgment obtained under a Delaware statute which had been on the books since early colonial days and with origins going back to the ancient custom of London. In this case he adumbrated what was to become the major theme in his constitutional jurisprudence—judicial self-restraint. The correction of outmoded processes ought to be left, he contended, to legislatures rather than assumed by courts.[5]

This principle of judicial self-restraint he had invoked earlier in a verbal tussle with sociologist and reformer Ed-

[3] *Ibid.*, 59.
[4] *Ownbey* v. *Morgan*, 256 U.S. 94 (1921).
[5] For discussion of the case, see my *Harlan Fiske Stone*, 184–88.

ward Devine.[6] In 1912, Devine, an editor of *The Survey*, was casting about for causes to explain the waning respect for law. The editor cited as the most important single factor judicial obtuseness to the modern shift from sterile legalism to the urgent demand for social justice. Though Stone did not oppose social justice as a crusader's warcry, he took strong exception to Devine's contention that a statute's economic and social *desirability* was conclusive in determining its constitutionality.

The book in which Stone incorporated these ideas has since been regarded as conservative, even reactionary.[7] But when, as a Supreme Court Justice, he was equally harsh in his attack on the antithetical idea—that judicial *distrust* of social legislation was enough to condemn it— he was hailed as a liberal. The stand he took as a Supreme Court Justice is entirely consistent with his opposition to Devine's indiscriminate clamor for social justice. Neither conservative nor liberal tags afford the clue to Stone's constitutional jurisprudence. Such labels were, he thought, inappropriate for a judge. Against judicial obstructionists and judicial activists alike he urged the doctrine of judicial self-restraint.

It seems ironical that Stone, a solid, peace-loving man, should have been in the crossfires of controversy throughout his judicial career. On Taft's Court, and during a good part of Chief Justice Hughes's regime, he differed from colleagues on the Right who interposed their own social and economic predilections under the guise of interpreting the Constitution. During his own Chief Justiceship, Stone was at odds with colleagues on the Left who were equally set on using their judicial office to further some social or political preference.

Stone's moderate approach is revealed in his considera-

[6] *Ibid.*, 116–18.
[7] The book is entitled *Law and Its Administration*.

tion of governmental immunities from taxation—a vexing problem throughout the Chief Justiceships of Taft and Hughes. Rejecting the facile reciprocal immunities doctrine, established in *McCulloch* v. *Maryland* and *Collector* v. *Day*, he held that the federal system does not establish a "total want" of power in one government to tax the instrumentalities of the other. There is "no formula by which that line (which separates those activities having some relation to government from those which are immune) may be plotted in advance. . . . Neither government may destroy the other nor curtail in any substantial manner the exercise of its power." For him the extent and locus of the tax burden are the important considerations. No formula, no facile "black and white" distinction sufficed to resolve the issue.[8] Similarly in cases dealing with state regulation of economic affairs and state taxation affecting interstate and foreign commerce, no question-begging formula as to "business affected with a public interest," or as to the direct and indirect effects, was considered adequate. Here, as in the inter-governmental immunities tax cases, he insisted that the legislation be subjected to factual analysis.

Though an habitual Republican, Stone knew that increased use of government power is a necessary concomitant of twentieth-century conditions. "Law functions best only when it is fitted to the life of a people," he said. This conviction usually aligned him with Holmes and Brandeis. Uniting the triumvirate was their conviction that a Justice's personal predilections must not thwart the realization of social democracy.

Stone's constitutional jurisprudence, long in the mak-

[8] These ideas are elaborated in *Helvering* v. *Gerhardt*, 304 U.S. 405 (1938) and *Graves* v. *New York*, 306 U.S. 466 (1939). For a good estimate, see Samuel Hendel, "Chief Justice Stone and Judicial Review," 6 *Lawyers Guild Review* (July–August, 1946), 529–36.

ing, crystallized during 1936, the heyday of the Court's resistance to Franklin D. Roosevelt's sponsorship of government control and regulation. In the leading case of *United States* v. *Butler*,[9] the Court voted 6 to 3 to outlaw the Agricultural Adjustment Act. Justice Roberts, the majority's spokesman, and Justice Stone, dissenting, were about equally skeptical of the AAA in terms of policy. Their differences concerned the scope of national power, and the Court's role in the American system of government. Stone thought that the majority (which in this case included Chief Justice Hughes) had come to believe that any legislation that majority considered "undesirable" was necessarily unconstitutional. The Court had come, as Stone said, to think of itself as "the only agency of government that must be assumed to have capacity to govern."[10] Justice Roberts raised the forbidding spectacle of "legislative power without restriction or limitation." The majority was haunted by the possibility that Congress might become "a parliament of the whole people, subject to no restrictions save such as are self-imposed."[11] But, Justice Stone countered, consider the status of our own power. The executive and Congress are restrained by "the ballot box and the processes of democratic government," and "subject to judicial restraint; the only check upon our own exercise of power is our own sense of self-restraint."[12] Precisely because it is unfettered, Stone reasoned, judicial power should be exercised more circumspectly. Roberts' suggestion that congressional action, unless "curtailed by judicial fiat," might be abused was dismissed as hardly rising to "the dignity of argument."[13]

[9] 297 U.S. 1 (1936).
[10] *Ibid.*, 87.
[11] *Ibid.*, 78.
[12] *Ibid.*, 79.
[13] *Ibid.*, 87.

"Such suppositions," Stone declared, "are addressed to the mind accustomed to believe that it is the business of courts to sit in judgment on the wisdom of legislative action. . . . Congress and the courts both unhappily may falter or be mistaken in the performance of their constitutional duty. But interpretation of our great charter of government which proceeds on any assumption that the responsibility for the preservation of our institutions is the exclusive concern of any one of the three branches of government, or that it alone can save them from destruction, is far more likely, in the long run, 'to obliterate the constituent members' of 'an indestructible union of indestructible states' than the frank recognition that language, even of a Constitution, may mean what it says. . . ." [14]

This was not the first time a dissenter expressly accused the Court of "torturing" the Constitution under the guise of interpreting it. But no other Justice had used such strong language in condemning the practice. "Never before," Professor Howard L. McBain commented in a magazine article published shortly after the AAA decision came down, "has a dissenting minority gone quite so far toward calling into question the motives of the majority and clearly implying that they have abused their judicial prerogative." [15] Stone promptly clarified his position: "I thought your article in yesterday's *New York Times* very interesting and able, but perhaps I should enter one disclaimer. I do not question the motives of my brethren, and did not intend to do so in the vigorous language which I used in my dissenting opinion. I do question a *method of thinking* which is perhaps the greatest stumbling-block to the right administration of judicial review of legislation." Stone stated his position at length:

[14] *Ibid.*, 87–88.
[15] Howard Lee McBain, "The Issue: Court or Congress," *New York Times Magazine*, January 19, 1936, p. 2.

We see it frequently enough in the common untrained mind, which is accustomed to think that legislation which it regards as bad or unwise must necessarily be unconstitutional. Where there is a choice of interpretations of a constitutional provision, such a habit of thought is very likely to make a choice of the interpretation which would lessen the possibility of enacting a bad law. The difficulty with this method is that lessening the power to enact bad laws likewise lessens the power to enact good ones, and the judgment of what is bad or good, which is essentially a legislative function, is likely to be affected by the passions and prejudices of the moment. Such an approach to constitutional construction tends to increase the dead areas in the Constitution, the lacunae in which no power exists, neither state nor national, to deal with the problems of government.

"If judges can be brought to understand," Stone told McBain, "what I conceive to be the true nature of the judicial function I can think of no institution likely to be of more enduring value." [16]

A few months later Stone reaffirmed his indictment in the formal context of a dissenting opinion.[17] Sharply denouncing the majority's substitution of "personal economic predilections" for the Constitution, he commented:

It is not for the courts to resolve doubts whether the remedy by wage regulation is as efficacious as many believe, or is better than some other, or is better even than the blind operation of uncontrolled economic forces. The legislature must be free to choose unless government is to be rendered impotent. The Fourteenth Amendment has no more embedded in the Constitution our preference for some particular set of economic beliefs, than it has adopted, in the name of liberty, the system of theology which we may happen to approve.[18]

Frontal attack on judicial usurpation by one of the Court's most highly respected members could not be

---

[16] Quoted in my *Harlan Fiske Stone,* 411–12.
[17] *Morehead* v. *Tipaldo,* 298 U.S. 587 (1936).
[18] *Ibid.,* 636.

safely ignored. Justice Sutherland, champion of the majority, deplored Stone's telltale revelations, criticizing his advocacy of judicial self-restraint as "ill-considered and mischievous." Though the Court's own decisions had wiped out the distinction which judges were accustomed to make between judgment and will, Justice Sutherland boldly reiterated it. " 'Courts . . . declare the law as written,' " he asserted, citing the weighty authority of Thomas M. Cooley.[19]

"The check upon the judge," Sutherland explained, "is that imposed by his oath of office, by the Constitution and by his own conscientious and informed convictions; and since he has the duty to make up his own mind and adjudge accordingly, it is hard to see how there could be any other restraint. . . . If the Constitution . . . stands in the way of desirable legislation, the blame must rest upon that instrument and not upon the court for enforcing it according to its terms. The meaning of the Constitution does not change with the ebb and flow of events." [20]

Sutherland's claim of utter helplessness recalls Cardozo's words: "Judges march at times to pitiless conclusions under the prod of remorseless logic which is supposed to leave them no alternative. They deplore the sacrificial rite. They perform it none the less, with averted gaze, convinced as they plunge the knife that they obey the bidding of their office. The victim is offered up to the gods of jurisprudence on the altar of regularity." [21]

Stone had been guilty of an unforgivable sin. The former law school teacher had lifted the veil from mystery, revealing behind judicial pageantry nine human beings, all participants in the governing process, no nearer the source

[19] *West Coast Hotel* v. *Parrish,* 300 U.S. 379 (1937).
[20] *Ibid.,* 402, 404.
[21] B. N. Cardozo, *The Growth of the Law,* 66.

of ultimate wisdom than are others. The great vice of Stone's revelation that judges might, by the exercise of self-restraint, construe the Constitution so as to uphold undesirable legislation was that in destroying the hard and fast distinction between *judgment* and *will*, he endangered public confidence in the judiciary. Once the mystery that surrounds judicial doings is penetrated, once the public recognizes the personal nature of judicial power, it would become difficult for the judiciary to function at all. Stone had done the Court an incalculable disservice in letting the judicial cat out of the theological bag. One recalls Hans Christian Andersen's fable of the royal robes which could be seen only by the loyal, the pure, and the righteous. Justice Stone was the urchin who blurted out the facts.

Sutherland's *de profundis* as to judicial impotence was not a pose.[22] At the height of the Court-packing struggle, North Carolina Senator Bailey made a radio speech delineating the Court's function as "truth and righteousness. . . . It has no earthly power. . . . Its decrees prevail only by reason of the spiritual appeal of justice to the human heart." Justice Sutherland promptly applauded the Senator: "I am unable to refrain from breaking the silence which is supposed to enshroud the judiciary to tell you how deeply your words have moved me. I am quite

---

[22] But he was indulging in mythical thinking. "All judges exercise discretion, individualize abstract rules, make law," Judge Frank declares. "The fact is, and every lawyer knows it, that *those judges who are most lawless, or most swayed by the 'perverting influences of their emotional natures,' or most dishonest, are often the very judges who use most meticulously the language of compelling mechanical logic, who elaborately wrap about themselves the pretense of merely discovering and carrying out existing rules, who sedulously avoid any indication that they individualize cases.*" Jerome Frank, *Law and the Modern Mind* (New York, 1949), 137–38.

sincere in saying that in my judgment there never has been a better speech." [23]

In his war on the recalcitrant four (sometimes joined after 1930 by Hughes and Roberts) Stone was frequently allied with Holmes and Brandeis. But they were not always in complete agreement. Though the divergence was less than that separating Stone from his right- and left-wing colleagues, the Illustrious Three were not entirely one as to the nature of the judicial function or how it should be exercised. Holmes, Brandeis, and Stone were all the stronger as a team for differences between them of background, philosophy, and technique. They might indeed be thought of as typifying the American dream of unity in diversity. Each brought a unique contribution to their joint attack on government by judiciary; each pursued a distinct course in driving the assault forward.

Chief among points of agreement was their recognition of the need for a living law, their understanding that judicial decisions based on rigid formulae were "a slumber, that prolonged means death." All three were acutely aware that the judiciary was most often wounded "in the house of its own guardians." The essence of their creed was judicial self-restraint, recognized as a desirable, rather than a realizable, goal. Judge Learned Hand, summing up their essential agreement, writes:

These men believed that democracy was a political contrivance by which the group conflicts inevitable in all society should find a relatively harmless outlet in the give and take of legislative compromise after the contending groups had a chance to measure their relative strength; and through which the bitterest animosities might at least be assuaged, even though that reconciliation did not ensue which sometimes follows upon an open fight. They had no illusion that the outcome would necessarily be the best obtainable, certainly

[23] Quoted in J. Francis Paschal, *Mr. Justice Sutherland: A Man Against the State* (Princeton, 1951), 201–202.

not that which they might themselves have personally chosen; but the political stability of such a system, and the possible enlightenment which the battle itself might bring, were worth the price. . . . Statutes were not to be held invalid, so long as anyone could find a reasonable basis for not ascribing them purely to envy or greed; and, as it was seldom, if ever, that this could not be done with any confidence, most statutes were upheld.[24]

The bonds uniting them strengthened as the majority's doctrinaire approach became increasingly out of tune with the tenor of the times. Yet differences were continuously evidenced by the fact that they often filed separate opinions in support of the same decision. In dissent Holmes, addicted to generalization and gifted as an essayist, tended to avoid the tough issues and failed to meet the majority on its own ground. "This is a pretty good opinion on the point he decides," Stone remarked on one occasion, "but the old man leaves out all the troublesome facts and ignores all the tough points that worried the lower courts." "I wish," he once said in grudging admiration, "I could make my cases sound as easy as Holmes makes his." [25] So, even when agreeing with his elder colleague, Stone sometimes went to the trouble of writing his own opinion.

Stone's divergence from Brandeis is likewise most vividly portrayed in dissent. When the Court struck down legislation Brandeis favored in terms of policy, the erstwhile People's Attorney did not hesitate to utilize the Court as a forum to persuade others of its wisdom. "I told him [Brandeis] long ago," Holmes commented in 1930, "that he really was an advocate rather than a judge. He is affected by his interest in a cause, and if he feels it he is not

[24] Learned Hand, "Chief Justice Stone's Conception of the Judicial Function," loc. cit., 697.
[25] Alfred McCormack, "A Law Clerk's Recollections," 46 Columbia Law Review (1946), 714.

detached." [26] Stone took specific exception to Brandeis'
judicial activism. In reply on March 1, 1933, to a note
in which Brandeis invited concurrence with his Florida
chain store [27] dissent, Stone said:

> Your opinion is a very interesting and powerful document.
> But . . . it goes further than I am inclined to go, because I
> do not think it necessary to go that far in order to deal with
> this case. . . . I think you are too much an advocate of this
> particular legislation. I have little enthusiasm for it, although
> I think it constitutional. In any case I think our dissents are
> more effective if we take the attitude that we are concerned
> with power and not with the merits of its exercise. . . .
> Inquiry must be made whether the condition imposed is un-
> constitutional, and that requires examination of the question
> whether it [the statute] is unduly discriminatory, because its
> method of graduation is unreasonable. My preference is to
> deal with the latter question as the more immediate, and as
> requiring no departure from the method of treatment em-
> ployed in earlier cases.

The popular notion, vigorously advanced in certain
quarters, that Holmes and Brandeis were the "pacemak-
ers," and Stone a sort of judicial "me-too," is not borne
out by the record. Nor is it in accord with the encomiums
close students of the Court lavish on Stone and his work.
When, in 1937, the liberal position gained the ascendency
it was the dissenting opinions of Stone and Cardozo that
provided the constitutional rationale for positive government.

"When the time comes," Professor Karl Llewellyn
wrote Justice Stone on May 18, 1936, apropos of the Car-
dozo-Stone dissent in the Guffey Coal case, "and the attitude you express becomes the law of the majority attitude,
the case should be clear, with the first victory, that (1) a

[26] Quoted in Bickel, *The Unpublished Opinions of Mr. Justice
Brandeis*, 222.
[27] *Liggett* v. *Lee*, 288 U.S. 517 (1933).

whole new line of doctrine, and perhaps even (2) a whole new body of recorded precedent come into alternative being together."

The record confirms Llewellyn's prediction. Without minimizing the great contributions of Holmes and Brandeis, it is fair to conclude that in a logical as well as a chronological sense, Stone was the one who, in both the old and the new Court, carried the Holmes-Brandeis tradition to fulfillment. Perforce it fell to him, as his former law clerk Professor Herbert Wechsler says, "to carry through the victory and consolidate the gain." [28]

Going beyond Holmes and Brandeis, Stone built by precept and example an impressive catechism for judges. He took seriously the "aphorisms of his trade." This meant thorough probing of the historical roots of ambiguous statutes for the intent of the legislator; it meant according legislation he distrusted the full benefit of the "presumption of constitutionality." Nothing delighted Stone more than to take a morass of conflicting decisions, sort them all out, and then restate the rule with reasons having solid substance. His skillful trimming, elaborating, and blending of the Brandeis and Holmes approach makes him one of the great creative judges of our time.

Alarmed by the fresh constitutional foundations Stone used to lay in his opinion, Taft paid high tribute to his pioneering even as he warned of the danger implicit in the former law teacher's methods. Said Taft: "he is quite disposed to be discursive and to write opinions as if he were writing an editorial or a comment for a legal journal, covering as much as he can upon a general subject and thus expressing opinions that have not been thought

[28] Herbert Wechsler, "Stone and the Constitution," 46 *Columbia Law Review*, 771. For illustration of Stone's creative power, as discerned by Karl Llewellyn and Wechsler, see my *Harlan Fiske Stone*, Chapters 30, 31, and 33.

out by the whole Court. He is a learned lawyer in many ways but his judgments I do not altogether consider safe, and the ease with which he expresses himself and his interest in the whole branch of the law in which he is called upon to give an opinion on a single principle makes the rest of the Court impatient and doubtful. . . . Without impeaching at all his good faith in matters of that sort, we find we have to watch closely the language he uses." [29]

"He was," Judge Learned Hand commented in 1951, "a thorough craftsman as a judge. He steered a course at times very difficult and he had the right—absolutely right —measure of the Court's limitation on constitutional questions, which appears in danger of being lost again." [30]

Among other results of the 1937 revolution was the abandonment of judicial guardianship of property as a sort of preferred freedom. Soon thereafter the judiciary began propounding another category of preferred freedoms. Having adopted self-restraint as to regulatory commercial legislation, would the same narrow concept of the judicial power apply to enactments allegedly infringing freedom of speech, thought, and religion? For reasons suggested by Justice Jackson this question had no easy answer.

The task of translating the majestic generalities of the Bill of Rights, conceived as part of the pattern of liberal government in the eighteenth century, into concrete restraints on officials dealing with problems in the twentieth century, is one to disturb self-confidence. These principles grew in soil which also produced a philosophy that the individual was the center of society, that his liberty was attainable through mere absence of governmental restraints, and the government should be entrusted with few controls and only the mildest supervision over men's affairs. We must transplant these rights into a soil in which the laissez-faire concept or principle of non-

[29] W. H. Taft to Charles P. Taft, May 12, 1929 (Taft Papers).
[30] Learned Hand to A. T. Mason, August 22, 1951.

interference has withered at least as to economic affairs, and social advancements are increasingly sought through closer integration of society and through expanded and strengthened government controls. These changed conditions often deprive precedents of reliability and cast us more than we would choose upon our own judgment.[31]

For certain judges the Bill of Rights, especially those enumerated in the First Amendment, constitute the basis of all our civil and political institutions. Their protection by the judiciary is considered an essential aspect of "free government." Other Justices are disinclined to accord a preferred position to any particular category of rights. Viewing Stone's dissent in *United States* v. *Butler* as "a lodestar for due regard between legislative and judicial powers," [32] Justice Frankfurter appears to interpret the 1937 judicial revolution as signifying well-nigh complete withdrawal of the Court from the governing process. At first glance, it does seem paradoxical that Justice Stone, who led the campaign for judicial self-restraint in cases involving government regulation of economic affairs, should have articulated the so-called preferred freedoms doctrine.

The notion of a preferred position for civil liberties in the American political tradition is implicit in the free speech opinions of Holmes and Brandeis. In the Abrams[33] case Holmes declared that the theory of our Constitution is that the ultimate good is better reached through "free trade in ideas." In the Pierce case,[34] Brandeis spoke of a fundamental right of free men to strive for improved conditions through "new legislation and new institutions."

[31] *West Virginia State Board of Education* v. *Barnette,* 319 U.S. 624 (1943), 639–49.
[32] Frankfurter to Stone, May 27, 1940. Quoted in my *Security Through Freedom* (Ithaca, 1955), 220.
[33] *Abrams* v. *U.S.,* 250 U.S. 616 (1919), 630.
[34] *Pierce* v. *U.S.,* 252 U.S. 239 (1920), 273.

The consequences of the doctrine were never spelled out, nor the full implications faced by either Justice.

Chief Justice Hughes saw many of the Holmes-Brandeis minority opinions on civil liberties become the majority view. Beginning with *Near* v. *Minnesota*,[35] legislation affecting free speech and press was, in fact, no longer presumed constitutional. Characteristically, Hughes never formulated this approach in a doctrinal way, nor attempted to state his views definitively,[36] as Brandeis had done in the Whitney case.[37] After the doctrine gained majority support, the obligation to articulate an underlying theory became more compelling. It was not, however, until 1938 that the rationale of preferred freedoms was formulated.

In the otherwise obscure case [38] of *United States* v. *Carolene Products Co.*,[39] Stone suggested in the body of the opinion that he would not go so far as to say that no economic legislation would ever violate constitutional restraints, but he did indicate that in this area the court's role would be strictly confined. As to commercial regulations, in other words, the rule henceforth was judicial laissez faire. Attached to this proposition is the now-famous footnote suggesting special judicial responsibility in the orbit of civil rights. Stone's language is suggestive and tentative:

There may be narrower scope for operation of the presumption of constitutionality when legislation appears on its face to be within a specific prohibition of the Constitution,

[35] 283 U.S. 697 (1931).

[36] The closest approximation of a statement of the doctrine is *DeJonge* v. *Oregon*, 299 U.S. 353 (1937), 365.

[37] *Whitney* v. *California*, 274 U.S. 357 (1927), 374–75.

[38] But the case was not without significance, for it "marked the demise of *Hammer* v. *Dagenhart*, though the event was not officially noted until [the Darby case, 312 U.S. 100, 1941] several years later." W. O. Douglas, *We the Judges* (Garden City, N.Y., 1956), 199.

[39] 304 U.S. 144 (1938)

such as those of the first ten amendments, which are deemed equally specific when held to be embraced within the Fourteenth. . . .

It is unnecessary to consider now whether legislation which restricts those *political processes which can ordinarily be expected to bring about repeal of undesirable legislation,* is to be subjected to *more exacting judicial scrutiny* under the general prohibitions of the Fourteenth Amendment than are most other types of legislation. . . .

Nor need we enquire whether similar considerations enter into review of statutes directed at particular religions, . . . or national, . . . or racial minorities, . . . whether prejudice against discrete and insular minorities may be a special condition, which tends seriously to *curtail the operation of those political processes* ordinarily to be relied upon to protect minorities and which may call for a correspondingly more searching judicial inquiry.[40]

Less than two years after these words were written Hitler unleashed the Nazi forces. With Europe aflame in World War II, the judicial stage was set for a significant debate on the Court's role as guardian of First Amendment freedoms. In the grip of fear as to security, men have ever seemed ready, as de Tocqueville reminds us, "to fling away their freedom at the first disturbance . . . before they discover how freedom itself serves to promote it." [41] The Court, illustrating de Tocqueville's point, voted 8 to 1 to uphold Pennsylvania's compulsory flag salute as applied to Jehovah's Witnesses. In justifying his stand the Court's spokesman, Justice Frankfurter, explained that "time and circumstances are surely not irrelevant considerations in resolving the conflicts that we do have to resolve in this particular case. . . . [I]t is relevant to

[40] *Ibid.,* 152–54. Italics added. The elaborate documentation in the note has been omitted.

[41] Quoted by Henry Steele Commager, "Democracy in America: One Hundred Years After," *New York Times Magazine,* December 15, 1935, p. 15.

make the adjustment that we have to make within the framework of present circumstances and those that are clearly ahead of us." [42]

For Frankfurter "the ultimate foundation of a free society is the binding tie of cohesive sentiment. . . . Except where the transgression of constitutional liberty is too plain for argument, personal freedom is best maintained—so long as the remedial channels of the democratic process remain open and unobstructed—when it is ingrained in a people's habits and not enforced against popular policy by the coercion of adjudicated law." "The precise issue . . . for us to decide," Frankfurter wrote for the majority,

is whether the legislatures of the various states and the authorities in a thousand counties and school districts of this country are barred from determining the appropriateness of various means to evoke that unifying sentiment without which there can ultimately be no liberties, civil or religious. To stigmatize legislative judgment in providing for this universal gesture of respect for the symbol of our national life in the setting of the common school as a lawless inroad on that freedom of conscience which the Constitution protects, would amount to no less than the pronouncement of pedagogical and psychological dogma in a field where Courts possess no marked and certainly no controlling competence. . . . So to hold would in effect make us the school board for the country. That authority has not been given to this Court, nor should we assume it.

"Judicial review," Frankfurter concluded, "itself a limitation on *popular government,* is a fundamental part of our constitutional scheme. But to the legislature no less

[42] For the full text of Frankfurter's letter, see my *Security Through Freedom,* 217–20. See *West Virginia State Board of Education* v. *Barnette,* 319 U.S. 624 (1943), 646–47, for an illustration of how a judicial predilection can be disguised as "judicial humility," how "independence of the judiciary is jeopardized when Courts become embroiled in the passions of the day."

than to courts is committed the guardianship of deeply cherished liberties. . . . Where all the effective means of inducing political changes are left free from interference, education in the abandonment of foolish legislation is itself a training in liberty." [43]

In taking this line, the Court's spokesman assumed he was following Stone's rule of judicial self-restraint, as well as the fundamentals of our political tradition. In a five-page letter to Stone, Frankfurter spelled out his thought:

All my bias and pre-disposition are in favor of giving the fullest elbow room to every variety of religious, political, and economic view. . . . [But] I want to avoid the mistake comparable to that made by those whom *we* criticized when dealing with the control of property. . . . My intention . . . was to use this opinion as a vehicle for preaching the true democratic faith of not relying on the Court for the impossible task of assuring a vigorous, mature, self-protecting and tolerant democracy by bringing the responsibility for a combination of firmness and toleration directly home where it belongs—to the people and their representatives themselves.[44]

"We are not," Frankfurter emphasized, "the primary resolver of the clash. What weighs strongly on me in this case is my anxiety that, while we lean in the direction of the libertarian aspect, we do not exercise our judicial power unduly, and as though we ourselves were legislators by holding with too tight a rein the organs of popular government."

Stone, quite unconvinced, dissented—alone. Any "vulgar intrusion" of the legislators into the domain of conscience, he countered, imposes on the Court a larger responsibility than in passing on statutes which regulate property. Jehovah's Witnesses constituted an unpopular minority subject to prejudice. Corrective political proc-

[43] *Minersville School District* v. *Gobitis,* 310 U.S. 586 (1940), 597–600 *passim.*
[44] Quoted in my *Security Through Freedom,* 217–20 Italics added.

esses could not be effectively invoked in their behalf. If the Justices stood aloof, as the majority decreed, numerically inconsequential groups might become helpless victims of overpowering legislative majorities. The situation was precisely that which he had suggested in the Carolene Products footnote.

"I am truly sorry not to go along with you," Stone wrote Frankfurter. "The case is one of the relative weight of imponderables and I cannot overcome the feeling that the Constitution tips the scales in favor of religion." [45]

Nor was the majority opinion consistent, as Justice Frankfurter supposed, with what Justice Stone had said in his AAA dissent. With specific reference to Frankfurter's assumption that he was following his colleague's own prescriptions, Stone observed: "I am not persuaded that we should refrain from passing upon the legislative judgment as long as the remedial channels of the democratic process remain open and unobstructed. This seems to me no less than the surrender of the constitutional protection of the liberty of small minorities to the popular will." [46] As for Justice Frankfurter's notion that liberty is best maintained when instilled in the habits of the people and left to the "forum of public opinion," Stone commented: "The Constitution expresses more than the conviction of the people that democratic processes must be preserved at all costs. It is also an expression of faith and a command that freedom of mind and spirit must be preserved, which government must obey, if it is to adhere to that justice and moderation without which no *free government* can exist." [47]

Underlying the cleavage between Stone and Frank-

[45] Handwritten, undated note from Stone to Frankfurter. For this I am indebted to Justice Frankfurter.

[46] 310 U.S. 586, pp. 605–606.

[47] *Ibid.*, 606–607 Italics added.

furter are basic differences as to the meaning and requirements of the American system of government. Frankfurter
thinks of judicial review as limiting *popular government*.[48]
In support of his view, he invokes the authority of Jefferson. Certainly Jefferson, on occasion, said some harsh
things about judicial aggrandizement. But Frankfurter's
blanket statement that "Jefferson *all of his life* thought of
the Court as 'an irresponsible body' " [49] is somewhat misleading. To Jefferson the idea that paramount law carries
with it a duty in the Court to declare invalid all laws in
conflict with it was entirely congenial. One of his recommendations for improving the Virginia State Constitution
was that of making it paramount over "the powers of the
ordinary legislature so that all acts contradictory to it may
be adjudged null." [50] Two years later he considered it ax-
iomatic that "the judges would consider any law as void,
which was contrary to the Constitution." [51] On receiving
a copy of the proposed federal Constitution Jefferson responded, December 20, 1787: "I like the negative given to
the Executive, conjointly with a third of either House;
though I should have liked it better, had the judiciary
been associated for that purpose, or invested separately
with a similar power."

Writing Madison on March 15, 1789, Jefferson expressly endorsed judicial review with reference to the enforcement of the Bill of Rights: "In the arguments in favor
of a declaration of rights, you omit one which has great
weight with me; the legal check which is put into the

[48] For Frankfurter judicial review appears tainted, "nondemo-
cratic," "inherently oligarchic," *AFL* v. *American Sash and Door Co.*,
335 U.S. 538 (1949), 555.

[49] *Ibid.*

[50] Jefferson to Edmund Pendleton, May 25, 1784, in Julian P.
Boyd (ed.), *The Papers of Thomas Jefferson* (Princeton, 1950——),
VII, 293.

[51] Boyd (ed.), *The Papers of Thomas Jefferson*, X, 18.

hands of the judiciary. This is a body, which if rendered independent and kept strictly to their own department, merits great confidence for their learning and integrity. In fact, what degree of confidence would be too much, for a body composed of such men as Wythe, Blair and Pendleton. On characters like these, the *'civium ardor prava jubentium'* [frenzy of the citizens bidding what is wrong] would make no impression." [52]

Jefferson opposed judicial usurpation, judicial pre-eminence. So did Holmes, Brandeis, Stone, and many other Justices. Jefferson did not oppose judicial review. What he, and many others after him, deplored was the inclination among judges to demonstrate the maxim that "it is the office of a good judge to enlarge his jurisdiction." "The [judges] are in the habit of going out of the question before them, to throw an anchor ahead and grapple further hold for future advances of power." "Jefferson lived to conclude," Arthur Krock has noted "that, far from keeping to their own department, the justices were enlarging 'judicial review' to 'judicial supremacy.' . . ." [53] "I cannot find," Professor Corwin writes, "that Jefferson ever actually denied the right of the Supreme Court to judge the validity of acts of Congress." [54] Jefferson's quarrel was with John Marshall and his alleged judicial usurpations, not with judicial review as such.

Perhaps the clearest statement of Jefferson's position occurs in a letter to Mrs. Abigail Adams, September 11, 1804, with reference to the Sedition Act: "The Judges be-

[52] *The Writings of Thomas Jefferson,* edited by Andrew A. Lipscomb (Memorial ed.; 20 vols.; Washington, D.C., 1905), VII, 309. Quoted in Edmund Cahn, "The Firstness of the First Amendment," 65 *Yale Law Journal* 464 (1956), 466.

[53] Krock, *New York Times Magazine,* October 28, 1956, p. 6.

[54] Corwin, "The Supreme Court and Unconstitutional Acts of Congress," 4 *Michigan Law Review* (June, 1906), 629.

lieving the law constitutional, had a right to pass a sentence of fine and imprisonment; because that power was placed in their hands by the Constitution. But the Executive, believing the law to be unconstitutional, was bound to remit the execution of it; because that power had been confided to him by the Constitution. That instrument meant that its co-ordinate branches should be checks on · each other. But the opinion which gives to the judges the right to decide what laws are constitutional, and what not, not only for themselves in their own sphere of action, but for the legislature and executive also in their spheres, would make the judiciary a despotic branch." [55]

Jefferson, like Madison and Hamilton, realized that "popular assemblies" are "frequently subject to the impulses of rage, resentment, jealousy, avarice, and the other irregular and violent propensities" (*Federalist* No. 6, p. 22). An independent judiciary was an essential safeguard in the functioning of "free government." The contemporary record, especially *The Federalist,* exhibits an opinion directly opposite Justice Frankfurter's—that a "democracy need not rely on the courts to save it from its own unwisdom." [56]

For Madison (*Federalist* No. 51), "a dependence on the people" was only the "primary control" on government. For Frankfurter such dependence, at times, comes close to being the exclusive means of "obliging the government to control itself."

"Free speech cases," Frankfurter observes, "are not an exception to the principle that we are not legislators, that direct policy making is not our province." "How best to reconcile competing interests" is the function of the legis-

[55] For the manuscript copy of this letter I am indebted to Dr. Julian P. Boyd, editor of *The Jefferson Papers.*
[56] 335 U.S. 538, p. 556.

lature and "the balance they strike is a judgment not to be displaced by us but to be respected unless outside the pale of fair judgment." [57]

In *Stein* v. *New York* Frankfurter remarked, somewhat self-consciously, perhaps, that the "duty of deference cannot be allowed imperceptibly to slide into abdication." [58]

The Constitution establishes not popular government[59] (the expression is Frankfurter's) but free government. The founding fathers insisted that the dependence of government on the people must not be carried to the point where individual rights are left unprotected. "A dependence on the people," Madison commented in *Federalist* No. 51, "is, no doubt, the primary control on the government, but experience has taught mankind the necessity of auxiliary precautions." Unless the Court invokes its authority against the majority to preserve the freedoms essential to the functioning of the political process, "no free government can exist." As Madison explained in piloting the Bill of Rights through the first Congress:

The prescriptions in favor of liberty ought to be levelled against that quarter where the greatest danger lies, namely, that which possesses the highest prerogative of power. But this is not found in either the Executive or Legislative departments of Government, but in the body of the people, operating by the majority against the minority. . . . If they [the Bill of Rights] are incorporated into the Constitution, independent tribunals of justice will consider themselves in a peculiar manner the guardians of those rights; they will be an impenetrable bulwark against every assumption of power

[57] *Dennis* v. *U.S.*, 341 U.S. (1950), 539–40. Compare the position of the *Federalist* as explored in Gottfried Dietze, "Hamilton's *Federalist*—Treatise for Free Government," 307–28; and, by the same author, "Madison's *Federalist*—A Treatise for Free Government," 46 *Georgetown Law Journal* 21 (1957).

[58] 346 U.S. 156 (1953), 200.

[59] For light on the sense in which this term is used see *The Federalist*, Nos. 12, p. 55; 18, p. 86; 83, p. 427.

in the Legislative or Executive; they will be naturally led to resist every incroachment upon rights, expressly stipulated for in the Constitution by the declaration of rights.[60]

Judicial review is not at war with the principles of "free government"; it is, on the contrary, essential to its implementation. "When it is said," Samuel Konefsky writes, "that judicial review is an undemocratic feature of our political system, it ought also to be remembered that the architects of that system did not equate constitutional government with unbridled majority rule. Out of their concern for political stability and security for private rights, particularly property, they designed a structure the keystone of which was to consist of barriers to the untrammeled exercise of power by any group." [61]

With the triumph of judicial self-restraint in 1937, government won power to advance the cause of economic security. In the altered context of 1940, might not the Court be expected to safeguard national security by upholding the First Amendment freedoms? Stone believed that the legislature was free to regulate but not repress. To achieve this balance a positive duty of infinite complexity rests squarely on the judiciary. He put it this way: "Where there are competing demands of the interests of government and of liberty under the Constitution, and where the performance of governmental functions is brought into conflict with specific constitutional restrictions there must, when that is possible, be reasonable accommodation between them so as to preserve the essentials of both, and . . . it is the function of this Court to determine whether such accommodation is reasonably possible." [62]

[60] *Annals of Congress,* 1st Congress, 1st Session (June 8, 1789), Vol. 1, pp. 454–55, 457.
[61] *The Legacy of Holmes and Brandeis,* 293.
[62] 310 U.S. 586 (1940), p. 603.

The presumption of constitutionality—a practical rule of government holding that the people and their representatives should be allowed to correct their own mistakes wherever possible—simply does not apply in a situation where, for one reason or another, the legislature cannot be expected to correct its mistakes. The Court cannot, under the preferred freedoms doctrine, avoid responsibility for the result. It must be alert to legislative intrusions that prevent effective functioning of the political processes; it must extend its benefits to the novel, the unpopular, the unorthodox. "If only popular causes are entitled to enjoy the benefit of constitutional guaranties," Stone observed, "they serve no purpose and could as well not have been written." [63] By fastidiously standing aloof, as in the flag salute case, the Court in effect sanctioned the authoritarian policy of coercion in the delicate realm of civil rights.

"The greater the importance of safeguarding the community from incitements to the overthrow of our institutions by force and violence," Chief Justice Hughes declared in 1937, "the more imperative is the need to preserve inviolate the constitutional rights of free speech, free press and free assembly in order to maintain the opportunity for free political discussion, to the end that government may be responsive to the will of the people, and that changes, if desired, may be obtained by peaceful means. Therein lies the security of the Republic, the very foundation of constitutional government." [64] Those who won our independence and framed the Constitution believed that the only security worth having is built on freedom.

[63] From Stone's draft of an undelivered dissenting opinion in *Martin* v. *City of Struthers,* 319 U.S. 141 (1943). Stone's unpublished opinion became, in substance, Justice Black's opinion for the majority.

[64] *DeJonge* v. *Oregon,* 299 U.S. 353, p. 365.

It would be hard to cite a more glaring example of personal and emotional predilection parading under the verbal guise of judicial self-restraint than the majority opinion in the first flag salute case. Three years later, when the Court reversed its decision, Justice Frankfurter, in a remarkable personal testimonial, indicated his own emotional involvement.[65]

Stone won this battle. By 1943 three of the Justices (Hugo Black, W. O. Douglas, and Frank Murphy) who had joined the majority upholding the compulsory flag salute against solemnly avowed religious conviction, changed their minds,[66] and two new appointees (Jackson and Wiley Rutledge) agreed with Stone's dissent, thus transforming what was formerly a vote of 8 to 1 in favor of the compulsory flag salute into a vote of 6 to 3 against it.[67] Speaking for the Court in this remarkable about-face, Justice Jackson maintained that national unity may be fostered by persuasion and example, not by coercion.[68] By this reversal a conspicuous addition was thus made to the ever-lengthening list of "self-inflicted wounds" and, along with it, a blow without precedent was struck at Chief Justice Hughes's highest value—stability of judicial decision.

Stone has been accurately described as "one of the great architects of civil liberties," as "a substantial but not a

[65] See *West Virginia State Board of Education* v. *Barnette,* 646–47.

[66] Since these Justices had joined the majority in the Gobitis case, and now had misgivings, they thought the occasion appropriate to state their belief that the Gobitis case had been "wrongly decided." "The First Amendment," they declared, "does not put the right freely to exercise religion in a subordinate position. We fear, however, that the opinions in these and in the Gobitis case do exactly that." *Jones* v. *City of Opelika,* 316 U.S. 584 (1941), 624.

[67] *West Virginia State Board of Education* v. *Barnette,* 319 U.S. 624 (1943), 641.

[68] "Those who begin coercive elimination of dissent soon find themselves exterminating dissenters. Compulsory unification of opinion achieves only the unanimity of the graveyard."

groundbreaking adherent to the rights of man." [69] In 1919 he wrote a fresh and perceptive treatment[70] of the ages-old problem of conscientious objectors and thus laid the foundation for his opinion in the first flag salute case. He was often, but not invariably, joined with Holmes and Brandeis in defense of individual freedom. On the delicate problem of whether pacifists must take an oath to bear arms as a condition of naturalization, he wavered incredibly.[71] In certain of the most hotly contested cases during his Chief Justiceship, including *Bridges,*[72] *Schneiderman,*[73] and *Yamashita,*[74] he was on the side of restriction. In full flower Stone refused to endorse the preferred freedoms doctrine itself.

Stone's conception of this doctrine in the Carolene Products footnote was phrased tentatively. He merely raised the question whether, in the case of legislation touching rights protected by the First Amendment, there may be "narrower scope for the operation of the presumption of constitutionality" and whether such legislation might not be "subjected to more exacting judicial scrutiny." He first used the expression in *Jones* v. *Opelika.* "The Constitution, by virtue of the First and Fourteenth Amendments, has put those freedoms [speech and religion] in a preferred position. Their commands are not restricted to cases where the protected privilege is sought out for attack. They extend at least to every form of taxation which, because it is a condition of the exercise of the privilege, is capable of being used to control or suppress

[69] John P. Frank, "Harlan Fiske Stone: An Estimate," 9 *Stanford Law Review* 621 (1957), 624.

[70] H. F. Stone, "The Conscientious Objector," *Columbia University Quarterly,* October, 1919.

[71] See my *Harlan Fiske Stone,* Chapter 31 and pp. 804–06.

[72] *Bridges* v. *California,* 314 U.S. 252 (1941).

[73] *Schneiderman* v. *U.S.,* 320 U.S. 118 (1943), 170.

[74] *In re Yamashita,* 327 U.S. 1 (1946).

it." [75] The Court presumed unconstitutionality in this case because the statute was void "on its face." Four years later, when the preferred freedoms doctrine was carried to the point where invalidity was presumed against all legislation relating to First Amendment freedom, Stone dissented.

The case *Thomas* v. *Collins*[76] involved a Texas law requiring union organizers to register and obtain an organizer's card from the Texas secretary of state. R. J. Thomas, later defeated by Walter Reuther for president of the United Auto Workers, came to Texas to speak on behalf of his union. Not having registered as an organizer, he was served with a restraining order prior to his speech. He persisted and, to test the constitutionality of the law, solicited one Pat O'Sullivan during his address. The Texas statute, a regulation on the border between free speech and economic endeavor, was held invalid as extending into the domain of freedom of speech, where infringement of individual rights is contingent upon a clear and present danger. This case, Justice Rutledge observed in the opinion for the Court, requires a line to be drawn between individual freedom and state power. "Choice in that border, now as always delicate, is perhaps more so where the usual presumption supporting legislation is balanced by the preferred place given in our scheme to the great, the indispensable democratic freedoms secured by the First Amendment. . . . That priority gives these liberties a sanctity and sanction not permitting dubious intrusions. And it is the character of the right, not of the limitation, which determines what standard governs the choice." [77]

The fact that the act was, on the face of it, an economic regulation did not protect the law. The right infringed

[75] 316 U.S. 584 (1942), 608.
[76] 323 U.S. 515 (1945).
[77] *Ibid.*, 529–30.

was one of personal liberty. Rutledge went so far as to suggest that "as a matter of principle a requirement of registration of labor organizers would seem generally incompatible with an exercise of . . . free speech and assembly," and cited Stone's Carolene Products footnote as authority. Yet Stone himself, joined by Roberts, Stanley Reed, and Frankfurter, dissented. For them, this was an economic regulation and therefore not within the scope of the preferred freedoms doctrine. Speaking for the minority, Justice Roberts used language reminiscent of Stone's own AAA dissent: "We may deem the statutory provision under review unnecessary or unwise, but it is not our function as judges to read our views of policy into a Constitutional guarantee, in order to overthrow a state policy we do not personally approve, by denominating that policy a violation of free speech." [78]

The next year, 1946, when the Court, speaking through Justice Black,[79] upheld the right to distribute religious literature in a company town, Stone joined Justice Burton in a vigorous dissent by Justice Reed. Evidently the doctrine of preferred freedoms, as Stone understood it, had been transformed.

By 1950, with the change of judicial personnel (particularly the passing of Justices Murphy and Rutledge), the outbreak of the Korean War, and the rise of Senator McCarthy to power, the preferred freedoms doctrine

[78] *Ibid.*, 557.

Roberts made similarly pointed remarks as to Justice Murphy's activistic approach: "The question for decision in this case should be approached not on the basis of any broad humanitarian prepossessions we may all entertain, not with desire to construe legislation so as to accomplish what we deem worthy objects, but in the traditional and, if we are to have a government of laws, the essential attitude of ascertaining what Congress has enacted rather than what we wish it had enacted." *Tennessee Coal, Iron & Railroad Co.* v. *Muscoda Local No. 123*, 321 U.S. 590 (1944), 606.

[79] *Marsh* v. *Alabama*, 326 U.S. 501 (1946).

fell into a sort of constitutional limbo. Not explicitly approved in recent years by any majority opinion, it has been explicitly disapproved only by Justice Frankfurter.[80]

[80] Frankfurter launched an all-out attack in *Kovacs* v. *Cooper* (336 U.S. 77 [1949], 91–97), denouncing the preferred freedoms doctrine as a "mischievous" phrase, a "deceptive formula," a reversion to "mechanical jurisprudence." Stone is credited with having first introduced the idea. To make matters worse he had done so through the medium of a footnote which (to Frankfurter) "hardly seems to be an appropriate way of announcing a new constitutional doctrine." Frankfurter went on to deny that a majority of the Court had ever subscribed to the view that any legislation is "presumptively unconstitutional which touches the field of the First Amendment and the Fourteenth Amendment, insofar as the latter's concept of 'liberty' contains what is specifically protected by the First. . . ."

Though this is true, Justice Rutledge denied it: "I think my brother Frankfurter demonstrates the conclusion opposite to that which he draws, namely, that the First Amendment guaranties, the freedoms of speech, press, assembly and religion, occupy preferred position not only in the Bill of Rights but also in repeated decisions of this Court" (p. 106). Frankfurter and Rutledge were, of course, talking about different things. The preferred freedoms doctrine, as Stone formulated it in the Carolene Products footnote, meant only that legislation interfering with the First Amendment freedoms should be subjected to "more exacting judicial scrutiny" than that regulating ordinary commercial relations. Neither Stone nor a majority of the Court carried the doctrine so far as to presume the *unconstitutionality* of legislation interfering with the First Amendment freedoms.

Looking back in 1951, Justice Frankfurter took a less restrictive view of the Court's position on "preferred freedoms": ". . . in recent decisions we have made explicit what has long been implicitly recognized. In reviewing statutes which restrict freedoms protected by the First Amendment, we have emphasized the close relation which those freedoms bear to maintenance of a free society. . . . Some members of the Court—and at times a majority have done more" (*Dennis* v. *U.S.*, 341 U.S. 494 [1951], 526).

Frankfurter continued his campaign against preferred freedoms in *Ullman* v. *U.S.*, 350 U.S 422 (1956). Upholding the constitutionality of the 1954 Immunity Act, he inserted in an opinion for the court the dictum, "as no constitutional guarantee enjoys preference so none should suffer subordination or deletion" (p. 428). This did not escape the alert eye of Justice Reed who, in concurring with the

Dennis v. *United States* dealt the doctrine (at least as interpreted by Justice Rutledge and his supporters) a serious blow. Yet even after the Dennis case some substance of the doctrine remained. The "clear and present danger" test, in the altered form given it in that decision, continued to be applied in First Amendment cases.[81] Even where the Court seemed to sanction the "reasonableness" approach to First Amendment freedoms, it cautioned that freedoms of speech and press must weigh heavily in the scales.[82] In short, despite the ground lost in the Dennis case, the preferred freedoms doctrine, as Stone formulated it, was not without validity. Dissenting in the Dennis case, Justice Black expressed the hope "that in calmer times, when present pressures, passions and fears subside, this or some later Court will restore the First Amendment liberties to the high preferred place where they belong in a free society." [83] Though often the decisions have been reached by a 5 to 4 margin, Black's hope is now close to realization.

The Court's decision on June 17, 1957, dismissing five West Coast communists and ordering a new trial for nine others represents a significant step toward the fulfillment of Black's forecast. All the California communists had been convicted under the Smith Act, which forbids conspiracies to teach or advocate the violent overthrow of the government. Making an approach to the construction of

---

judgment, took exception to "the statement that no constitutional guarantee enjoys preference" (p. 439). In support of this proposition, Reed cited *Murdock* v. *Penna.,* 319 U.S. 105 (1943), 115; *Thomas* v. *Collins,* 323 U.S. 516 (1945), 530; *Kovacs* v. *Cooper* (1949), 88.

[81] For the different standard applied in substantive due process cases, see *Wieman* v. *Updegraff,* 344 U.S. 183 (1952); *American Communications Ass'n* v. *Douds,* 339 U.S. 382, 391–92 (1950).

[82] See 339 U.S. 382, pp. 399–400; *Communist Party* v. *Subversive Activities Control Bd.,* 223 F. 2d 531, 544–46, 554–57 (D.C. Cir. 1954), *cert. granted,* 349 U.S. 943 (1955).

[83] *Dennis* v. *U.S.,* 341 U.S. 494 (1951), 581.

the Smith Act markedly different from that followed by Chief Justice Fred Vinson's opinion in the Dennis case, Justice Harlan ruled: "We are thus faced with the question whether the Smith Act prohibits advocacy and teaching of forcible overthrow as an abstract principle, divorced from any effort to instigate action to that end, so long as such advocacy or teaching is engaged in with evil intent. We hold that it does not. . . . The statute was aimed at the advocacy and teaching of concrete action for the forcible overthrow of the Government, and not of principles divorced from action." [84] One cannot be sure that Chief Justice Stone would have joined in this opinion. His Schneiderman dissent makes it at least doubtful.

Stone's guiding rule was judicial self-restraint, not judicial self-abnegation. Except for the short period between 1937 and 1941, he was destined to invoke this principle against the dominant tides of his time. Before 1937 he criticized right-wing colleagues who equated what they considered economically undesirable legislation with invalidity. After the Court was reconstructed in 1941 he was at loggerheads with judges, especially those on the extreme left, equally intent, he thought, on reading their preferences into the Constitution.

As leader of the Roosevelt Court, the Chief Justice met new antagonists on all sides. His convictions about the Constitution and judging induced him to call a halt somewhat in advance of a tenuous, unstable majority of his colleagues. Examples of this divergence are numerous. In the familiar field of intergovernmental tax immunities, he would not sanction Justice Frankfurter's formula forbidding merely discriminatory federal taxation—that is, except where the tax hits the "state as a state." Preferring now, as in the past, "to deal with the matter empirically," Stone refused to go along. Holmes was "plainly

[84] *Yates* v. *U.S.*, 354 U.S. 1356 (1957), 1374–76.

mistaken," Stone informed Frankfurter, when he (Holmes) intimated that courts could invalidate federal taxes simply because they were destructive.

"Are you intending to suggest," the Chief Justice asked Frankfurter, "that the rule is different where such a tax is imposed on a state, as well as the citizen, without discrimination?" Stone had no doubt Congress might lawfully destroy liquor traffic by exorbitant taxation and, taking this tack, he shredded Frankfurter's argument by pointed queries: "Would such a tax be invalid if levied on a liquor business conducted by a state? If it would be valid, why cite Justice Holmes' statement? If it would be invalid, then what becomes of your thesis that a tax laid upon a state in the same way that it is laid on ordinary taxpayers, is not invalid?" Frankfurter's whole argument thus boiled down to "another way of saying that states may have an implied immunity from taxation which private individuals may not claim, and we are left where we began." [85] Reiterating the stand he had taken on the Taft Court, the Chief Justice said:

The problem is not one to be solved by a formula, but we may look to the structure of the Constitution as our guide to decision. In a broad sense, the taxing power of either government, even when exercised in a manner admittedly necessary and proper, unavoidably has some effect upon the other. The burden of federal taxation necessarily sets an economic limit to the practical operation of the taxing power of the states, and vice versa. . . . But neither government may destroy the other nor curtail in any substantial manner the exercise of its powers. Hence the limitation upon the taxing power of each, so far as it affects the other, must receive a practical construction which permits both to function with the minimum of interference each with the other; and that limitation cannot be so varied or extended as seriously to impair either the taxing power of the government imposing the

[85] H. F. Stone to Felix Frankfurter, Dec. 21, 1945.

tax . . . or the appropriate exercise of the functions of the government affected by it.[86]

Stone also called a halt when his colleagues carried "to absurd lengths the deference which courts must pay to the rulings of administrative agencies." "It is just ridiculous," he exploded on one occasion, "to say that the money collectors in the Treasury Department know better than we or the federal courts what Congress intended to do by the legislation here involved." Far more than his colleagues he was inclined to scrutinize National Labor Relations Board rulings. In advising Justice Jackson to include in an opinion the exact wording of a modified board order, he warned: "Otherwise interpretation of what you have said will become a subject of debate and the National Labor Relations Board, with its usual tendencies, will reframe the order to suit its own purposes."

During the early years of labor's march to power Stone was able to move forthrightly because he felt that both Constitution and legislation clearly sustained the workingman's claim. But when the cases became more subtle, and the National Labor Relations Board reached out for authority not plainly written into the statute, the Chief Justice retreated from the thesis he had advanced in his Harvard Tercentenary address of 1936 as to the judge's responsibility for rounding out statutory law.[87] Repeated conflicts with Black and Douglas, whom he felt were prone to resolve all doubts in labor's favor, alienated him, and led him to believe that he was again, as in 1928 and 1936, confronted with judges too anxious to write their predilections into law. Though he left the qualification

[86] *New York* v. *U.S.*, 326 U.S. 571 (1945), 589.
[87] "The Common Law in the United States," an address delivered at the Harvard Tercentenary Celebration. Published in the *Harvard Law Review*, November, 1936.

of labor's great gains largely to others, the record discloses diminishing sympathy with the majority views.

Stone and the newer Justices generally were agreed that the Court might use its power to rectify mistaken constitutional judgments. The more radical went further, insisting that the Court drastically revise previous interpretations of major congressional enactments, such as the Sherman Act. Stone disagreed. In notable cases, such as Apex and South-Eastern Underwriters, he demanded that the Justices leave undisturbed the old Court's constructions. Stone expressed this idea in 1940 when, in *Apex Hosiery Co.* v. *Leader*,[88] he pointed out that several court decisions had been responsible for the ruling that "to some extent and in some circumstances" labor unions were subject to the antitrust laws. He had long before voiced his doubt as to the correctness of this view. But Congress had not seen fit, as it might have done, to reject it. This failure was "persuasive of legislative recognition that the judicial construction is the correct one." [89] The Court, under the doctrine of self-restraint, was therefore barred from doing that which Congress, for whatever reasons, had failed to do.

Justice Stone upheld the same idea four years later in opposition to the powerful championship of Justice Black. Like judges of the old school, Black did not hesitate to correct nearly "a century of error." [90] In the face of a seventy-five-year-old precedent,[91] he held that the insurance business is within federal authority under the commerce clause, and hence subject to the Sherman Act. Stone dissented. The net of his argument was that back in 1869 the Court had repulsed an effort to interpose the com-

[88] 310 U.S. 469 (1940).

[89] *Ibid.*, 487–88.

[90] See *Pollock* v. *Farmers' Loan and Trust Co.*, 158 U.S. 601 (1895).

[91] *Paul* v. *Virginia*, 8 Wallace 168 (1869).

merce clause against the exercise of state power to regulate
the insurance business. Then the Court had held that the
states could regulate insurance because it was not commerce. Succeeding Justices faithfully adhered to this decision. On this understanding a vast and complicated
structure of state regulation had grown up. On this understanding, too, the Sherman Act had been passed. In
view of the long history of state regulation and in accord-
ance with the doctrine of self-restraint, the legislature
rather than the Court should take the first step in nation-
alizing insurance controls.

The very last day the Chief Justice sat on the bench, his
famous dictum, "Courts are not the only agency of government that must be presumed to have capacity to govern,"
resounded as a grim valedictory.[92]

Under the naturalization act of 1948, the oath of
citizenship requires the applicant "to support and defend
the Constitution." Should this provision be interpreted
so as to bar anyone who refuses the oath to bear arms? In
three previous cases the Court had turned down pacifists'
pleas for citizenship on just this ground. In two of them
Stone himself had dissented. Should the Court or Congress
correct this judicial "error" in the construction of the naturalization laws. A majority claimed this authority for the
Court. Stone dissented.

"With three other Justices of the Court," he observed,
"I dissented in the Macintosh and Bland cases, for reasons
which the Court now adopts as grounds for overruling
them." A majority had then rejected his arguments. Now,
he said, "the question, which for me is decisive in the present case, is whether Congress had likewise rejected that construction by its subsequent legislative action." The record
clearly indicated to him a negative answer. Therefore, he
concluded:

[92] *Girouard* v. *U.S.*, 328 U.S. 61 (1946).

It is the responsibility of Congress, in reenacting a statute, to make known its purpose in a controversial matter of interpretation of its former language . . . it is not lightly to be implied that Congress has failed to perform it and has delegated to this Court the responsibility of giving new content to language deliberately readopted after this Court has construed it. For us to make such an assumption is to discourage, if not to deny, legislative responsibility.[93]

Stone was creative, John P. Frank has written, "within the boundaries of the known." Any marked departure from existing principles left him "a little hurt, a little bewildered and sometimes even a little angry." [94] When, in 1945, he found himself pitted against judicial activists on the Left, he dolefully reminisced:

My more conservative brethren in the old days enacted their own economic prejudice into law. What they did placed in jeopardy a great and useful institution of government. The pendulum has now swung to the other extreme, and history is repeating itself. The Court is now in as much danger of becoming a legislative Constitution-making body, enacting into law its own predilections, as it was then. The only difference is that now the interpretations of statutes whether "over-conservative" or "over-liberal" can be corrected by Congress.[95]

Stone's conception of judicial conduct was almost monastic. He strove against nearly insuperable odds to keep the Court within what he considered appropriate bounds. A judge should limit himself precisely to the issue at hand. Contradictory precedents should usually be specifically overruled. The Court ought, he said, to "correct its own errors, even if I helped in making them." Each case should

[93] *Ibid.,* 72–73, 76.
[94] Frank, "Harlan Fiske Stone: An Estimate," *loc. cit.,* 625.
[95] Stone to Irving Brant, August 25, 1945.

Writing in 1965 Thomas Reed Powell said: "Four of the Roosevelt appointees were as determined in *their* direction as four of their predecessors were determined by attraction to the opposite role." Powell, *Vagaries and Varieties in Constitutional Interpretation,* 82.

be dealt with in the light of precedent, facts, legislative intent, and the judge's own reason and values. Stone's judicial technique, in essence, stressed complexity. To oversimplify was convenient for the pedagogue, but disastrous for the judge. In constitutional law the "perpetual question" is where to draw the line between a variety of competing interests—between individual liberty and government action for the larger public good, between state policy designed to promote local interests and the larger welfare which the Constitution commits to the federal government. The judge must make an appraisal of the past and of the present. He must open his eyes to all the conditions and circumstances. His own idea of reasonableness will inevitably enter into the calculation. He would do well to set all this against "a considered judgment of what the community may regard as within the limits of the reasonable." In a process so intricate, the judge who rests on formula risks disaster. Life does not conform to legal categories or even to judicial decisions of the Supreme Court. The "sober second thought of the community," Stone said, "is the firm base on which all law must ultimately rest." [96]

The overall appraisal of one privileged to observe Justice Stone in action is that he was "a careful and wise judge, who after two industrious decades has left the mark of his wisdom on almost every type of case which comes before the Supreme Court." [97] As Chief Justice, Stone was less impressive. For a great variety of reasons he experienced difficulty in "massing" the Court—a possibility Chief Justice Taft had clearly foreseen. The bench Stone headed was the most frequently divided, the most openly quarrelsome in history. If success be measured by the

[96] See H. F. Stone, "The Common Law in the United States," *Harvard Law Review,* November, 1936.

[97] Warner Gardner, "Mr. Chief Justice Stone," 59 *Harvard Law Review* 1203 (1946), 1208.

Chief's ability to maintain the *appearance* of harmony, he certainly was a failure. There can be little doubt that his solid convictions handicapped him. He refused to use the high-pressure tactics of Taft and Hughes. Nor would he resort to ingenious reasoning, good fellowship, the caucus, or other familiar political devices useful in keeping the Court united; much less would he try to create that impression. The contrast with Hughes is particularly striking. A law teacher who has carefully explored the differing methods of Hughes and Stone is not convinced that the superiority often accorded the former can be justified. "I wonder," he writes,

whether the virtues of Hughes as a leader of the Court are not overstated; or whether some of the changes in the Court's behaviour were not changes for the better rather than for

Berryman in the Washington Evening Star, *February, 1944*

the worse. When Hughes was in the saddle the Court did
. . . get through its Saturday conferences in four hours; and
sometimes, under Stone, the conferences continued for four
days. But I am not prepared to say that this was an undesirable development. I am shocked by the decisional process in
the Supreme Court of the United States as it proceeded under
Hughes. The judges heard arguments throughout the week
on cases that had been for the most part carefully selected as
the sort of cases that required the judgment of our highest
Court. Few of the judges made any extensive notes about the
cases they had heard; few of them made any careful study of
the records or briefs of the cited authorities before they went
to conference. Then in the space of four hours the Court
decided not only the cases that it had heard, but also voted
on the pending petitions for certiorari, jurisdictional statements, and other materials on the docket. This meant that
the discussion in conference was perforce a statement of conclusions more than an exchange of mutually stimulating
ideas. Some of the apparent unanimity in the Hughes Court
derived, in my estimation, from the superficiality of the discussion which glossed over rather than illuminated difficulties
in the path. If judging is as important a governmental task
as we lawyers assert it to be, I am not at all inclined to say
that extended conferences about the matters being judged
should be viewed as a deficiency in a Court. . . . Hughes
used to believe in the appearance of unanimity regardless of
the reality. As a consequence of his policy, opinions were
often published without the actual but with the apparent
concurrence of the brethren. Hughes himself often switched
his own vote in order to give a larger measure of apparent
support to an opinion with which he did not in fact agree.
I am dubious that this sort of intellectual flexibility is a sign
of better judging than would be a more candid reflection
of division when division exists.[98]

Stone had an abiding faith in "free government" and
in judicial review as an essential adjunct to its operation.

[98] Quoted in Frank, "Harlan Fiske Stone: An Estimate," *loc. cit.*,
629n.

For a detailed comparison of the contrasting methods of Hughes
and Stone, see my *Harlan Fiske Stone,* Chapter 47.

He believed that radical change is neither necessary nor generally desirable. Drastic change could be avoided, he believed, "if fear of legislative action, which Courts distrust or think unwise, is not over-emphasized in interpreting the document." [99] A free society, he held, needs continuity, "not of rules but of aims and ideals which will enable government, in all the various crises of human affairs, to continue to function and to perform its appointed task within the bounds of reasonableness." [100]

Stone urged "restraint," not because he believed a judge's preference should not enter law, but precisely because it inevitably did. The sharp barbs of his thought were intended for the flesh of judges, both Right and Left, who, without taking the trouble to weigh social values, *prematurely* enforced private convictions as law. Awareness of the subjective element in judging must end in curbing it. He strove not to eliminate subjectivity, but to tame it. Recognition of self was to him the first step toward judicial self-control.

"Men whose fashion is to press their power to the utmost," Herbert Wechsler has observed, "will never understand how much there was of self-subordination in his great work." [101]

To certain students of his career Stone's distrust of extremes made him seem lacking in courage. His friend Thomas Reed Powell once described him "as a person who turned neither to partiality on the one hand nor impartiality on the other." [102] It seems more likely that his

[99] Stone to Duane R. Dills, January 22, 1936 (Stone Papers).

[100] Stone, "The Common Law in the United States," *loc. cit.*

[101] "In Memoriam, Harlan Fiske Stone," remarks of Herbert Wechsler, November 12, 1947, *Proceedings of the Bar and Officers of the Supreme Court of the United States*, 46.

[102] Credited to Thomas Reed Powell in Felix Frankfurter, "Harlan Fiske Stone," *Year Book of the American Philosophical Society*, 1946, p. 339.

arduous search was due to a sophisticated understanding of our political heritage, a wide knowledge of our country's vast complexity, and an acute awareness of the role the Court must and should play in the American scheme of government.

CHAPTER 5

Toward Positive Responsibility

JUDICIAL retreat in 1937 shocked a minority which so recently had been a majority, and confounded conservative legalism generally. An enlarged concept of public power over economic affairs suggested "a ramp, with no convenient landings for a logical mind . . . to rest on." [1] "Almost anything," Justice McReynolds blustered in his Jones and Laughlin dissent—"marriage, birth, death—may in some fashion affect commerce." [2] Nor were the Justice's fears ungrounded. In rapid succession old landmarks were effaced. "The plain result . . . is," President Frank J. Hogan of the American Bar Association commented on the disrupting consequences, "no lawyer can safely advise his client what the law is; no business man, no farmer, can know whether or not he is breaking the law, for if he follows established principles he is likely to be doing exactly that." Disregard of the venerable *stare decisis* principle had replaced stability with instability, substituted uncertainty for certainty. Plenary power had superseded limitations upon power, so that "most if not all activities of the Nation" were centered in Washington.

[1] Charles P. Curtis, *Lions under the Throne* (Boston, 1947), 175.
[2] *National Labor Relations Board* v. *Jones and Laughlin Steel Corp.*, 301 U.S. 1 (1937), 99.

174

"The conclusion to be drawn from all of this," Hogan declared with resignation, "is that reliance against the exercise of arbitrary power must be placed by the people henceforth in the legislative rather than in the judicial department of the National Government. . . . Legislative independence and legislative wisdom are America's almost sole reliance for the continuance of that security of the blessings of liberty for which the Constitution was framed and the Government of the United States of America created." [3]

President Hogan misinterpreted 1937. The constitutional decisions overturned were of recent creation; their rejection involved a return "to first principles, as early pronounced by Marshall and others." [4] By hoisting the flag of self-restraint the Justices signaled retreat, not surrender. During the years since 1937, Americans have not been entirely at the mercy of legislative wisdom, legislative independence. Hogan exaggerated the role the Court was intended to play in the governing process. Dependence on the people was, and is, "the primary control" on government; judicial review is an "auxiliary" check. Judicial preeminence, a comparatively recent development dating from about 1890, had reversed the order and scope of these controls.

Chief Justice Marshall had been content to rely on the "wisdom and discretion of Congress," along with the usual political restraints.[5] Half a century later, Chief Justice

[3] An address by Frank J. Hogan, "Shifts in Constitutional Doctrines," *Legal Intelligencer*, July 22, 1939, p. 8. Also in *Reports of the American Bar Association*, 64 (1939), 498–500.

[4] Douglas, *We the Judges*, 431.

[5] "The wisdom and discretion of Congress," he declared in 1824, "their identity with the people, and the influence which their constituents possess at elections, are . . . in many . . . instances, as that, for example, of declaring war, the *sole restraints* on which they have relied, to secure them from its [Congress'] abuse. They are the restraints on which the people must often *rely solely, in all representa-*

Waite emphatically told aggrieved litigants to "resort to the polls, not the courts," when seeking judicial correction of alleged wrongs inflicted by a state legislature.[6] Justice Bradley [7] voiced these same sentiments in 1890. By that time, however, judicial aggrandizement had reached such a pitch as compelled him to do so in dissent, and thus initiate a plaintive note which became a resounding refrain later on in dissenting opinions by Justices Holmes, Brandeis, and Stone.

Judicial surrender of lawmaking power in the economic sphere has been compared to the British king's strategy in 1832. William IV relinquished his power in order to keep his place and, so we are told, the Justices yielded under

---

tive governments. . . ." Gibbons v. *Ogden,* 9 Wheaton 1 (1821), 197 Italics added.

[6] *Munn* v. *Illinois,* 94 U.S. 113 (1877). The entire passage reads: "For our purposes, we must assume that, if a state of facts could exist that would justify such legislation, it actually did exist when the statute now under consideration was passed. . . . We know that this is a power which may be abused; but that is no argument against its existence. For protection against abuses by legislatures the people must resort to the polls, not to the courts" (pp. 132, 134).

[7] Joined by Justices Horace Gray and Joseph Lamar, Bradley, charging that the Court "practically over-rules" *Munn* v. *Illinois,* reasoned: "It is complained that the decisions of the board are final and without appeal. So are the decisions of the courts in matters within their jurisdiction. There must be a final tribunal somewhere for deciding every question in the world. Injustice may take place in all tribunals. All human institutions are imperfect— courts as well as commissions and legislatures. . . . It may be that our legislatures are invested with too much power, open, as they are, to influences so dangerous to the interests of individuals, corporations and society. But such is the Constitution of our republican form of government; and we are bound to abide by it until it can be corrected in a legitimate way." *Chicago, Milwaukee and St. Paul R.R.* v. *Minnesota,* 134 U.S. 418, pp. 465–66. Justice Stone echoed Bradley's plaint in 1936 (*U.S.* v. *Butler,* 297 U.S. 1, pp. 87–88). The medium for expressing it was still a dissenting opinion.

pressure of President Roosevelt's threats. The parallel is suggestive but not entirely apt. The Court gave up power which it had itself previously usurped. When Stone accused his colleagues of governing by judicial fiat, he did not hint at self-abnegation, much less judicial abdication.

The Court's reversion to the Madison idea (that dependence on the people is America's primary safeguard against abuses of government power) suggested need of special alertness to any legislation possibly impairing the political process or hindering the effectiveness of its operation. As a sort of corollary to judicial self-restraint, Justice Stone invoked the doctrine of political restraints. Again, as in enunciating the preferred freedoms concept, he used a footnote as the vehicle of its expression.

In 1933 the general assembly of South Carolina prohibited use on its highways of trucks exceeding ninety inches in width and twenty thousand pounds. Stone, speaking for a unanimous court in *South Carolina* v. *Bramwell,* upheld the legislation. In the text of his opinion he wrote that "while the constitutional grant to Congress of power to regulate interstate commerce has been held to operate of its own force to curtail state power in some measure, it did not forestall all State action affecting interstate commerce." Attached to this proposition is the suggestive footnote:

State regulations affecting interstate commerce, whose purpose or effect is to gain for those within the state an advantage at the expense of those without, or to burden those out of the state without any corresponding advantage to those within, have been thought to impinge upon the constitutional prohibition even though Congress has not acted.

Underlying the stated rule has been the thought, often expressed in judicial opinion, that when the regulation is of such a character that its burden falls principally upon those without the state, legislative action is not likely to be subjected to those political restraints which are normally exerted on legislation where it affects adversely some interests within the state.[8]

This was precisely the situation created by the South Carolina statute. Judicial review was therefore auxiliary to political restraints. Put in another way, it is one thing for the Court to endorse congressional action, presumably enacted in the national interest and subject to approval or rejection by the voters in all the states; it is something else to uphold state regulations burdening those without the state, those to whom the usual political restraints are not available. As to restrictions of the latter sort, the Court's responsibility is correspondingly increased.

Stone's doctrine of political restraints, like that of preferred freedoms, has deep roots in the past.[9] Chief Justice Marshall suggested it as the rationale justifying the immunity of federal instrumentalities from state taxation. The states could not claim a similar immunity, Marshall said, because "the two cases are not on the same reason."

The people of all the States have created the general government, and have conferred upon it the general power of taxation. The people of all the States, and the States themselves, are represented in Congress, and, by their representatives, exercise this power. When they tax the chartered institutions of the States, they tax their constituents; and these taxes must be uniform. But, when a state taxes the operations of the government of the United States, it acts upon institutions

[8] *South Carolina* v. *Bramwell Bros.*, 303 U.S. 177 (1937), 184 n.2.

Stone expressed the same doctrine in *McGoldrick* v. *Berwind-White Coal Mining Co.*, 309 U.S. 33 (1940). Once again he resorted to a footnote for stating it. See footnote 2, pp. 45–46. The best discussion of judicial review vis-à-vis the doctrine of political restraints is Noel T. Dowling, "The Methods of Mr. Justice Stone in Constitutional Cases," 41 *Columbia Law Review* 1160 (November, 1941), especially 1171–81.

[9] See Dowling, "The Methods of Mr. Justice Stone in Constitutional Cases," *loc. cit.*, 1172–75.

created, not by their own constituents, but by people over whom they claim no control. It acts upon the measures of a government created by others as well as themselves, for the benefit of others in common with themselves. The difference is that which always exists, and always must exist, between the action of the whole on a part, and the action of a part on the whole—between the laws of a government declared to be supreme, and those of a government which, when in opposition to those laws, is not supreme.[10]

Stone argued that a federal tax on a state instrumentality does not have the same defect as a state tax on federal instrumentalities. For in "laying a Federal tax on state instrumentalities the people of the states, acting through their representatives, are laying a tax on their own institutions and consequently are subject to political restraints which can be counted on to prevent abuse. State taxation of national instrumentalities is subject to no such restraint, for the people outside the state have no representatives who participate in the legislation; and in a real sense, as to them, the taxation is without representation." The national taxing power is therefore "subject to a safeguard which does not operate when a state undertakes to tax a national instrumentality." [11] It is not enough, however, to uphold duly asserted national power. Chief Justice Marshall's nationalist proposition—a part cannot be permitted to control the whole—has an equally explicit corollary—Congress cannot be completely entrusted with the care of local interests. Stone rejected, as we have seen, the syncretic nationalist–laissez-faire theory Justice Frankfurter advanced in *New York* v. *United States*.

The doctrine of political restraints has given rise to harsh criticism. In 1945, when the Court set aside the statutory limit Arizona placed on the length of trains, Justice Black dissented vehemently. For him the commerce

[10] *McCulloch* v. *Maryland,* 435.
[11] *Helvering* v. *Gerhardt,* 412.

clause meant that Congress could regulate commerce and the Court could not. To him the 1937 "revolution" meant that the Justices had virtually surrendered their power as arbiters of the federal system. Said Justice Black: "The determination of whether it is in the interest of society for the length of trains to be governmentally regulated is a matter of public policy. Someone must fix that policy— either the Congress, or the State, or the courts. A century and a half of constitutional history and government admonishes this Court to leave that choice to the elected representatives of the people themselves, where it properly belongs both on democratic principles and the requirements of efficient government." [12]

Within a decade after victory for judicial self-restraint Justice Black felt constrained to reiterate the charge that the Court, speaking through Justice Stone, was "assuming the role of a 'super-legislature' in determining matters of governmental policy." [13] It was the same indictment that Stone himself had brought against his right-wing colleagues prior to 1937.

"The judicially directed march of the due process philosophy as an emancipator of business from regulation," the New Deal Justice remarked in 1949, "appeared arrested a few years ago. That appearance was illusory. That philosophy continues its march. The due process clause and commerce clause have been used like Siamese twins in a never-ending stream of challenges to government regulation." [14]

Justice Black's drive for judicial abnegation in this field has not prevailed. In the absence of congressional action the Court has the responsibility of protecting the federal system. What Justice Jackson aptly characterized as the

[12] *Southern Pacific Co.* v. *Arizona,* 325 U.S. 761 (1945), 789.
[13] *Morgan* v. *Virginia,* 328 U.S. 373 (1946), 387.
[14] *Hood* v. *Du Mond,* 336 U.S. 525 (1949), 562.

"great silences" of Congress have become the basis of a
positive responsibility, a source of judicial power. Stone
stated the now dominant view: "For a hundred years, it
has been accepted constitutional doctrine that the commerce clause, without the aid of Congressional legislation, thus affords some protection from state legislation
inimical to the national commerce, and that in such cases,
where Congress has not acted, this Court, and not the state
legislature, is under the commerce clause the final arbiter
of the competing demands of state and national interests. . . ." [15]

Not even Justice Douglas, then usually a Black sup-
porter, always endorsed the former senator's version of judicial self-restraint in cases involving federalism. Referring
in 1955 to the barriers states may place on national commerce, Douglas observed: "Congress, of course, could
have removed those barriers and probably would have
done so. But the judiciary has moved with speed. As a
result of the case by case approach, there has been no
great lag between the creation of the forbidden barrier or
burden and its removal by the judiciary." [16]

Justice Holmes gave the rationale of the positive task
the federal system imposes on the Supreme Court: "I do
not think the United States would come to an end if we
lost our power to declare an Act of Congress void. I do
think the Union would be imperiled if we could not make
that declaration as to the laws of the several States. For
one in my place sees how often a local policy prevails with
those who are not trained to national views and how often
action is taken that embodies what the Commerce Clause
was meant to end." [17]

Nor is the Court's responsibility confined to safeguard-

---

[15] *Southern Pacific Co.* v. *Arizona,* 325 U.S. 761, p. 769.
[16] Douglas, *We the Judges,* 254.
[17] Holmes, *Collected Legal Papers,* 295–96.

ing from state interference the power of Congress to regulate commerce. It must also protect the sovereignty of the
states. Chief Justice Stone made his position clear in 1941
when a majority ruled that in enacting the Pure Food and
Drug Act, Congress had so occupied the field as to preclude all state regulation. "It is one thing," he said, "for
courts in interpreting an Act of Congress regulating matters beyond state control to construe its language with a
view to carrying into effect a general though unexpressed
congressional purpose. It is quite another to infer a purpose, which Congress has not expressed, to deprive the
states of authority which otherwise constitutionally belongs to them, over a subject which Congress has not undertaken to control. Due regard for the maintenance of
our dual system of government demands that the courts
do not diminish state power by extravagant inferences
regarding what Congress might have intended if it had
considered the matter, or by reference to their own conceptions of a policy which Congress has not expressed
and is not plainly to be inferred from the legislation which
it has enacted." To restrict state power beyond the point
required by the statute is, Stone said, "to condemn a working harmonious federal-state relationship for the sake of
a sterile and harmful insistence on exclusive federal
power." [18]

Clearly the Court-packing struggle produced "no permanent reconciliation between the principles of representative government and the opposing principle of judicial authority." [19] Solution of baffling problems growing
out of federalism was still a judicial responsibility. Yet
Justice Roberts' words of 1951 merely echo what Frank
Hogan had said in 1939:

[18] Dissenting in *Cloverleaf Butter Co.* v. *Patterson,* 315 U.S. 148
(1942), 176–77.
[19] Jackson, *The Struggle for Judicial Supremacy,* vi.

The Supreme Court has limited and surrendered the role the Constitution was intended to confer on it. *Vox populi, vox Dei* was not the theory on which the charter was drawn. The sharp division of powers intended has become blurred. . . . It seems obvious that doctrines announced as corollaries to express grants of power to the Congress have more and more circumscribed the pristine powers of the states, which were intended to be reserved to them by the Constitution. . . .[20]

Roberts seems too pessimistic. The federal government, it is true, might almost completely supersede the states, but Congress has not often seen fit to go so far. Speaking for the Court in 1949, Justice Jackson declared:

While the Constitution vests in Congress the power to regulate commerce among the states, it does not say what the states may or may not do in the absence of congressional action, nor how to draw the line between what is and what is not commerce among the states. Perhaps even more than by interpretation of its written word, this Court has advanced the solidarity and prosperity of this Nation by the meaning it has given to these great silences of the Constitution. . . .[21]

What Metternich said about Austria after Waterloo might be said about the Supreme Court in the American political system today. "If there were no Supreme Court, somebody would have to invent one." The constitutional design of the framers embraces both a national and a local scheme of political activity. The Court is under obligation to preserve the integrity of the local within the general supremacy of the national. In the event of conflict between the legitimate interests of these two spheres of government, it is the Court's responsibility to correct such state action as cannot be reconciled with the national interest.

[20] Roberts, *The Court and the Constitution*, 95.
[21] *Hood* v. *Du Mond*, 534–35. For further discussion of this problem see *Bethlehem Steel Co.* v. *NLRB*, 330 U.S. 767 (1947) and *Castle* v. *Hayes Freight Lines*, 348 U.S. 61 (1954).

Before the judicial revolution of 1937 the Court acted, as it were, as a policeman over both federal and state legislatures, using the truncheon of "dual federalism" to enforce the dogma of laissez faire. Since 1937 the Court's function is more like that of a traffic cop—to see that our multiple legislatures, in their many activities, do not collide, to make sure that the road is kept free for national power, which, under the rules laid down in 1789, has the right of way. In case of state action unduly burdening interstate commerce, the Court must augment political restraints lest outlanders be left unprotected.

Self-restraint, in the sense of judicial hands-off, is difficult if not impossible to maintain. In 1821 counsel for Virginia contended that the Supreme Court could not take jurisdiction of a case on appeal from a sovereign state court. "They maintain," Chief Justice Marshall noted, "that the Constitution of the United States has provided no tribunal for the final construction of itself, . . . but that this power may be exercised in the last resort by the courts of every state of the Union." To Marshall such an oversight was unthinkable. Vesting final authority to interpret the Constitution in the state courts would create "a hydra in government, from which nothing but contradiction and confusion can proceed." [22] Chief Justice Roger Taney agreed: "So long . . . as this Constitution shall endure, this tribunal must exist with it, deciding in the peaceful forms of judicial proceeding the angry and irritating controversies between sovereignties, which in other countries have been determined by the arbitrament of force." [23] The segregation issue today, enmeshed as it is in politics, human rights, and deep-rooted emotional factors, highlights the Court's role in the struggle.

The Court's duty is equally imperative in case of con-

[22] *Cohens* v. *Virginia,* 6 Wheaton 264 (1821), 377, 415.
[23] *Ableman* v. *Booth,* 21 Howard 506 (1859), 521.

flicts between political organs of the national government. Differences among these power-wielding authorities are inevitable, and when they occur, judicial responsibility for their solution cannot easily be sidestepped.[24] The point was dramatically illustrated in the Youngstown Steel case, outlawing President Truman's seizure of company property.

Under the Taft-Hartley Act, Congress tried to provide a method of meeting emergency situations such as are often brought about by labor disputes. On April 8, 1952, during the Korean War, President Truman, to head off a threatened steel strike, issued an executive order directing the Secretary of Commerce to seize and operate the steel mills. "A work stoppage," the President's order declared, "would immediately jeopardize and imperil our national defense and the defense of those joined with us in resisting aggression, and would add to the continuing danger of our soldiers, sailors, and airmen engaged in combat in the field." Did the President have the power to choose, as his action clearly implied, means other than those provided in the Taft-Hartley Act of dealing with such an emergency? As to this the two political branches of the federal government were disagreed. What responsibility, if any, did the Justices have to resolve the clash?

While teaching at the Harvard Law School, Professor Frankfurter recognized that "the Supreme Court has always been arbiter of issues intrinsically political." Determination of political issues was then considered "pre-

[24] "The judicial power of the Supreme Court," the late Justice Jackson said in lectures prepared for delivery at Harvard University, "does extend to all cases arising under the Constitution, to controversies to which the United States is a party, and to those between two or more states. Thus, the Court must face political questions in legal form, for surely a controversy between two separately organized political societies does present a political question, even if waged with the formalities of a lawsuit." *The Supreme Court and the American System of Government,* 55.

eminently the characteristic of the Court's business." [25] As a Supreme Court Justice, however, he holds that the judiciary is not the "resolver of the clash" and ought, if possible, to find ways of avoiding a decision.

The Framers . . . did not make the judiciary the overseer of our government. . . . A basic rule is the duty of the Court not to pass on a constitutional issue at all, however narrowly it may be confined, if the case may, as a matter of intellectual honesty, be decided without even considering delicate problems of power under the Constitution. It ought to be, but apparently is not a matter of common understanding that clashes between different branches of the government should be avoided if a legal ground of less explosive potentialities is properly available.[26]

But here our political system impales the Justice on the horns of a dilemma. The Court "ought" to surrender its power. But to whom? Confronted with an important political issue, a judicial decision in favor of Congress or the President or no decision at all is a political determination. Finding no way to avoid it, Frankfurter shoulders the responsibility placed upon him by the Constitution. "And so," he comments helplessly, "with the utmost unwillingness, with every desire to avoid judicial inquiry into the powers and duties of the other two branches of the government, I cannot escape consideration of the legality of Executive Order No. 10340." [27]

Justice Frankfurter, the most articulate exponent of judicial self-restraint on the bench, joined in invalidating the President's seizure order, thereby asserting a power over a political branch of government it had previously shunned. Since Congress had not authorized it, the seizure was invalid. With the banner "self-restraint" still flying,

[25] Frankfurter, "The United States Supreme Court Moulding the Constitution," *loc. cit.*, 236.

[26] *Youngstown Sheet & Tube Co.* v. *Sawyer*, 343 U.S. 579 (1952), 594–95.

[27] *Ibid.*, 596.

the Court made it clear that Presidential action is not immune to judicial review. As to this bold stroke, the London *Economist* commented: "the Supreme Court, although it does not possess and never has possessed any means of enforcing its decisions, has once more brought to heel the mighty: the President, the union, the industry, and Congress. All that was needed to produce this effect was the knowledge that the Court had seen and was ready to do its constitutional duty." [28]

Other responsibilities rest heavily on the Court. The judiciary is "expected to maintain . . . the most delicate, difficult and shifting of all balances—that between liberty and authority." [29] Of all the civil rights, equal access to the ballot box is, of course, the most basic. The Court has a peculiar responsibility as protector of minorities singled out for attacks and unable to appeal effectively to the political processes. This task conforms to democratic precepts, for when some groups are permanently barred from access to the polls, the Court performs a democratic function in demanding that the integrity of the electoral process be preserved. Judicial intervention to safeguard voting rights does not run counter to the self-restraint recognized as appropriate for commercial regulations. Rather, it derives logically from it. If judicial deference is justified on the basis of the political restraints available against the legislature, the Court has a special role in relation to the political process by which the legislature is kept in its "proper place." "Reliance upon the operation of normal political processes," Professor Noel T. Dowling writes, "to obviate the need of judicial checks on other governmental powers may well be thought to impose a special responsibility on the Court to see to it, as far as the judicial de-

[28] *The Economist,* May 10, 1952, p. 371. Quoted in Schwartz, *The Supreme Court,* 5.
[29] Jackson, *The Supreme Court in the American System of Government,* 75.

vices permit, that those processes are adequately safe-guarded." [30]

In 1940 Stone recalled how "we have previously pointed to the importance of a searching judicial inquiry into the legislative judgment in situations where prejudice against discrete and insular minorities may tend to curtail the operation of those political processes ordinarily to be relied on to protect minorities." [31] When minority groups are kept permanently from exercising the right to vote, the political process is obviously obstructed. What respon-sibility rests on the Court in this situation? "There is no agency here available," John Raeburn Green contends, "to protect minorities when the majority does err, except the courts."

The limitations which the Constitution, and in particular the Bill of Rights, impose, were and are an exercise of self-restraint by a national majority, intended to be permanent until changed by a subsequent national (not local) majority. So long as they remain unchanged, they may fairly be taken to reflect the continuing and present popular will of the nation, much more accurately than a school board's regula-tion, a town's ordinance, or even a State's statute. The es-sential principle of the Bill of Rights is certainly that the protection of the fundamental rights of minorities is a matter of national concern, necessary, as Mr. Chief Justice Hughes said, "in order to save democratic government from destroy-ing itself by the excesses of its own powers." . . . In other words, the majority which makes and continues the consti-tutional compact . . . is not identical with the local majority which . . . has indicated its will by local legislation. In a clamor of conflicting commands, ought not the Court, when it is ultimately required to act in a litigated matter, to make some inquiry as to which is the authentic voice of the people? [32]

[30] Dowling, "The Methods of Mr. Justice Stone in Constitutional Cases," *loc. cit.*, 1175.
[31] 310 U.S. 586, p. 606.
[32] John Raeburn Green, review of Henry Steele Commager, *Ma-*

A series of important Supreme Court decisions gives an affirmative answer to Green's query. The 1954 decision outlawing racial segregation in public schools—one of the boldest judicial ventures in American history—did not come as a bolt from the blue. A series of cases between 1948 and 1950, marked by the forward-looking opinions of Chief Justice Fred Vinson, clearly indicated that the "separate but equal" doctrine was living on borrowed time. *Sipuel* v. *University of Oklahoma* (332 U.S. 631 [1948]) held that qualified Negroes must be admitted to a state law school or be furnished equivalent education within the state. *McLaurin* v. *Oklahoma State Regents* (339 U.S. 637 [1950]) nullified a state effort to segregate the scholastic activities of a Negro student admitted to the graduate school of the University of Oklahoma pursuant to a Federal Court order. In *Sweatt* v. *Painter* (339 U.S. 629 [1950]) the Justices voted 9 to 0, throwing down a direct challenge to segregated education. Sweatt had been denied admission to the Texas Law School solely on the basis of color, instruction being made available to him in the recently established law school for Negroes. Chief Justice Vinson could not find "substantial equality in the educational opportunities offered white and Negro law students by the State." The Texas Law School possessed to a "far greater degree those qualities which are incapable of objective measurement but which make for greatness in a law school, . . . reputation of the faculty, experience of the administration, position and influence of the alumni, standing in the community, traditions and prestige." It was but a short step from Chief Justice Vinson's sentiments to Chief Justice Warren's dictum of 1954—"separate educational facilities are inherently unequal." Moreover, the Justices might have taken this step without annexing the

---

jority Rule and Minority Rights, 32 *California Law Review* 111 (1944), 117.

controversial footnote containing several references to supporting psychological knowledge and modern sociological authority.

Foundations had already been laid for the assertion of enlarged judicial responsibility in other areas. In certain Southern states the White Primary was long a permanent bar against Negro participation in voting. The Democratic primary being in fact the election, Negroes denied the right to vote therein were in effect eliminated from the governing process. The Supreme Court ignored this fact by the convenient fiction that elections in the constitutional sense do not include the party primaries.[33] In 1941, however, a case arose in Louisiana involving the alleged failure of election officials to count ballots properly in a congressional primary. Justice Stone, writing for the Court in *United States* v. *Classic*,[34] maintained that the primary was in fact the election and therefore came under aegis of federal control. The primary was not a private affair in Louisiana, Stone ruled, because it represented, essentially, the election for federal office. "Here," he said, "even apart from the circumstance that the Louisiana primary is made by law an integral part of the procedure of choice, the right to choose a representative is in fact controlled by the primary because, as is alleged in the indictment, the choice of candidates at the Democratic primary determines the choice of the elected representative. . . ."[35]

The Classic decision set the stage for the death knell of the White Primary. In 1944, less than a decade after the

[33] *Newberry* v. *U.S.*, 256 U.S. 232 (1921). In *Grovey* v. *Townsend*, 295 U.S. 45 (1935), the Court held that political parties were free to define the conditions of party membership to be met by voters in primaries, and that such action was not "state action," despite the fact that the state accepted the primary results.
[34] 313 U.S. 299 (1941).
[35] *Ibid.*, 318–19.

Court had accepted the primary as a sort of private game immune from federal control, Lonnie Smith, a Negro citizen of Texas, barred from participation in the Texas Democratic primary on the basis of a party resolution, sued Allwright, the election official, for damages. The Supreme Court, upholding Smith's claims, justified its decision in terms of the American theory of "constitutional democracy." Said Justice Reed:

> It may now be taken as a postulate that the right to vote in such a primary for the nomination of candidates without discrimination by the State, like the right to vote in a general election, is a right secured by the Constitution. . . . By the terms of the Fifteenth Amendment that right may not be abridged by any State on account of race. Under our Constitution, the great privilege of the ballot may not be denied a man by the State because of his color. . . .
>
> The United States is a constitutional democracy. Its organic law grants to all citizens a right to participate in the choice of elected officials without restriction by any State because of race. This grant to the people of the opportunity for choice is not to be nullified by a State through casting its electoral process in a form which permits a private organization to practice racial discrimination in the election. Constitutional rights would be of little value if they could be thus indirectly denied.[36]

The primary was as much the election in Texas in 1935 as in 1944 when the Smith case was decided. The words of the Constitution had not been changed. The Fifteenth Amendment remained the same for all the White Primary cases. Nor had the facts been substantially altered. Changed were the Justices' views as to the actual situation and their own constitutional responsibilities thereto. The shift was a positive performance as creative as that of the legislature.

The White Primary cases vividly illustrate the wide

[36] *Smith* v. *Allwright*, 321 U.S. 649 (1944), 661–62, 664.

range of lawmaking activity open to the Court and expose the exercise of power a century and a half of denials has not been able to cloak. In 1946 one writer envisioned in the Classic opinion "several untapped potentialities." He saw it as opening up "breath-taking vistas," as indicating the assumption of even broader judicial responsibility— the obligation to protect civil rights from "vicious private interference" generally. As the shenanigans of party officials in the South show, freedom can be infringed by the action of private individuals and groups. Does government have authority to protect political freedoms from such individual action? The Civil Rights cases of 1883 held that the Fourteenth Amendment applies only to state action, not to individual injustices. Recently, however, the Court has expanded its definition of state action. In *Shelley* v. *Kraemer* [37] the Court held that a restrictive covenant could not be judicially enforced, since such sanction would cloak private action with officiality and thus deprive a person of equal protection of the law. The implications are far-reaching.

"If," Alexander Pekelis has written, "the outcome of a private primary is in fact determinative of the result in the official elections, . . . then the constitutional requirement of fairness in the elections extends further to the private game which really counts." "I submit," Pekelis continues, "that the right to keep the political processes free from private interference, the doctrine asserted in the *Classic* case, is a broad formula that must cover, to mean what it says, freedom from vicious private interference with political education and the formation of opinion, and freedom from economic obstacles in its expression." [38]

Pekelis' forecast was borne out in the decision of 1953

[37] 334 U.S. 1 (1948).
[38] Alexander H. Pekelis, *Law and Social Action* (Ithaca, 1950), 113–14.

holding that the action of self-styled private citizens, making rules for the conduct of "private," all-white primary elections, was subject to the same constitutional controls that might be imposed if it were the action of Texas public officials.[39] The possibilities this writer discerned in the Classic opinion of 1941 may be further realized in judicial reaction to various proposals for circumventing the desegregation decisions of 1954. The Court's decision in the *Civil Rights Cases* of 1883 still stands as a bar against direct national regulation of nongovernmental education and of "private" racial injustice. But Justice Harlan's dissenting opinion that this seventy-five-year-old ruling rested "upon ground entirely too narrow and artificial" [40] may yet prevail.

The Court has not always acted to keep the political process pure and unimpeded. A glaring inequity in our electoral system, by which certain groups are permanently

[39] *Terry* v. *Adams,* 345 U.S. 461 (1953).

[40] *Civil Rights Cases,* 109 U.S. 3 (1883), 26. Continuing, Harlan said: "Constitutional provisions, adopted in the interest of liberty, and for the purpose of securing, through national legislation, if need be, rights inhering in a state of freedom, and belonging to American citizenship, have been so construed as to defeat the ends the people desired to accomplish, which they attempted to accomplish, and which they supposed they had accomplished by changes in their fundamental law. . . .

"Exemption from race discrimination in respect of the civil rights which are fundamental in *citizenship* in a republican government is a . . . new right, created by the nation, with express power in Congress, by legislation, to enforce the constitutional provision from which it is derived. . . .

"What I affirm is that no State, nor the officers of any State, nor any corporation or individual wielding power under State authority for the public benefit or the public convenience, can, consistently either with the freedom established by the fundamental law, or with that equality of civil rights which now belongs to every citizen, [under the Thirteenth, Fourteenth, and Fifteenth amendments] discriminate against freemen or citizens, in those rights because of their race, or because they once labored under the disabilities of slavery imposed upon them as a race" (pp. 26, 56, 59).

kept from full participation in the political process, has resulted from the unwillingness of state legislatures to reapportion election districts to accord with the actual distribution of population. The voter in a district of rapid population growth will have a much smaller voice in elections than the voter from the district of steady or declining population. When this "system" works, as it often does, to give certain areas having less than a majority of the population permanent control over the state legislature, or over the state's congressional delegation, the practical result is a proportionate disenfranchisement of those in the rest of the state. Furthermore, the control over the legislature by the representatives of these rotten boroughs not only perpetuates the situation but also prevents the normal political process from providing a corrective.

This condition in Illinois was notorious. Congressional districts had not been reapportioned since 1901. The largest district had nine times the population of the smallest. In *Colegrove* v. *Green* the disenfranchised voters finally challenged the Illinois "system." But no help was forthcoming from the Supreme Court. The issue facing the Justices, Frankfurter declared, was "of a peculiarly political nature and therefore not meet for judicial determination. . . . From the determination of such issues this Court has traditionally held aloof. It is hostile to a democratic system to involve the judiciary in the politics of the people. And it is not less pernicious if such judicial intervention in an essentially political contest be dressed up in the abstract phrases of the law." [41]

"Strange language," Bernard Schwartz comments somewhat derisively, "from a tribunal that has, from the very nature of its constitutional function, been making political decisions from the very beginning of its history! Strange timidity from a Court that has since become embroiled,

[41] 328 U.S. 549 (1946), 552–54 *passim*.

via its school segregation decisions, in one of the most significant political issues of our times!" [42] The contradiction is even more "strange" when one puts Frankfurter's fastidious pronouncements of 1946 alongside what he wrote in 1930. As a professor of law he led his students to believe that "the cases before the Supreme Court . . . in essence . . . involve the stuff of politics." [43]

The Colegrove case is similar in certain respects to the White Primary case of *Smith* v. *Allwright*. In both, a minority was barred from full participation in the political process. Both involved issues of a "peculiarly political nature"; both brought the Court "into immediate and active relations with party contests"—as, indeed, have scores of other important judicial decisions. In both cases the Constitution had expressly authorized Congress to correct the abuses complained of. In the White Primary cases the Court stepped in and corrected the "system." In the Illinois apportionment case, however, Justice Frankfurter applied (or misapplied) the doctrine of judicial self-restraint.

"The remedy ultimately," Frankfurter declared, "lies with the people. . . . The remedy for unfairness in districting is to secure State legislatures that will apportion properly, or to invoke the ample powers of Congress." [44] Such deference to the legislature illustrates the logical inconsistency of the application of judicial self-restraint in cases affecting political rights. To say that the only remedy lies with the body that perpetuates the abuse is to admit that there is no remedy. To avoid the issue because it

[42] Schwartz, *The Supreme Court,* 149–50.

An even more extreme case of judicial obtuseness to the constitutional guarantee to the states of a republican government is *South* v. *Peters* (239 U.S. 276, 1950) repulsing an effort by Georgia voters to destroy the so-called county unit system.

[43] Frankfurter, "The Supreme Court and the Public," *loc. cit.,* 330.

[44] 328 U.S. 549, pp. 554, 556.

is a "political question" is, as the dissenters pointed out ". . . a mere 'play upon words.' " It is to maintain that "courts have nothing to do with protecting and vindicating the right of a voter to cast an effective ballot"—the most elementary right in a free society, and essential to the functioning of free government.[45]

Voting is only the end result of a long political process —the product of a complex political choice. Even if the voting system is kept free and open to all, effective political choice would be impossible if the climate of opinion were such as to discourage free and effective interchange of ideas among the contesting parties. If the suffrage nominally open to all qualified voters is exercised in an atmosphere of apprehension, does the Supreme Court have responsibility to correct this condition? That is to say, does the Court have any obligation to guarantee conditions prerequisite to the operation of political processes? What responsibility rests on it to safeguard that "freedom of mind and spirit . . . without which no free government can exist?"

Freedom of speech, press, and assembly, the high notes in countless patriotic speeches, are concepts whose meaning is far from clear. In the abstract, all Americans defend freedom; and for himself, each American endorses it as absolutely necessary. But the question of free speech for the other fellow, especially when his views are unorthodox, elicits a variety of responses, among laymen and Supreme Court Justices alike.

For certain Justices, as we have seen, the First Amendment freedoms are "preferred"—as sacred as those of property and contract had been to members of an earlier bench. In the case of the former, the preference seems more solidly grounded, for in the regulation of property, "due process of law" is the only constitutional bar. First Amend-

[45] *Ibid.*, 573–74.

ment freedoms, on the other hand, are protected from legislative encroachment not only by the due process requirement but also by the injunction that "Congress shall make *no* law . . . abridging the freedom of speech, or of the press; or the right of the people peaceably to assemble. . . ." The Constitution does not embody, as Holmes said, any particular *economic* philosophy, but it does seem to incorporate a particular political theory. Central to that theory are the freedoms listed in the First Amendment. Self-restraint does not mean that the Court is paralyzed. "It simply conserves its strength," as Attorney-General Jackson put it, "to strike more telling blows in the cause of a working democracy." [46]

"The very purpose of a Bill of Rights," Justice Jackson wrote in the second flag salute case, "was to withdraw certain subjects from the vicissitudes of political controversy, to place them beyond the reach of majorities and officials and to establish them as legal principles to be applied by the courts. . . . We cannot, because of modest estimates of our competence in such specialities as public education, withhold the judgment that history authenticates as the function of this Court when liberty is infringed." [47]

Shortly before his death, Jackson qualified his earlier view that the Court by "intervening" in cases affecting civil rights "restores the processes of democratic government." In his last pronouncement he assailed the "vicious teaching" of that "cult of libertarian judicial activists" who wish to use the Court as a check on the legislature in political matters. Said Jackson:

The question that the present times put into the minds of thoughtful people is to what extent Supreme Court interpretations of the Constitution will or can preserve the free gov-

[46] Jackson, *The Struggle for Judicial Supremacy,* 285.
[47] *West Virginia State Board of Education* v. *Barnette,* 319 U.S. 624 (1943), 638, 640.

ernment of which the Court is a part. A cult of libertarian judicial activists now assails the Court almost as bitterly for renouncing power as the earlier "liberals" once did for assuming too much power. This cult appears to believe that the Court can find in a 4,000-word eighteenth-century document or its nineteenth-century Amendments, or can plausibly supply, some clear bulwark against all dangers and evils that today beset us internally. This assumes that the Court will be the dominant factor in shaping the constitutional practice of the future and can and will maintain, not only equality with the elective branches, but a large measure of supremacy and control over them. I may be biased against this attitude because it is so contrary to the doctrines of the critics of the Court, of whom I was one, at the time of the Roosevelt proposal to reorganize the judiciary. But it seems to me a doctrine wholly incompatible with faith in democracy, and in so far as it encourages a belief that the judges may be left to correct the result of public indifference to issues of liberty in choosing Presidents, Senators and Representatives, it is a vicious teaching.[48]

Nor has the preferred position Justice Jackson once accorded First Amendment freedom been generally acceptable to a majority of the Court. Differences center not so much on the abstract value of these rights as on the responsibility the judiciary is under in relation to them.

"In our system," Justice Rutledge maintained, "where the line can constitutionally be placed presents a question this Court cannot escape answering independently, whatever the legislative judgment, in the light of our constitu-

[48] Jackson, *The Supreme Court in the American System of Government,* 57–58. Taking essentially Jackson's revised position, one writer characterizes the "preferred freedoms" doctrine as "that *beau geste* which would give Americans 'better' government than they are at the moment able to give themselves and take from them (perhaps merely dilute) moral responsibility for their acts, which is the indispensable matrix of human freedom." Wallace Mendelson, "Mr. Justice Rutledge's Mark on the Bill of Rights," 50 *Columbia Law Review* 48 (1950), 51.

tional tradition. . . . And the answer, under that tradition, can be affirmative, to support an intrusion upon this domain, only if grave and impending public danger requires this." [49]

Justice Frankfurter, on the other hand, persists somewhat intermittently in his advocacy of a highly restricted role for the Court, whatever the rights at stake. The concept of "preferred position of freedom of speech" he castigates as "a phrase that has uncritically crept into some recent opinions of this Court. I deem it a mischievous phrase, if it carries the thought, which it may subtly imply, that any law touching communication is infected with presumptive invalidity." [50] Courts should, Frankfurter believes, stand aloof from any responsibility of weighing the competing interests of free speech in a democratic society and the interests of national security.

Full responsibility for the choice cannot be given to the courts. Courts are not representative bodies. They are not designed to be a good reflex of a democratic society. Their judgment is best informed, and therefore most dependable, within narrow limits. Their essential quality is detachment, founded on independence. History teaches that the independence of the judiciary is jeopardized when courts become embroiled in the passions of the day and assume primary responsibility in choosing between competing political, economic and social pressures.[51]

[49] *Thomas* v. *Collins,* 323 U.S. 516 (1945), 531–32. Black's position is indistinguishable: "I view the guaranties of the First Amendment as the foundation upon which our governmental structure rests and without which it could not continue to endure as conceived and planned. Freedom to speak and write about public questions is as important to the life of our government as is the heart to the human body. In fact, this privilege is the heart of our government. If that heart be weakened, the result is debilitation; if it be stilled, the result is death." Dissenting, *Milk Wagon Drivers' Union* v. *Meadowmoor Co.,* 312 U.S. 287 (1941), 301–302.

[50] *Kovacs* v. *Cooper,* 336 U.S. 77 (1949), 90.

[51] *Dennis* v. *U.S.,* 341 U.S. 494 (1951), 525.

The "libertarian activists"—Black, Rutledge, Murphy, and Douglas—on the other hand, accord free speech practically absolute protection against legislative encroachment. Dissenting in the Dennis case, Justices Douglas and Black called for restoration of the First Amendment freedoms to their preferred standing. For them "free speech is the rule, not the exception. The restraint to be constitutional must be based on more than fear, on more than passionate opposition against the speech, on more than a revolted dislike for its contents. There must be some immediate injury to society that is likely if speech is allowed. . . . The First Amendment makes confidence in the common sense of our people and in their maturity of judgment the great postulate of our democracy." [52]

The Smith Act case and certain other important decisions handed down during the 1956–1957 term represented a step toward acceptance of this philosophy. In the scales on which liberty and authority are balanced, the pendulum has swung toward freedom's side. Chief Justice Warren and newly appointed Justice Brennan have joined such veteran supporters of civil liberties as Black and Douglas in asserting the Court's role as protector of American liberties. It is significant, however, that in the case of the West Coast Communists, Justice Black wrote a concurrence reiterating his belief that the Smith Act is itself unconstitutional. Neither the majority opinion in this case, nor in any of the other 1957 rulings, justifies the fear aroused in certain quarters that the Justices will presume unconstitut*onality of legislation touching the First Amendment freedoms. The decisions do indicate quite conclusively that the Warren Court, far more than that headed by Chief Justice Vinson, is disposed to subject

[52] Language of Justice Douglas, 341 U.S. 494, pp. 585, 590. The position of the judicial activists is essentially the same as that of Alexander Meiklejohn. See Douglas, *We the Judges,* 310.

legislation restricting freedom of mind and spirit to "more searching judicial inquiry." [53] The Court under Chief Justice Warren, Thurman Arnold declares, is becoming "unified," "a Court of inspired choice and policy . . . rather than a Court of law as we used to know it." [54] It is no longer fair to conclude, as did Bernard Schwartz in 1957, that "only Justices Black and Douglas are still partisans of a preferred status for First Amendment rights." [55]

Minority rights by definition limit majority rule. In his First Inaugural Address, Jefferson admonished all "to bear in mind this sacred principle, that though the will of the majority is in all cases to prevail, that will to be rightful must be reasonable, that the minority possess their equal rights which equal law must protect and to violate which would be oppression." "Free government," Abel P. Upshur wrote in 1837, "so far as its protecting power is concerned, is made for minorities alone." [56] Can the Supreme Court block the will of the majority in the name of minorities and still remain a democratic institution? When the minority rights protected are those of property, the answer is probably "no." Between 1890 and 1937, the Supreme Court actually retarded the growth of democracy. When, on the other hand, judicial review serves to give a minority, otherwise barred, access to the political process, it implements rather than limits free govern-

[53] Even Justice Frankfurter has said that "those liberties of the individual which history has attested as the indispensable conditions of an open as against a closed society come to this Court with a momentum for respect lacking when appeal is made to liberties which derive merely from shifting economic arrangements." *Kovacs v. Cooper,* 336 U.S. 77 (1949), 95.

[54] Quoted in *Business Week,* July 6, 1957, p. 34.

[55] Schwartz, *The Supreme Court,* 239. See Anthony Lewis, "Four Justices Setting Tone for High Court," *New York Times,* Dec. 29, 1957.

[56] Abel P. Upshur, *The Federal Government, Its True Nature and Character* (New York, 1868), 232.

"Can You See Me Now?"

Herblock in the Washington Post, *June 18, 1957*

ment.[57] Majorities—and this is a key point of democratic theory—are in flux. Tomorrow's majority may have a different composition as well as different goals. Defense of the political rights of minorities thus becomes, not the antithesis of majority rule, but its very foundation. The majority must leave open the political process by which

[57] For an excellent discussion of this thesis, see Eugene Rostow, "The Democratic Character of Judicial Review," 66 *Harvard Law Review* (1952), 193–224.

it can be replaced when no longer able to command majority support.

It is not enough to maintain merely the forms of free government. Equally necessary is such a climate of freedom as will create confidence that the established machinery will work for the good of all. As Louis Lusky has written:

There is a national interest not only in preserving a form of government in which men can control their own destinies, but in enabling the common man to see its advantages and know its feasibility. It is an interest in quelling doubts as to the practical efficacy of our system to accomplish essential justice. It is an interest in preventing deviations from our national ideal, . . . because deviations create such doubts. In short, it is an interest in making a belief in our system a part of the American creed.

The Court [Lusky continues] thus performs an important part in the maintenance of the basic conditions of just legislation. By preserving the hope that bad laws can and will be changed, the Court preserves the basis for the technique of political obligation, minimizing extra-legal opposition to the government by making it unnecessary. . . . Where the regular corrective processes are interfered with, the Court must remove the interference; where the dislike of minorities renders those processes ineffective to accomplish their underlying purpose of holding out a real hope that unwise laws will be changed, the Court itself must step in.[58]

The function of the Supreme Court is not to determine what decisions can be made by political processes, but to prevent the mechanism from breaking down. Under this theory the legislature can control the wages and hours of workers; it cannot limit the right to vote with respect to race or color. Congress can regulate agricultural production; it cannot control the content of newspapers. The state can demand that children attend school; it cannot

[58] Louis Lusky, "Minority Rights and the Public Interest," 52 *Yale Law Journal* (1942), 18–21.

compel them to participate in political ceremonies that violate their religious convictions. Judicial hands-off in economic matters is perfectly consistent with judicial activism designed to preserve the integrity of the political process.

"There is nothing covert or conflicting," Justice Jackson commented the year he was appointed to the bench, "in the recent judgments of the Court on social legislation and on legislative repressions of civil rights. The presumption of validity which attaches in general to legislative acts is frankly reversed in the case of interferences with free speech and free assembly, and for a perfectly cogent reason. Ordinarily, legislation whose basis in economic wisdom is uncertain can be redressed by the processes of the ballot box or the pressures of opinion. But when the channels of opinion or of peaceful persuasion are corrupted or clogged, these political correctives can no longer be relied on, and the democratic system is threatened at its most vital point. In that event the Court, by intervening, restores the processes of democratic government; it does not disrupt them." [59]

An appointive body, such as the Supreme Court, exercising political control in a system of government whose powers are supposed to derive from the people, has, as we have seen, sometimes been considered an alien offshoot from an otherwise democratic polity. The dilemma was once resolved by invoking the fiction that the Court had no power—that it merely applied the Constitution which, in some mystical way, is always the highest expression of the people's will. Though this ancient theory still shows signs of vitality, it is not altogether satisfying. The real problem is to protect individuals and minorities without thereby destroying capacity in the majority to govern. The Supreme Court alone cannot solve this impondera-

[59] Jackson, *The Struggle for Judicial Supremacy*, 284–85.

ble, but it can contribute toward a solution. It may do so by guaranteeing all minority groups free access to the political process and the instruments of political change, while at the same time allowing the majority government—as long as the political process is open and untrammeled—to rule.

CHAPTER 6

By the Light of Reason

L ET us face the fact," Professor Frankfurter proclaimed in 1930, "that five Justices of the Supreme Court *are* moulders of policy, rather than impersonal vehicles of revealed truth." [1] Others have suggested that the Court might use its political power for wholesome social purposes. "Conservative majorities in past Courts have always legislated in the interests of the business community," Arthur Schlesinger, Jr., points out. "Why should a liberal majority tie its hands by a policy of self-denial?" [2]

Evidence mounts that Chief Justice Earl Warren's Court is alert to positive responsibilities. The Warren Court began the task of applying "to ever changing conditions the never changing principles of freedom" [3] on May 17, 1954. On that historic day the Justices handed down their unanimous decision in the school segregation cases. The anxiously awaited judgment was short and incisive. Chief Justice Warren found neither history nor precedent an adequate guide. Special studies of the intention of the framers of the Fourteenth Amendment were

[1] Frankfurter, "The Supreme Court and the Public," *loc. cit.*, 334.

[2] Arthur Schlesinger, Jr., "The Supreme Court, 1947," 35 *Fortune* 73 (Jan. 1947), 202.

[3] Earl Warren, "The Law and the Future," *Fortune*, Nov. 1955, p. 107.

inconclusive. Nor did previous Court rulings in this genre suffice. In these, the Court had not considered the validity of the "separate but equal" formula per se; it chose to rule on other grounds. For all these reasons, the Justices now had to look at the educational system itself.

"In approaching this problem," the Chief Justice remarked, "we cannot turn the clock back to 1868, when the Amendment was adopted, or even to 1896 when *Plessy* v. *Ferguson* [4] was written. We must consider public education in the light of its full development and its present place in American life throughout the Nation."

Education, the Court ruled, "is the very foundation of good citizenship." Segregated schools, by that fact alone, tend to retard the educational and mental development of Negro children. "To separate them from others of similar age and qualifications solely because of their race generates a feeling of inferiority as to their status in the community that may affect their hearts and minds in a way unlikely ever to be undone." [5] In support of these propositions the Court cited the "modern authority" of six sociological and psychological texts, concluding that "separate educational facilities are inherently unequal" and, therefore, violate the equal protection clause of the Fourteenth Amendment.

With this decision certain of the most sacred temples in the realm of judicial witchcraft crumbled. Exorcism was out of style. Even the observance of *stare decisis* was rudely shaken; the notion that social facts are meet for the legislature but not for the Court was ignored; the distinction between *judgment* and *will*, already tenuous, was honored only in the breach.

Public reaction to the Court's ruling was electric and

[4] 163 U.S. 537.
[5] *Brown* v. *Board of Education,* 347 U.S. 483 (1954), 492–94 *passim.*

widely divergent. Certain observers marked the case as denoting judicial statesmanship of the first order; others denounced it as judicial usurpation. Much of the discussion centered (it still does) on the merits of the issue—that is, whether public schools should be desegregated. For those whose interests are less parochial, the decision raises basic questions concerning the Court's place in American life and politics.

On all sides a strangely archaic note is sounded. "Was the Court legislating?" Yes, say opponents of integration. Instead of following the constitutional mandate, law was made out of whole cloth. The Court's defenders maintain, on the other hand, that the Justices merely followed the clear wording of the Constitution. Being helpless to do otherwise, they should not be criticized. Still others hold that, though the Court was justified in ignoring a fifty-year-old precedent, it did it the wrong way. Instead of relying on solid legal arguments, Chief Justice Warren had based his opinion on the quicksands of social psychology. If the Court had grounded the case in its own precedents, the argument runs, it would have been "less vulnerable to criticisms to the effect that the decision was sheer judicial legislation." [6]

Any disinclination now to recognize the fact that the Court makes law seems extraordinary. Robert H. Jackson, later Associate Justice, once described the Court as a sort of "continuous constitutional convention which, without submitting its proposals to any ratification or rejection, could amend the basic law." [7] Jackson was only reporting what official Court reports reveal. The segregation cases reaffirm the fact that judges do make and unmake law.

[6] Robert J. Harris, "The Constitution, Education, and Segregation," 29 *Temple Law Quarterly* 409 (1956), 432.

[7] Jackson, *The Struggle for Judicial Supremacy*, x–xi.

The knowledge that judges are "willing, purposeful creatures" is now an open secret, Professor Robert Mc-Closkey commented. In the summer of 1956 *Time* magazine blithely informed its readers that the present Chief Justice "views his role as steering the law rather than being steered by it." [8] The Chief Justice did not, as we have seen, state his views quite so cavalierly. The segregation decision is nevertheless a conspicuous example of how an unelected, politically non-responsible body can accomplish what Congress was "powerless" to achieve. "What has occurred," Robert J. Harris explains, "has been the atrophy of the fifth section of the fourteenth amendment [9] as a result both of judicial decisions and of the continuing influence of John C. Calhoun, whose mischievous device of the concurrent veto finds current expression in the Senate filibuster and the seniority rule in the organization of congressional committees, either of which is a sufficient barrier to legislative implementation of the fourteenth amendment. If the fourteenth amendment is to have meaning, the Court must provide it, and, in doing so, it must have regard to all relevant factors." [10]

"The Court," Harris observes, "has never been more

[8] Robert G. McCloskey, "The Supreme Court Finds a Role: Civil Liberties in the 1955 Term," 42 *Virginia Law Review* (October 1956), 736.

[9] "The Congress shall have power, by appropriate legislation, to enforce the provisions of this article."

The civil rights legislation enacted in 1957, 1960, 1964, and 1965, though short of what its advocates sought, sets up non-jury-trial civil-contempt sanctions to protect the most basic of civil rights— the right to vote. This legislation is significant as representing the first civil rights legislation since the Reconstruction. So, despite the practical obstacles in the way of implementing the Fourteenth and Fifteenth amendments, Congress may yet come to the aid of the Court.

[10] Harris, "The Constitution, Education, and Segregation," *loc. cit.*, 432.

candid in basing a reversal of precedent on changing conditions and new developments alone than it was here." [11] Yet judicial lawmaking must still be either denounced or denied. Though none may believe it, the doctrine that judges *will* nothing lingers on. Robeism is still with us.

How is the Court to fulfill the statesmanlike role the present Chief Justice envisages for it amid professions of adherence to an exploded myth? An unfortunate aspect of the pre-1937 Court was that it not only legislated in favor of a particular set of values but shamelessly mouthed the fiction of powerlessness to do so. With eyes thus closed to reality, the Justices intoned esoteric phrases of a meaning, as the inconsistent pattern of judicial decisions shows, apparent only to themselves. Surely if the Court is to step into the role spelled out for it by that three-pronged Carolene Products footnote, if it is to apply to "ever changing conditions the never changing principles of freedom," it must do so firmly and with clear recognition of what it is doing.

Revival of myth, stimulated by controversy over the segregation issue, highlights the need for better understanding of the Supreme Court. This education can best be furthered by the knowledge that judges, like other human beings, are influenced by political and personal factors. "When I woke up one morning a federal court judge," Jerome Frank commented in 1945, "I found myself about the same person who had gone to bed the night before an S.E.C. Commissioner." "It is not good, either for the country or the Court," Frankfurter insisted during his pre-Court years, "that the part played by the Court in the life of the country should be shrouded in mystery." The Court, he emphasized, "exercises essentially political functions. . . . So long as this power of judicial review exists, its true nature should be frankly recognized by the

11 *Ibid.*, 431.

public and by the Court." [12] These ideas were, perhaps, mildly shocking in 1930. Though rather commonplace today, the argument in their support has strengthened through the years.

Recognition of the Court's actual policy-making function might help the Justices themselves as well as further public understanding of the judicial function. Consider the matter of *stare decisis,* of stability—an historical value of first importance in jurisprudence. The legal lexicon defines *stare decisis* as "a doctrine giving to precedent the authority of established law." Following this definition is the somewhat waggish qualification—"not, however, always followed." Nor should it be slavishly adhered to in constitutional cases. The high court outlawed the exclusion of Negroes from voting in primary elections, reversing a fresh precedent of only a few years. It forbade racial segregation in public schools after sticking to the "separate but equal" doctrine for nearly two generations. Charles Evans Hughes's test of stability suggests that these decisions should have been avoided or explained away, lest it be revealed that judges make and unmake law. Other Justices feel no such compulsion.

"*Stare decisis,*" Brandeis explained, is not a universal, inexorable command. It "does not command that we err again when we have occasion to pass upon a different statute." [13] "The Court bows to the lessons of experience and the force of better reasoning, recognizing that the process of trial and error, so fruitful in the physical sciences, is appropriate also in the judicial function." [14] "The doctrine of *Swift* v. *Tyson,*" he wrote in a significant judicial upset (quoting Holmes), "is 'an unconstitutional

[12] Frankfurter, "The Supreme Court and the Public," *loc. cit.,* 329–34 *passim.*
[13] *Di Santo* v. *Pennsylvania,* 273 U.S. 34 (1927), 42.
[14] *Burnet* v. *Coronado Oil & Gas Co.,* 285 U.S. 393 (1932), 407–408.

assumption of power by courts of the United States which no lapse of time or respectable array of opinion should make us hesitate to correct.' " [15] "If we would guide by the light of reason, we must let our minds be bold."

Stare decisis, Justice Stone commented, "gives to our institutions a certain stability and continuity of great practical worth." But rigid, mechanical observance of the rule is not required. Querying Hughes's test of stability, Stone suggestively wondered "whether continuity of legal doctrine is worth the price which, in some periods of our legal history, we have paid for it." [16]

"When convinced of former error," Justice Reed declared in 1944, "this Court has never felt constrained to follow precedent. In constitutional questions, where correction depends upon amendment and not upon legislative action this Court throughout its history has freely exercised its power to re-examine the basis of its constitutional decisions. This has long been accepted practice, and this practice has continued to this day." [17] Reed made this declaration regarding a current case which had reversed a comparatively recent decision outlawing the White Primary. Justice Roberts, dissenting, was outraged. Reed's cavalier disregard of *stare decisis* put adjudications of the Supreme Court "into the same class as a restricted railroad ticket, good for this day and train only." [18]

In 1944 Justice Roberts' statement must have seemed extreme even to himself. His words became virtually a statement of fact in 1957, when the Court reversed a ruling of the previous year in which the Justices upheld court martial conviction of wives of soldier husbands for

[15] *Erie Railroad Co.* v. *Tompkins,* 304 U.S. 64 (1938), 79.
[16] H. F. Stone, "The Common Law in the United States," *loc. cit.,* 7.
[17] *Smith* v. *Allwright,* 321 U.S. 649 (1944), 665.
[18] *Ibid.,* 669.

having murdered their husbands.[19] Nor was this the only injury inflicted on the *stare decisis* principle. To Chief Justice Warren's Court "stability" evidently means keeping up with the country—indeed with the world— not blindly or ambiguously adhering to outmoded precedent. This is but a part of the "continuous problem" which the Supreme Court is bound to resolve. Nor is the disruptive effect necessarily harmful.

"Much of the uncertainty of law," Judge Jerome Frank observed, "is not an unfortunate accident; it is of immense social value. . . . When men are free of childish compulsions away from or toward the traditional, it will be possible for them to have an open mind on the question of the advisability of radical alterations of law." [20] A Court facing up to its lawmaking function might appraise the principle of *stare desisis* in the realistic terms suggested by judicial activist William O. Douglas:

From age to age, the problem of constitutional adjudication is the same. It is to keep the power of the government unrestrained by the social or economic theories that one set of judges may import into the Constitution. It is to keep one age unfettered by the fears or limited vision of another. In that connection, there is a fundamental tenet of faith that evolved from our long experience as a nation. It is this: If the social and economic problems of state and nation can be kept under political management of the people, there is likely to be long-run stability. It is when a judiciary with life tenure seeks to write its own social and economic creed into the Charter that

[19] *Reid* v. *Covert*, 354 U.S. 1 (1957), reversing *Kinsella* v. *Krueger*, 351 U.S. 470, decided June 11, 1956. The vote to reverse was 6 to 2. The majority was made up of Warren, Black, and Douglas, who dissented in the first opinion. Justice Harlan changed his vote, Justice Frankfurter voted for the first time, and Justice Brennen, a new appointee, joined the majority. Burton and Clark, holding fast to their earlier view, dissented.

[20] *Law and the Modern Mind* (New York, 1949), 7, 251.

instability is created. For then the nation lacks the adaptability to master the sudden storms of an era.[21]

"Frank recognition" of the Court's policy-making function might be helpful in other ways. The Justices who deny most vigorously their lawmaking power have usually looked with disdain on any tendency to stray beyond law books into the mundane realm of facts. "Under elementary and elemental law," a critic of the segregation decision insists, "a court may not consider treatises in a field other than law, unless the treatises themselves are the very subject of inquiry. The doctrine of judicial notice extends only to those things of common knowledge that lie without the realm of science, or to that one science in which judges are presumed to be learned or experts themselves —the science of law." [22] Such self-imposed blinders seem unfortunate for, as Lester Ward commented many years ago, "but for the narrow 'special' and superficial education which officers of the law receive, courts would embody the highest wisdom of society." [23]

The situation is worsened by the custom which decrees that the Supreme Court shall be composed only of lawyers. "Those lawyers on the bench," the late Robert H. Jackson pointed out, "will hear only from lawyers at the bar. If the views of the scientist, the laborer, the business man, the social worker, the economist, the legislator, or the government executive reach the Court, it is only

[21] Douglas, We the Judges, 429–30.

[22] Eugene Cook and William I. Potter, "The School Segregation Cases: Opposing the Opinion of the Supreme Court," 42 American Bar Association Journal 313 (April, 1956), 315. Similarly Justice Roberts, in 1930, scathingly denounced a district court for "resorting to 'political science,' the 'political thought' of the times, and a 'scientific approach to the problem of government.'" United States v. Sprague, 282 U.S. 716 (1930), 730.

[23] Lester Ward, Dynamic Sociology (2 vols.; New York, 1883), II, 573.

through the lawyer, in spite of the fact that the effect of the decision may be far greater in other fields than in jurisprudence. Thus government by lawsuit leads to a final decision guided by the learning and limited by the understanding of a single profession—the law." [24]

The doctrine of "judicial notice," combined with the exclusion of non-lawyers from the judicial process, serves to heighten the relevance of facts. "I hate facts," Justice Holmes told his friend Pollock. Yet the Justice grudgingly conceded that it would be good for his "immortal soul to plunge into them, good also for the performance of my duty." [25] As a lawyer, Brandeis introduced the factual brief to demonstrate, against a presumption to the contrary, that a relation did in fact exist between social legislation and the power of the state to promote the health, safety, morals, and general welfare. As a Supreme Court Justice, however, he was content, except in dissent,[26] to follow "traditional policy"—"to presume in favor of constitutionality until violation of the Constitution is proved beyond all reasonable doubt." Burden of proof to the contrary was thus thrown on the defendant. The fullest statement of his position occurs in *Jay Burns Baking Co.* v. *Bryan* in which the Court set aside a Nebraska standard-weight statute, designed to protect buyers from short weights and honest bakers from unfair competition. Dissenting, Brandeis said:

[24] Jackson, *The Struggle for Judicial Supremacy,* 291.

[25] O. W. Holmes, *Holmes-Pollock Letters,* edited by Mark DeWolfe Howe (2 vols.; Cambridge, Mass., 1946), II, 13–14.

[26] The Court's decision (*Adams* v. *Tanner,* 244 U.S. 590, 1917) evoked from him the view that "whether a measure relating to the public welfare is arbitrary or unreasonable, whether it has no substantial relation to the end proposed is obviously not to be determined by assumptions or by *a priori* reasoning. The judgment should be based upon a consideration of relevant facts, actual or possible—*Ex facto oritur.* That ancient rule must prevail in order that we may have a system of living law" (p. 600).

Put at its highest, our function is to determine, in the light of all facts which may enrich our knowledge and enlarge our understanding, whether the measure, enacted in the exercise of an unquestioned police power and of a character inherently unobjectionable, transcends the bounds of reason. That is, whether the provision as applied is so clearly arbitrary or capricious that legislators acting reasonably could not have believed it to be necessary or appropriate for the public welfare.

To decide, as a fact, that the prohibition of excess weights "is not necessary for the protection of the purchasers against imposition and fraud by short weights"; that it "is not calculated to effectuate that purpose"; and that it "subjects bakers and sellers of bread" to heavy burdens, is, in my opinion, an exercise of the powers of a super-legislature—not the performance of the constitutional function of judicial review.[27]

Those inclined to cite Brandeis as authority for the Court's reliance on extralegal data in the segregation decisions may have less support in his constitutional jurisprudence than is usually supposed. Facts were, he agreed, important considerations in the decision-making process. He would therefore open "the priestly ears" to the call of extralegal voices.[28] He doubtless would have concurred in Stone's judgment of 1936 as to the need for "an economic service—a small group of men, who have had some training as economists and statisticians, who would be qualified to assemble material for use of the Court." [29] But in man's eternal pursuit of the more exact, Brandeis recognized that there are facts and facts. For him the economic and

[27] *Jay Burns Baking Co.* v. *Bryan,* 264 U.S. 504 (1924), 534.

[28] B. N. Cardozo, *The Growth of Law* (New Haven, 1924), 66. See, in this connection, my "The Case of the Overworked Laundress," in John A. Garraty (ed.), *Quarrels That Have Shaped the Constitution* (New York, 1964), 176–91.

[29] H. F. Stone to W. Z. Ripley, April 6, 1937 (Stone Papers).

Justice Frankfurter strikes a somewhat skeptical note as to the relation of social data to law. "The Constitution does not require legislatures to reflect sociological insight, or shifting social standards, any more than it requires them to keep abreast of the latest scientific standards." *Goesaert* v. *Cleary,* 335 U.S. 464 (1948), 466.

social sciences were "largely uncharted seas." [30] Since government was not "an exact science, prevailing public opinion concerning the evils and the remedy is among the important facts deserving consideration." [31] In the formulation and adjudication of public policy a more certain measure than "what the crowd wants" is obviously needed. The essence of improvement, however, demands only that we be as accurate as we can. Overwhelming factual demonstrations alone do not account for the intensity of Brandeis' reformist zeal. "Mr. Brandeis, how can you be so sure of your course of action?" a friend once asked him. "When you are 51% sure, then go ahead," the Justice replied.

Whether or not segregated schools can be equal was a question of fact. The science of law, which does not exist in any real sense, provided no adequate answer. Segregation requirements could not be tested in a vacuum. One writer suggests that the sociological question was "inherent in the terms of the Fourteenth Amendment." [32] Justice Sutherland, it will be recalled, brushed aside extralegal data as irrelevant, but he conceded that factual demonstration of the relation between the minimum wage for women and their health and morals was "proper enough for the consideration of law-making bodies"— proper enough for the Court too, presumably, if lawmaking be frankly recognized.

"Even if new law has to be made today," Alexander Pekelis commented in 1946, "why should judges directly predicate the changes upon welfare, instead of using, as the old wise men used to do, the persuasive symbols of ju-

[30] *New State Ice Co.* v. *Liebmann,* 310.

[31] *Truax* v. *Corrigan,* 257 U.S. 312 (1921), 357.

[32] Arthur E. Sutherland, Jr., "The American Judiciary and Racial Segregation," 20 *The Modern Law Review* 201 (May, 1957), 208. See also Morroe Berger, "Desegregation, Law, and Social Science," *Commentary,* May, 1957, pp. 471–77.

dicial astrology? Is it not true that in many situations people would fare better if they were convinced that mediocre decisions reached by judges are the inevitable result of
the dictates of The Law, produced *jure ac necessitate dic-
tantibus,* than if they were faced with excellent decisions,
avowedly grounded in the judges' freely chosen conception of welfare?" [33] "Whether or not such a close relation
between the bench and public opinion is desirable,"
Pekelis continues, "historical forces have brought it about.
. . . It seems futile to attempt a return to the esoteric
solemnities of the past." [34] Yet he recognizes that certain
judges still behave as if no one knew their "priestly
secrets." [35]

The judicial robe works a miracle.[36] Great precaution is

[33] Alexander H. Pekelis, *Law and Social Action,* 30–31.

[34] *Ibid.,* 32.

[35] *Ibid.*

[36] "There is a good deal of shallow talk," Justice Frankfurter has
written, "that the judicial robe does not change the man within
it. It does. The fact is that on the whole judges do lay aside private
views in discharging their judicial functions." *Public Utilities Commission* v. *Pollak,* 343 U.S. 451 (1952), 466.

"Does a man become any different when he puts on a gown?"
Frankfurter observed on another occasion. "I say, 'If he is any good,
he does.'" *Of Law and Men* (New York, 1956), 133.

Former Justice Ferdinand Pecora of the Supreme Court, State of
New York, entertains sentiments more in accord with those voiced
by Professor Frankfurter before the latter was transformed. "As one
who is privileged to wear the judicial robe, let me assure you that
there is no magic in the robe. It does not invest its wearer with qualities he did not possess before the robe was draped about his shoulders. It does not endow him with an intellectuality or spirituality not
his previously. It does not transform his personality. It does not
enable him to step out of that personality and assume a new one.
If he lacked humanity before he donned the robe, his understanding
is not leavened with that virtue by it." Statement before Senate
Judiciary Committee, *Reorganization of the Judiciary,* 75th Congress, 1st Session, Part 2 (1937), 422–23.

The late Judge Jerome Frank believed that "much harm is done
by the myth that, merely by putting on a black robe and taking the
oath of office as a judge, a man ceases to be human and strips himself

necessary lest the public be disabused of such fancies. To safeguard the Court's prestige, the claims of history must be narrowly circumscribed. A compelling reason for adherence to *stare decisis* is that the public might begin to suspect that "changes in the Court's composition and the contingencies in the choice of successors" [37] are a determining factor in judicial decision. It is further suggested that any publication that reveals the internal workings of the Court might not only mar the Court as America's esoteric symbol of ultimate wisdom and eternal law, but also seriously disrupt the Justices' routine work. The prospect, it is feared, that what the Justices do and how they do it may be opened to public gaze will perhaps make them hesitate freely to communicate with each other, or drive them to burn their papers.[38]

Why should the procedures whereby the Court hammers out opinions, vitally affecting the lives of all, be screened from public view? Close study of a Supreme Court Justice's files over two of the most crucial decades in its history affirms emphatically that the Justices have nothing to hide. Knowledge of the decision-making process at the highest level reinforces Brandeis' judgment

of all predilections, becomes a passionless thinking machine." *Law and the Modern Mind* (New York, 1949), Preface to 6th ed., xx.

[37] Justice Frankfurter, dissenting in *United States* v. *Rabinowitz,* 339 U.S. 56 (1950), 86.

[38] See Edmond Cahn, "Eavesdropping on Justice," *Nation,* January 5, 1957. For a relaxed comment, see James H. Duffy, *Nation,* February 2, 1957.

An untoward consequence of tailoring the record lest the revelations "discourage adequate discussion among the judges" is that a distorted or overly favorable biography may result. See my review, "Charles Evans Hughes: An Appeal to the Bar of History," 6 *Vanderbilt Law Review* (1952).

"The necessity of complying with times," Dr. Samuel Johnson observed, "and of sparing persons is the great impediment of biography." G. B. N. Hill, *The Wit and Wisdom of Samuel Johnson* (Oxford, 1888), 29.

that "the reason the public thinks so much of the Justices of the Supreme Court is that they are almost the only people in Washington who do their own work." [39] Far more substantial reasons have been put forward to justify penetration of the inner sanctum. In 1936, Professor Frankfurter regretted the lack of biographical studies of that comparatively small number of Supreme Court Justices who have had a major share in shaping constitutional doctrine—hence American constitutional law. Frankfurter then sounded sharp warning against "that pertinacious inquiry into the cultural and psychological roots of legal doctrine on which very little spade work has yet been undertaken."

At best [he wrote] we are likely to know much less of the forces that shaped the great judge and the development of his mind after he came to the Bench, than we know about distinguished statesmen. . . . The intimacies of the conference room—the workshop of the living Constitution—are illuminations denied the historian. . . . Divisions on the Court and clarity of view and candor of expression to which they give rise, are especially productive of insight. Moreover, much life may be found to stir beneath even the decorous surface of unanimous opinions.

"Until we have penetrating studies of the influence of these men," Frankfurter concluded, "we shall not have an adequate history of the Supreme Court, and, therefore, of the United States." [40]

The claims of history, great as they are, do not, of course, justify invasion of the conference room at the consultive stage of the Court's work. In determining what material shall be opened to the public after the decision-making process is passed, balance must be struck between the

[39] Quoted in Judge Charles E. Wyzanski, Jr., "Brandeis," *Atlantic,* November, 1956.

[40] Frankfurter, *The Commerce Clause under Marshall, Taney and Waite* (Chapel Hill, 1937), 7–9 *passim.*

rightful interest of succeeding generations in the workings of an institution affecting the lives of all, and the
observance of secrecy that must, for a while, veil the Justices' doings. The time-lapse factor has been suggested as
the criterion for determining the propriety of publication
of a Justice's papers. Difference of opinion as to what that
period should be—ten years, a generation, or a century—
is interminable. Assuming that papers have been placed by
responsible persons in the hands of a responsible scholar,
certain considerations governing their selection may perhaps meet the demands of both privacy and history, *viz:*
(a) exclusion of everything that descends to the level of
mere gossip; (b) inclusion of whatever contributes to an
understanding of the judging process and everything of
possible help in the Court's future deliberations; (c) inclusion of such material as appears meaningful in terms of
biography. If judicial procedures, the give and take of the
conference room, the compromises that a collective judgment inevitably entails, and the incidental revelations of
human frailties and strength, are so peculiarly immune to
the claims of history as to preclude the spadework necessary to an understanding of the Supreme Court, the Court
itself would be among the losers.

Greater knowledge of the Court's internal workings
might save Justices themselves from drawing erroneous inferences. In *U.S.* v. *Kahriger,*[41] Justice Frankfurter, dissenting, noted that Brandeis joined a majority of eight in
setting aside the Child Labor Tax Act.[42] Frankfurter naturally assumed that Brandeis considered the act unconstitutional—a "fact" of great significance for him. Bickel's
volume shows that Brandeis, in fact, had "no difficulty in
holding the act valid." [43] Considerations of judicial strat-

[41] 345 U.S. 22 (1953), 38.
[42] 259 U.S. 20 (1922).
[43] Bickel, *The Unpublished Opinions of Mr. Justice Brandeis,* 16–
19.

egy, rather than doubts as to the act's validity, dictated his stand.

Soon after his appointment in 1910 as an Associate Justice, Charles Evans Hughes said: "In the conferences of the Justices of the Supreme Court of the United States, there is exhibited a candour, a comprehensiveness, a sincerity, and a complete devotion to their task that I am sure would be most gratifying to the entire people of the Union, could they know more intimately what actually takes place." [44] The Stone papers, deposited in the Library of Congress, furnish numerous examples of dedication and rare open-mindedness. One is the Supreme Court decision in *Grosjean* v. *American Press Co.* (297 U.S. 233). At the behest of Huey Long, the Louisiana legislature passed a 2 per cent gross-receipts tax on newspapers with a circulation of more than 20,000 copies a week, a provision designed to hit twelve of thirteen newspapers openly opposed to Long. The Court set this gag law aside as an unconstitutional invasion of a free press. The wonder was that the Justices were not only unanimous, but that Justice Sutherland, appointed by President Harding, was the Court's spokesman. Justice Stone dispelled the mystery: "In conference, a majority voted to by-pass the issue of freedom of the press and annul the Statute as a commercial discrimination that denied the equal protection of the laws. Justice Sutherland wrote for the Court along that line. Justice Cardozo, who contended that freedom of the press was violated, put his own rejected oral argument on paper and circulated it as a concurring opinion. It proved so persuasive that the Court approved it; Justice Sutherland embodied it in his opinion and cut his original hold-

[44] Address to New York County Lawyers' Association, 1911, in William L. Ransom, *Charles E. Hughes: The Statesman as Shown in the Opinions of the Jurist* (New York, 1916), 13–14.

ing down to the remark that "we deem it unnecessary to consider the further ground assigned that it also constitutes a denial of the equal protection of the laws." Thus Justice Sutherland won plaudits that belonged to his colleagues, but demonstrated his own capacity for growth and submergence of pride." [45]

Self-appointed guardians, eager to shield the Court from the public eye, or from those who cannot be trusted to observe the mysterious ways of judges, their wonders to perform, do the honorable men who sit on the supreme bench an egregious disservice. The Court stands to gain rather than lose by informed and responsible disclosures of its internal workings. Not least among the advantages would be further to discredit the distorted picture one gets of the Court and its members from gossip books such as *Nine Old Men,* by Drew Pearson and Robert S. Allen. While revealing only normal human frailties, firsthand studies throw light on matters of solid substance: the complex doctrinal questions posed by the far-flung extension of government; the clashing notions of the judicial function; the dilemma of a bench that takes the risk of erasing the well-worn distinction between *will* and *judgment* in the judicial process. It will be seen that the give and take, the sensitivity to outside pressure and opinion, so characteristic of other organs of government, is not entirely absent from the councils of the judiciary.

The suggestion that any agency of government is beyond public scrutiny is to be deplored. Nothing of the sort was envisioned by the framers of the Constitution. Implicit in the system of government they designed is the basic premise that unchecked power in any hands whatsoever is intolerable.

James Wilson spoke of the people's power to scrutinize

[45] Irving Brant, *The Bill of Rights* (Indianapolis, 1965), 403.

and criticize the government as "the great panacea of human politics." "It is a power," Wilson said, "paramount to every Constitution, inalienable in its nature, and indefinite in its extent. For I insist, if there are errors in government, the people have the right not only to correct and amend them, but likewise totally to change and reject its form." [46] Only that power which is recognized can be effectively checked. Comparing European judicial anonymity with our own more or less uninhibited discussions of the judicial process, Edmund Cahn has written: "We insist that anonymous hands may become irresponsible hands and that no man is fit to judge unless the people can ultimately pass judgment on him." Judicial biographies, Professor Cahn continues, "furnish useful and often valuable aids in understanding the judicial function within the republic. While something can be said on behalf of the European way . . . , the American way has the supreme advantage of linking responsibility directly to the exercise of power." [47]

The Justices themselves have been less anxious to black out knowledge of the Court's activity than are certain of its self-appointed protectors. "It is a mistake to suppose," Justice David Brewer declared in 1898, "that the Supreme Court is either honored or helped by being spoken of as beyond criticism. On the contrary, the life and character of its justices should be the objects of constant watchfulness by all, and its judgments subject to the freest criticism. The time is past in the history of the world when any living man or body of men can be set on a pedestal and decorated with a halo. True, many criticisms may be, like their authors, devoid of good taste, but better all sorts of criticism than no criticism at all. The moving waters

[46] Farrand (ed.), *The Records of the Federal Convention of 1787*, III, 142.

[47] Cahn, "Eavesdropping on Justice," *loc. cit.*, 15.

are full of life and health; only in the still waters is stagnation and death." [48]

In 1930 Justice Stone was quite undisturbed by the close scrutiny the Senate gave Mr. Hughes's nomination. Stone regarded it as evidence of "wholesome interest in what the Court was doing." "I have no patience," the Justice commented, "with the complaint that criticism of judicial action involves any lack of respect for the courts. Where the courts deal, as ours do, with great public questions, the only protection against unwise decisions, and even judicial usurpation, is careful scrutiny of their action and fearless comment on it." Stone was not horrified in 1937 when President Roosevelt went on his court-packing spree. Then, as in 1928, he believed that even the unjust attacks on the Court had left "no scar," that "the only wounds from which it has suffered have been self-inflicted." [49]

Yet, the effort persists to maintain the law as an exclusively professional subject and to keep the Court above and beyond criticism. In 1956, when nearly one hundred Southern Congressmen criticized the Court's decision in the segregation cases, and issued a manifesto calling for reversal by "lawful means," certain members of the bar, professing grave concern, issued a statement condemning the manifesto as "reckless." [50] Refusal to obey the Supreme Court mandate is, of course, intolerable. One may go further and denounce the motives of those who signed the Southern manifesto; one may hold that the efforts called for neither will nor should succeed, and still defend the right of those who disagree with the segregation decisions to resort to "lawful means" (reversal or recourse to

[48] David J. Brewer, Lincoln Day Address of 1898. Quoted in Frankfurter, "The Supreme Court and the Public," *loc. cit.,* 334.

[49] Quoted in my *Harlan Fiske Stone,* 447.

[50] For the resolution and list of signers, see the *New York Times,* October 28, 1956.

constitutional amendment) of bringing about a change.
To deny this right appears not in keeping with the principles of a free society.

Should Lincoln have been muzzled for his attack on the
Dred Scott decision? After the Supreme Court had on two
occasions outlawed child labor legislation as beyond the
reach of congressional regulation, should the efforts of
those who deplored this impasse as unnecessary have been
stayed? Consistently, with the opprobrium heaped on the
heads of those who have criticized the Court's segregation
decision, President Roosevelt should have been impeached
for his ill-tempered assertion that the unanimous Schechter
decision, outlawing NIRA, took America back to the
"horse and buggy days."

Apropos of Lincoln's pointed criticism of the Dred
Scott decision, Professor John W. Burgess [51] of Columbia
University declared that "every person in a free country
may argue the question on its merits for the peaceable
purpose of inducing the court or the amending power in
the Constitution to reverse, revise or nullify the decision,
always obeying the same until such change shall have been
duly effected. Of course, this is even more applicable to
legislative and executive acts. This is sound to the very
core. It is the very foundation principle of American constitutional liberty." [52]

[51] *Reminiscences of an American Scholar* (New York, 1934), 310.

[52] In 1935 the Lawyers' Committee of the American Liberty
League declared, in advance of a Supreme Court ruling, the Wagner
Labor Relations Act "unconstitutional," and openly advised employers to ignore its provision. Though not analogous to the action
taken by the Southern senators, it indicates how far criticism has
gone. The contribution this group of distinguished lawyers made to
"law and order" is at least doubtful. See, in this connection, "Fifty-
six Unofficial Judges: Constitutional Lawyers Scan New Deal for
Liberty League," *Literary Digest*, Vol. 120 (August 31, 1935), 9; "A
Conspiracy by Lawyers," *Nation*, Vol. 141 (October 2, 1935); "Liberty League Lawyers," *New Republic*, Vol. 84 (October 2, 1935);

The Supreme Court is but one among several agencies empowered, within limits, to govern. The framers' design for obliging government to control itself was, as Madison put it, so to contrive its internal structure that "its several constituent parts may, by their mutual relations, be the means of keeping each other in their proper places." If the Court becomes "packed" with judges inclined to transcend the undefined bounds prescribed by the Constitution, the President's appointing power enables him to redress the balance. During the administrations of Jefferson, Jackson, Lincoln, Grant, and the two Roosevelts, when judges, ignoring professed self-restraint, interposed the judicial veto and impeded popular aspirations, Congress altered the size of the Court, or threatened to do so.[53] President Franklin D. Roosevelt, confronted with a stubbornly recalcitrant bench and amid crisis "more serious than war," invoked as a corrective the method made available to him by the Constitution itself. Yet lawyers and others rose up in an attitude of shock and horror, echoing the stale thesis (*American Bar Association Journal*, May, 1937) that "the Court in no sense exercises a veto." In cases involving the validity of legislation, the Justices merely measure the controverted act against the relevant constitutional provision. *"And this, and only this, is all the Supreme Court has ever done"* (emphasis in the original).

Roosevelt's "desecration" of the Court has been considered so outrageous that certain senators are determined that there shall be no repetition of it. In 1953 Senator

---

T. R. Powell, "Fifty-eight Lawyers Report," *New Republic,* Vol. 85 (December 11, 1935).

[53] Over the years Congress has changed the number of Justices several times—1789, six; 1801, five; 1802, six; 1837, nine; 1863, ten; 1866, seven; 1869, nine. For ninety-odd years there has been no change, by far the longest period in history without one.

Butler of Maryland, apparently resolved to remove the Court permanently from the political arena, proposed a constitutional amendment that would fix the composition and jurisdiction of the Supreme Court. The Butler amendment seems to rest on three assumptions: (a) Supreme Court Justices can do no wrong; they, unlike other agencies of government, never abuse their power. (b) The Court has not been in politics, except as drawn in by the political organs of government. (c) The proposed amendment, by increasing their political independence, would take the Justices out of politics. There is little or nothing in our experience to bolster these assumptions. On the contrary, history shows that the President's appointing power, along with congressional authority to determine the size of the Court and control its jurisdiction, are useful guns behind the door. The proposed amendment got exactly what it deserved—a quick legislative brush-off.

Vacancies on the supreme bench are not always the work of fate. Not every tired or disabled constitutional warrior is disposed to "bow to the inevitable" and retire promptly and unhesitatingly without regard to how his successor will vote on the crucial issues ahead. Judges have, in fact, displayed conspicuous determination and capacity to stay on pending political change—incumbency of a new President of the right political stripe. On more than one occasion, Presidents or Justices themselves have felt impelled to resort to the embarrassing task of advising a senescent judge to quit.

Though he felt his powers failing, John Marshall died in the center chair, because Jackson triumphed in the 1832 election.[54] In 1875 Justice Samuel Miller complained bitterly of his inability to induce colleagues "who

[54] Albert J. Beveridge, *The Life of John Marshall* (Boston, 1916), IV, 521.

are too old [to] resign." [55] Taft, mistaking Hoover for a "progressive," faced retirement with trepidation, and urged like-minded colleagues to hang on. Holmes, the most sophisticated of judges, acutely aware of his aging colleagues' tendency to stay on and on, had himself to be asked to step down. For five years after Franklin D. Roosevelt's election in 1932, the supreme bench, comprised of judges averaging age seventy-two plus, remained unchanged, one reason being their hope that the people would return to their senses and elect a Republican president. It seems probable that Chief Justice Stone continued on the bench longer than he might have done except for political considerations.

Time and again the President's power to change the composition of the bench has illustrated what Madison aptly called, the "matching of ambition against ambition." Some allowance must be made for play in the constitutional joints, even at the price of injecting politics into judicial appointments. Such flexibility is far more likely to achieve justice and moderation than the futile attempt, as in the Butler amendment, to create a Supreme Court independent of politics.

Destruction of magic and other practices of witchcraft is a calculated risk. To regard the Court as an instrument of political power might limit its effectiveness. Judicial decisions have been rendered more acceptable because of the belief that the Court merely pronounced the law, deciding nothing. Nine men are more vulnerable than "the Law" or "the Constitution." Candor, combined with a knowledge of unconcealed judicial disagreements, tends to rob the "Higher Law" of its dogmatic quality. Walter Bagehot reminds us that those elements in the governing

---

[55] Charles Fairman, *Mr. Justice Miller and the Supreme Court, 1862–1890* (Cambridge, Mass., 1939), 373.

process which "excite the most easy reverence" are *theatrical* elements— . . . that which is mystic in its claims; that which is occult in its mode of action." [56] The kingship and royalty—the "dignified" parts of the British Constitution— do in fact facilitate rulership. In America the judiciary occupies vis-à-vis the populace a position not unlike that of the British Crown.[57] The difference—and it is a big one—is that the Court has real power. Nor are Americans so dependent as the British on theatrical elements. "Americans will accept immense, almost autocratic power over them so long as they do not have to see in it a transcendent authority, and they will always attempt to 'humanize' such authority with the help of humor or incongruity. What they will always seek to cut down is not effective power but its awe-inspiring character." [58] Jerome Frank profoundly explored this problem and concluded:

[56] Walter Bagehot, *The English Constitution* (New York, 1914), 76.

[57] "The court is protected by the most powerful emotional support of any department of Government. It is far removed from the public gaze. It has been on the lips of everyone since childhood. Though seen by few, it is held in awe by everyone. Its public sessions are imposing and inspiring. Its troubles and bickerings within its conference room are never known. Its utterances are clothed in stately terms. Its members are men of learning and severe dignity who are rarely seen except on formal occasions. Their work is subtle and far removed from common understanding. They make few public speeches. The press reports concerning the Court, the judges, and their work are restrained and respectful. In every detail the Court, its members, and its work are portrayed to the country so as to create in the citizen profound respect and confidence. What the Supreme Court says and does carries the weight of authoritative finality. It is the Ark of the Covenant, the country's greatest symbol of orderly, stable, and righteous government." Testimony of Dean Leon Green before the Senate Judiciary Committee, *Reorganization of the Judiciary*, 75th Congress, 1st Session, Part 1 (1937), 233.

[58] Amaury Riencourt, *The Coming Caesars* (New York, 1957), 341. Robert H. Jackson points out, that though subject to attacks by strong Presidents throughout our history, "no substantial sentiment exists for any curtailment of the Court's powers. Even Presi-

Such men [Demogue and Wurzel] fail to speak out unequivocally because they, themselves, are still in some small part enthralled by the myths they have learned to see through. That those myths are shams they well know, but the fascination of the myths still continues and they are therefore not entirely ready to relinquish them. Their own need for authoritarianism is diminished, but, they say, the public cannot stand the full truth. What such men really mean is that they, themselves, cannot bear to have the shams utterly exposed, the superstitions totally destroyed. They find a lingering comfort in the spectacle of a public still under the spell. Such an attitude is not snobbery or esotericism. It is, perhaps, rather a remnant of childish fears, an attenuated father-worship.[59]

Judge Cardozo counseled that lawyers and laymen alike should understand the realities of the judicial process. Said Cardozo: "Magic words and incantations are as fatal to our science as they are to any other . . . We seek to find peace of mind in the word, the formula, the ritual. The hope is an illusion." [60]

"Only lawyers," Harold Laski used to say, "make law mysterious." [61] This idea, Judge Frank wrote in 1945, "should be rejected in toto. The courts should feel obligated to make themselves intelligible to the man on the street or in the subway." [62]

Everything considered, Judge Learned Hand's realistic

---

dent [F. D.] Roosevelt in the bitterest conflict with judicial power in our history suggested only change in the Court's composition, none in its constitutional prerogatives." *The Supreme Court in the American System of Government,* 26.

[59] Jerome Frank, *Law and the Modern Mind,* 235. See especially chapters entitled "Demogue's Belief in the Importance of Deluding the Public" and "Wurzel and the Value of Lay Ignorance," 222–31. Demogue (Bené) is a distinguished French jurist; Wurzel (Karl Georg) is a well-known Austrian writer.

[60] Cardozo, *The Growth of the Law,* 66–67.

[61] O. W. Holmes, *Holmes-Laski Letters,* edited by Mark DeWolfe Howe (2 vols.; Cambridge, Mass., 1953), I, 51.

[62] "The Cult of the Robe," *Saturday Review,* XXVIII (Oct. 13, 1945), 80.

approach seems more in keeping with the fundamentals of a free society. To uphold fiction on the ground that it will make the Court a more useful instrument of government is no more valid than to defend despotism because it acts more swiftly and unequivocally than free government.

In a free society the usefulness of an organ of government can never be defended solely in terms of its symbolic value. Even in the case of our Supreme Court its contribution consists rather in what it does, in the deliberate process that precedes judgment. The Court's decisions are likely to be more reliable than those of any other branch of government, not because its members are lawyers, but because the Court's action on all questions must be squared with reason and authority. "Nothing," said Lord Coke, "that is contrary to reason is consonant to law." The judiciary provides the final forum in which public policy is rationalized and vindicated. The statistic that only a relatively few congressional acts (eleven out of a total of eighty-eight)[63] have been set aside since 1937 affords an altogether misleading test of the value of judicial review. The Court legitimizes as well as restrains.[64]

The Court also performs an educational task of incalculable value, interpreting to us "our purposes and our meanings." A host of illustrations come readily to mind: the debate between Miller and Field in the Slaughter-House case (1873); Fuller and Harlan in the Sugar

[63] *Tot* v. *United States,* 319 U.S. 463 (1943); *United States* v. *Lovett,* 328 U.S. 303 (1946); *Toth* v. *Quarles,* 350 U.S. 11 (1955); *Reid* v. *Covert,* 254 U.S. 1 (1957); *Trop* v. *Dulles,* 356 U.S. 86 (1958); *Kennedy* v. *Mendoza-Martinez,* 372 U.S. 144 (1963); *Schneider* v. *Rusk,* 378 U.S. 163 (1964); *Aptheker* v. *Rusk,* 378 U.S. 500 (1964); *Lamont* v. *Postmaster General,* 381 U.S. 301 (1965); *United States* v. *Brown,* 381 U.S. 437 (1965); *Afroyin* v. *Rusk,* 18 L. ed., 2d 757. Decided May 29, 1967.

[64] B. N. Cardozo, *The Nature of the Judicial Process* (New Haven, 1921), 94.

Trust case (1895); Day and Holmes in the first child labor case (1918); Taft and Brandeis in *Truax* v. *Corrigan* (1921); Hughes and Sutherland in Minnesota's ban on mortgage foreclosures; Roberts and Stone in *United States* v. *Butler* (1936); Stone and Frankfurter in the first flag salute case (1941); Vinson and Black in the Dennis case (1950); Warren and Harlan in *Reynolds* v. *Sims* (1965). In these and scores of other major pronouncements, the Court explores and passes judgment on crucial issues, "not merely in the abstract but also in their bearing upon the concrete, immediate problems which are, at any given moment, puzzling and dividing us." [65] By precept and by example throughout the years, the Supreme Court shows us what free government means.

[65] Alexander Meiklejohn, *Free Speech and Its Relation to Self-Government* (New York, 1948), 32.

CHAPTER 7

Understanding the Warren Court

THE Warren Court (some call it the "Warren Revolution"), now entering its fifteenth year, continues unabated its myth-shattering, precedent-breaking course. Hamilton's relaxed portrayal of the judiciary as a weakling, along with Chief Justice Marshall's incredible description of the judicial function as involving only judgment, not will,[1] are revealed once again as gross misrepresentations. Jefferson and Madison anticipated with warm approval that the judiciary would participate creatively in the enforcement of the Bill of Rights. A Court of able and independent judges, empowered to enforce the Bill of Rights, Jefferson assured Madison, would not yield to a frenzied multitude demanding perverse things —"civium ardor prava jubentium." [2]

In America, all social and political issues sooner or later become judicial. Only the context in which judges operate changes. Courts do not and should not function in a

[1] Chief Justice Marshall in *Osborn* v. *U.S. Bank,* 9 Wheaton 738, 866 (1824). Symbolism and magic are, of course, useful in the governing process. But judges tend to insist on their impotence when they are making almost brazen use of their power. See my "Myth and Reality in Supreme Court Decisions," *Virginia Law Review,* XLVIII (1962), 1385–1406.

[2] Thomas Jefferson to James Madison, March 15, 1789, in Boyd (ed.), *The Papers of Thomas Jefferson,* XIV, 661.

vacuum. But the motives prompting judicial intervention are not inspired by equally valid or praiseworthy considerations. Warring against each other are differing concepts of judicial duty and judicial self-restraint. The point is dramatically illustrated by two historic examples—*Scott* v. *Sandford* [3] and *Brown* v. *Board of Education*.[4]

Separated by almost a century, judicial action in both these cases was obviously in response to time and circumstance. In words as applicable in 1954 as they were in 1857, Justice Wayne, concurring in *Dred Scott*, remarked: "[T]here had become such a difference of opinion that the peace and harmony of the country required the settlement of them [the slavery issues] by judicial decision. . . . In our action we have only discharged our duty as a distinct and efficient department of the Government, as the framers of the Constitution meant the judiciary to be . . ." [5] In 1857 extension of slavery had become a major issue; in 1954 racial discrimination was not only creating domestic unrest, but also projecting a highly unfavorable image of America to the entire world. In both instances, the Court attempted to settle a volcanic issue; in both, the opinions were less firmly grounded than seemed desirable in decisions so momentous. The justices split nine ways in *Dred Scott;* in *Brown* they were unanimous, allowing Chief Justice Warren to throw the full weight of his office and the prestige of the Court behind a ruling certain to provoke bitter controversy. Chief Justice Taney and his quarrelsome majority denied Congress a power it wanted to exert, an authority many felt it could properly exercise. The Warren Court asserted a power which Congress, under existing Senate rules, could not exercise even

[3] 60 U.S. (19 Howard) 393 (1857).
[4] 347 U.S. 483 (1954).
[5] *Scott* v. *Sandford,* 454–55 (concurring opinion).

if there had been the will to do so.[6] Taney raised an absolute bar against congressional action, ignoring precedents created by his own Court.[7] Though a line of decisions pointed in this direction, reaching a high point, ironically, during the quiescent years of Chief Justice Fred M. Vinson,[8] the Warren Court was careful not to overrule *Plessy* v. *Ferguson*[9] beyond the point necessary to abolish the "separate but equal" doctrine in the area of public education. Taney's unequivocal assertion that the Negro had no rights a white man was bound to respect crystallized the slavery issue, helping to bring on the Civil War, the Emancipation Proclamation, and the revolutionary Thirteenth, Fourteenth, and Fifteenth Amendments. *Brown* sparked the Negro revolution, stimulating Congress to pass the first civil rights legislation in almost a century—the civil rights acts of 1957, 1960, 1964, 1965, with other measures still pending. *Dred Scott* dealt a blow to the Court's prestige from which it did not recover for more than a generation; it was one of three notable instances Charles Evans Hughes singled out in which the Court "suffered severely from self-inflicted wounds." [10] Subjected to both praise and blame, *Brown* changed the image of America at home and abroad.

Certain commonplace lessons may be drawn from these explosive forays into judicial politics. Supreme Court justices may accelerate tendencies, but they cannot reverse them. Chief Justice Taney declared that "any change in

[6] R. J. Harris, "The Constitution, Education, and Segregation," *Temple Law Quarterly*, XXIX (1956), 409–33.

[7] See E. S. Corwin, *The Doctrine of Judicial Review* (Princeton, 1914), 134.

[8] See *Missouri* ex rel. *Gaines* v. *Canada*, 305 U.S. 337 (1938); *Sipuel* v. *Board of Regents*, 332 U.S. 631 (1948); *Sweatt* v. *Painter*, 339 U.S. 629 (1950); *McLaurin* v. *Oklahoma State Regents*, 339 U.S. 637 (1950).

[9] 163 U.S. 537 (1896).

[10] Hughes, *The Supreme Court of the United States*, 50.

public opinion or feeling, in relation to this unfortunate race" must under no circumstances be allowed to weigh in the balance. The Constitution "must be construed now as it was understood at the time of its adoption." [11] Chief Justice Warren was more realistic, as well as more creative. For him, as for Woodrow Wilson, the Constitution is "the vehicle of a nation's life." [12] In approaching racial segregation, the Justices refused to "turn the clock back to 1868 when the [Fourteenth] Amendment was adopted, or even to 1896 when *Plessy* v. *Ferguson* was written." [13] In both cases, the Court undertook to resolve a seething issue beyond the capacity of any or all other agencies of government. One was an abortive endorsement of slavery; the other, in accord with American ideals—a testimonial to what de Tocqueville called the "providential" drive for equality.

Implicit in *Dred Scott* is a theory of the union—"dual federalism"—the notion that the Constitution reserves certain subject matter, in this instance slavery, to the states, thus putting it beyond the reach of national control. *Brown*, exhibiting sensitivity to human values, asserted judicial supervision of them. In both instances the Court was criticized for making policy, for usurping the lawmaking function. Taney substituted his own conception of public policy for that declared by Congress. In 1954, Congress had not spoken on the subject of school desegregation. For practical reasons, implementation of the equal protection clause of the Fourteenth Amendment had been left to the courts.[14] Positive judicial responsibility had developed in this area. In 1857, Congress

[11] *Scott* v. *Sandford*, 393, 426.
[12] Woodrow Wilson, *Constitutional Government in the United States* (New York, 1917), 157.
[13] *Brown* v. *Board of Education*, 492.
[14] See Paul Freund, "Storm over the Supreme Court," *Modern Law Review*, XXI (1958), 351.

had acted; there was no need or justification for judicial policy-making. In 1954 there was every reason for it. The Court had written racial segregation into the Constitution. Under vastly changed conditions, the justices used their prerogative to read it out of our basic law.

Sometimes sharp divergence of judicial approach occurs in the same case, one stressing the negative, as in *Dred Scott*, the other the positive aspects exhibited in *Brown*. A good example of this historic dichotomy is *Baker* v. *Carr*,[15] the first in a series of judicial decisions[16] making rotten boroughs subject to judicial correction. "Courts ought not to enter this political thicket," Justice Frankfurter had warned in 1946. "It is hostile to a democratic system to involve the Judiciary in the politics of the people."

Justice Black, joined by Justices Douglas and Murphy, unpersuaded by Frankfurter's wariness lest the judicial activism in support of more equitable apportionment undermine our "democratic system," urged judicial action as "essential under a free government." Congressional districts should contain, they argued, as nearly as practicable an equal number of inhabitants.[17]

The Court's decision in *Baker*, March 26, 1962, holding that voters whose franchise is diluted by unfair, unequal, or discriminatory apportionment of legislative seats may seek relief in the federal courts, stimulated an illuminating exchange between Justices Frankfurter and Clark. Pleading for judicial self-restraint, Frankfurter deplored as "a massive repudiation of the experience of our whole past," the Court's belated assumption of responsibility for

[15] 369 U.S. 186 (1962).
[16] *Wesberry* v. *Sanders*, 376 U.S. 1 (1964); *Reynolds* v. *Sims*, 377 U.S. 533 (1964).
[17] *Colegrove* v. *Green*, 328 U.S. 549, 553–54, 556, 574 (1946).

a more equitable system of representation. Judicial invasion of this "political thicket" would, he suggested, "impair the Court's position as the ultimate organ of 'the supreme Law of the Land.' " [18] Justice Clark, moved by a sense of judicial duty, described Frankfurter's dissent as "bursting with words that go through so much and conclude with so little." [19] "I would not consider intervention by this Court," Clark observed, "into so delicate a field if there were any other relief available to the people of Tennessee. But the majority of the people of Tennessee have no practical opportunities for exerting their political weight at the polls." [20] As in 1946, Frankfurter's solution was an "informed, civically militant electorate [and] an aroused popular conscience." [21] But, Clark countered, these long continued electoral injustices do not, in fact, "sear 'the conscience of the people's representatives.' " [22] Reverting to Frankfurter's cherished principle of judicial self-restraint, Clark concluded: "It is well for this Court to practice self-restraint and discipline in constitutional adjudication, but never in its history have those principles received sanction where the national rights of so many have been so clearly infringed for so long a time." As for Frankfurter's concern lest the Court suffer a self-inflicted wound, Clark declared: "National respect for the courts is more enhanced through the forthright enforcement of those rights [equitable representation] rather than by rendering them nugatory through the interposition of subterfuges." [23]

Baker v. *Carr* and its progeny were prompted by neces-

---

[18] *Baker* v. *Carr,* 267 (dissenting opinion).
[19] *Ibid.,* 251 (concurring opinion).
[20] *Ibid.,* 258–59 (concurring opinion).
[21] *Ibid.,* 270 (dissenting opinion).
[22] *Ibid.,* 259 (concurring opinion).
[23] *Ibid.,* 262 (concurring opinion).

sity. Positive judicial action alone could fulfill the commitment of 1776. For the urban majority, long under the yoke of rural minorities, the reapportionment decisions recall Jefferson's famous lines: "Prudence will dictate that governments long established should not be changed for light and transient causes." The judicial corrective came only after "a long train of abuses and usurpations, pursuing invariably the same object." All such considerations left Justice Frankfurter unmoved. On the altar of federalism and judicial self-restraint, an urban majority must remain under the rural dominance of an unreformed legislature.

Justice Frankfurter's unsuccessful plea for judicial self-restraint on the reapportionment issue was destined to become his valedictory. Suffering a stroke in August, 1962, he retired. But his absence has not silenced intra-Court rumblings against the exercise of judicial duty imposed by the Bill of Rights. In 1964, Justice Harlan dubbed the ruling of the equal protection clause, requiring that seats in both houses of a bicameral state legislature be apportioned on a population basis, "an experiment in venturesome constitutionalism," "a radical alteration in the relationship between the states and the Federal Government," the substitution of the Court's view "of what should be so for the amending process." "The Constitution is not," he insists, "a panacea for every blot on the public welfare, nor should this Court, ordained as a judicial body, be thought of as a general haven for reform movements." [24] Harlan upbraids the majority generally for assuming that "deficiencies in society which have failed of correction by other means should find a cure in courts." [25]

[24] *Reynolds* v. *Sims,* 625.
[25] Address of John M. Harlan at the American Bar Center, Chicago, August 13, 1963.

I

The pattern of divergence in all these major decisions is the same—conflicting concepts of the judicial function, judicial self-restraint versus judicial duty. Justice Harlan's continuing complaint is that the Warren Court, enamored of the Bill of Rights and egalitarianism, "has forgotten the sense of judicial restraint which, with due regard for *stare decisis,* is one element that should enter into deciding whether a past decision of this Court should be overruled." [26]

Nor does Justice Harlan's charge of judicial usurpation stem solely from so-called neutralists. At the Court's session of June 7, 1965,[27] Justice Black, parting company with his erstwhile activist colleague, William O. Douglas, objected to reading the "Right to Privacy" into several provisions of the Bill of Rights. Recalling the Court's "proud pre-eminence" [28] before 1937, Black could find no more justification for embellishing the vague clauses of the Fourteenth Amendment with a liberalizing political theory than for enacting a restrictive economic dogma to safeguard economic privilege. General application of the constitutional right of privacy would, he said, "amount to a great unconstitutional shift of power to the Courts," [29] tending to break down separation of powers and federalism—doctrines of major concern to Justice Harlan.

[26] *Mapp* v. *Ohio,* 367 U.S. 643, 673 (1961).

[27] *Griswold* v. *Connecticut,* 381 U.S. 479 (1965).

[28] Language of Justice Gibson, criticizing the doctrine of judicial review, and described by Professor James Bradley Thayer as "the ablest discussion of the question which I have ever seen." *Eakin* v. *Raub,* 12 Sergeant and Rawle (Pa. Sup. Ct., 1825), 330. See, in this connection, Stanley I. Cutler, "John Bannister Gibson: Judicial Restraint and the 'Positive State,'" *Journal of Public Law,* XIV (1965), 181–97.

[29] *Griswold* v. *Connecticut,* 521.

These critical reactions, focusing especially on the reapportionment decisions and rulings extending, under the Fourteenth Amendment, an increasing number of bill-of-rights provisions to the states, recall earlier complaints. Belying Hamilton's prediction in *The Federalist,* No. 78, that the judiciary will always be "the weakest," the "least dangerous" branch, no Court in our history has escaped Jefferson's charge of working "like gravity" to enlarge its jurisdiction.[30] The same note—abuse of power, the peril of judges stepping into the shoes of legislators—has been sounded throughout our history: in the debates on repeal of the Judiciary Act of 1801;[31] in Justice John Bannister Gibson's powerful indictment of John Marshall and judicial review in 1825;[32] in Professor James Bradley Thayer's classic plea of 1893 for judicial self-restraint;[33] in President Roosevelt's impassioned radio "chat" of March 9, 1937, calling for reorganization of the judiciary;[34] in the abortive Jenner-Butler crusade of 1957, designed to clip judicial wings in the enforcement of certain bill-of-rights provisions;[35] in Senator Dirksen's repeated attempts to undo by constitutional amendment the 1964 "one-man, one-vote" ruling on state legislative apportionment.[36]

[30] Paul Leicester Ford (ed.), *The Works of Thomas Jefferson* (New York and London, 1904–1905), XII, 201–202.

[31] Beveridge, *The Life of John Marshall,* III, 50–100; Charles Warren, *The Supreme Court in United States History* (Boston, 1928), I, 188–230.

[32] See note 28.

[33] J. B. Thayer, "The Origin and Scope of the American Doctrine of Constitutional Law," *Harvard Law Review,* VII (1893), 129.

[34] Fireside Chat, March 9, 1937, in Samuel I. Rosenman (ed.), *The Public Papers and Addresses of Franklin D. Roosevelt* (New York, 1938–50), VI, 122–33.

[35] See Walter F. Murphy, *Congress and the Court: A Case Study in the American Political Process* (Chicago, 1962), 154–208.

[36] See "Legislative Apportionment: the latest proposal analyzed." Remarks of Senator Joseph D. Tydings, Oct. 5, 1965, in *Congressional Record,* 89th Congress, 1st Session, Appendix, 1–3; James

The indictment against judicial activism (or usurpation) reached ominous proportions in 1958 when the chief justices of forty-eight states voted 36 to 8 in support of a resolution condemning judicial policy-making in hasty decisions, "without proper judicial restraint." The attack was stepped up in 1962, when the Council of State Governments, seared by Supreme Court decisions upholding federal intervention into fields long considered immune—education, voting, representation, and the administration of criminal justice—proposed three far-reaching amendments.[37] One would permit state legislatures to amend the federal Constitution without consideration or discussion in any national forum. Another would make apportionment in the state legislatures immune to judicial action. The third would set up a super-Supreme Court—"Court of the Union"—consisting of the chief justices of the fifty states, empowered to overrule Supreme Court decisions in cases involving federal-state relations.

Within a few months, this triple threat—the most defiant assertion of state sovereignty since the Civil War—was endorsed in whole or in part by twelve states. Noting widespread public apathy, Chief Justice Warren struck back, prodded members of the bar to initiate a "great national debate": "If proposals of this magnitude had been made in the early days of the Republic, the great national debate would be resounding in every legislative hall and in every place where lawyers, scholars, and statesmen gather." [38]

Judicial history is repeating itself, but not precisely. The Warren Court's dramatic intervention in the govern-

---

C. Millstone, "Dirksen Hires Publicity Firm to Promote His Amendment," *St. Louis Post-Dispatch,* Feb. 5, 1966.

[37] For the full text of the proposed amendments, see *State Government,* XXXVI (1963), 1–15.

[38] *New York Times,* May 23, 1963.

ing process echoes 1920–36 in boldness. But in the ends served there is no parallel. More illuminating antecedents may be found in the constitutional jurisprudence of John Marshall.[39] Like the bench Chief Justice Marshall headed (1803–35), the Warren Court is stirring a powerful current in our politics. Just as Marshall's fervent nationalism evoked violent criticism among Democratic-Republicans, so the Warren Court's defense of basic freedoms rouses bitter denunciation from those inclined to equate security with repression.

Chief Justice Marshall lived and worked under Jefferson's unrelenting lash. When, at the end of his long judicial career, the Philadelphia Bar paid him homage, the Chief Justice used the occasion to comment on his judicial stewardship, boasting that his Court had "never sought to enlarge judicial power beyond its proper bounds, nor feared to carry it to the fullest extent duty requires." [40] Sensitive to the narrow line that separates judicial *review* and judicial *supremacy,* Marshall thought he had met the demanding requirements of both *self-restraint* and *duty.* The provisions of the Constitution must, he held, neither "be restricted into insignificance, nor extended to objects not comprehended in them nor contemplated by its framers." [41]

American constitutionalism embodies more than a prescription against the disease Lord Acton immortalized: "Power corrupts, absolute power corrupts absolutely." Judicial review, like the Constitution itself, affirms as well as negates; it is both a power-releasing and power-breaking function. "The restraining power of the judiciary," Judge Cardozo wrote, "does not manifest its chief worth

[39] See Fred Rodell, "It Is the Earl Warren Court," *New York Times Magazine,* March 13, 1966; McCloskey, "Reflections on the Warren Court," 1229–70.

[40] Beveridge, *The Life of John Marshall,* IV, 522.

[41] *Ogden* v. *Saunders,* 12 Wheaton 213, 332 (1827).

in the few cases in which the legislature has gone beyond the lines that mark the limits of discretion. Rather shall we find its chief worth in making vocal and audible the ideals that might otherwise be silenced, in giving them continuity of life and of expression, in guiding and directing choice within the limits where choice ranges." [42] John Marshall deserves to be remembered as much, if not more, for *McCulloch* v. *Maryland*,[43] in which the Court affirmed the power of Congress to incorporate a bank, nontaxable by the state, thus laying the foundations of national power, as for *Marbury* v. *Madison*[44] in which, for the first time, the Court set aside an act of Congress. Marshall did not repeat the prerogative he claimed for the judiciary. That remained for his successor, Chief Justice Taney, in the ill-fated *Dred Scott* case.

Jefferson fiercely denounced Marshall's constitutional jurisprudence, but not because the Chief Justice used the judicial axe against acts of Congress. On occasion, as in the Alien and Sedition Acts, he criticized the Court for not doing so. Jefferson complained angrily of Marshall's affirmative use of the Court as a forum from which to expound nationalist principles at the expense of the states, the effect being "to undermine the foundations of our confederated fabric, . . . construing our constitution from a co-ordination of a general and special government to a general and supreme one alone." [45]

Chief Justice Marshall, Jefferson to the contrary notwithstanding, exhibited remarkable sensitivity to the solemn duty judicial power imposes. Believing that the Constitution is the "creature of the people's will," "a very

[42] B. N. Cardozo, *The Nature of the Judicial Process* (New Haven, 1921), 94.

[43] 4 Wheaton 316 (1819).

[44] 1 Cranch 137 (1803).

[45] Jefferson to Thomas Ritchie, Dec. 25, 1820, in Ford (ed.), *The Works of Thomas Jefferson*, XII, 177.

great exertion" not "to be frequently repeated," [46] he identified the ballot box as the restraint on which "the people must rely solely, in all representative governments. . . ." [47] For him the question whether a law, national or state, is void was a matter of "much delicacy," seldom "to be decided in the affirmative, in a doubtful case." But when impelled by "duty" to render such a judgment, the Court would, he said, "be unworthy of its station," if it were "unmindful of the solemn obligations which that station imposes." [48]

Judicial duty required him to take, on appeal, state court decisions in cases arising under the Constitution or laws of the United States; otherwise America would suffer the chaos of "hydra in government. . . ." Each state would "possess a *veto* on the will of the whole. . . . We have no more right to decline the exercise of jurisdiction which is given," he declared, "than to usurp that which is not given. The one or the other would be treason to the Constitution." [49] Judicial duty commanded the Chief Justice to save the charter of Dartmouth College against New Hampshire's attempt to destroy it.[50] Precluding state action was not only the constitutional injunction against impairing the obligation of contracts in Article 1, Section

[46] *Cohens* v. *Virginia,* 6 Wheaton 264, 389 (1821); *Marbury* v. *Madison,* 176.

[47] *Gibbons* v. *Ogden,* 9 Wheaton 1, 197 (1824). Marshall applied the same standard to state acts: "The Constitution of the United States was not intended to furnish the corrective for every abuse of power which may be committed by the state governments. The interest, wisdom, and justice of the representative body, and its relations with its constituents, furnish the only security, where there is no express contract, against unjust and excessive taxation; as well as against unwise legislation generally." *Providence Bank* v. *Billings,* 4 Peters 514, 563 (1830).

[48] *Fletcher* v. *Peck,* 6 Cranch 87, 127 (1810).

[49] *Cohens* v. *Virginia,* 385, 415, 404.

[50] *Dartmouth College* v. *Woodward,* 4 Wheaton 518 (1819).

10—"a Bill of Rights for the people of each State," [51] he called it—but also the sanctity which enshrouds property and contract rights.

Marshall was as adept in fashioning political theory—"penumbra" to Mr. Justice Douglas, rights emanating from other rights—in defense of property as in support of his nationalist goals: "It may well be doubted whether the nature of society and of government does not prescribe some limits to the legislative power; and, if any be prescribed, where are they to be found, if property of an individual, fairly and honestly acquired, may be seized without compensation?" In the same case, Justice Johnson went further, finding limitations on legislative power resting "on a general principle, on the reason and nature of things: a principle which will impose laws even on the Deity." [52]

Chief Justice Marshall insisted that judicial duty is heightened when political checks are ineffective or unavailable. When a state, as in *McCulloch* v. *Maryland,* taxes an instrumentality of the national government, "it acts upon institutions created, not by their own constituents, but by people over whom they claim no control." [53] Since the people of the United States were not represented in the Maryland legislature which enacted the offending law, the usual political restraints for correcting abuse of power were not operative, hence an enlarged judicial responsibility. The burden of Chief Justice Marshall's constitutional jurisprudence throughout is that the Supreme Court's primary task is positive and creative. He deplored any construction which attempts "to explain away the Constitution," leaving "it a magnificent structure . . . to look at, but totally unfit for use." [54] The

[51] *Fletcher* v. *Peck,* 138.
[52] 6 Cranch 87, 135, 143 (1810).
[53] *McCulloch* v. *Maryland,* 435.
[54] *Gibbons* v. *Ogden,* 222.

judiciary, like other agencies of government, should facilitate achievement of the great objectives mentioned in the Constitution's Preamble.

Professor James Bradley Thayer, noting that constitutional law "is allied, not merely with history, but with Statecraft," singled out Chief Justice Marshall as one among a handful of American judges who were "sensible of the true nature of their work and of the large method of treatment which it required, who perceived that our constitutions had made them, in a limited and secondary way, but a real one, coadjutors with the other departments in the business of government; but many have fallen short of the requirements of so great a function." [55]

In the minds of many Americans, including certain Supreme Court justices, judicial review is essentially negative, limiting, and undemocratic. Whenever government enters a new field, the natural question is whether the action is constitutional. Deploring this emphasis, the late Justice Frankfurter observed: "Preoccupation by our people with the constitutionality, instead of with the wisdom of legislation or of executive action, is preoccupation with a false value. . . . Focusing attention on constitutionality tends to make constitutionality synonymous with wisdom." [56] It suggests that the brakes of our constitutional machinery are more important than the ignition— more essential than the Court's legitimizing function; it ignores the task Judge Cardozo stressed—that of upholding American ideals.

Judicial review, as a barrier against governing, reached a high point in the middle 1930's. Of the eighty-eight congressional statutes declared unconstitutional throughout our history, eleven fell under the judicial axe in 1935–

---

[55] J. B. Thayer, *Cases on Constitutional Law* (Cambridge, 1895), I, v–vi.

[56] *Dennis* v. *United States,* 341 U.S. 494, 556 (1951).

36.[57] The resulting impasse between Court and legislature, tying "Uncle Sam up in a hard knot," [58] as Justice Stone observed, provoked President Roosevelt's disingenuous war on the judiciary. The upshot was a sudden judicial about-face, marked by massive breakdown of constitutional limitations—separation of powers, federalism, "due process of law," judicial review itself—previously invoked against government regulation of the economy. Soon thereafter a new era emerged, stressing judicial duty and responsibility. Under Earl Warren, as during John Marshall's long regime, the Supreme Court has become a creative force in American life.

II

What happened in 1937 has gone down in history as a judicial revolution. But was it? In America, revolution is a loosely used word. The revolutionary principle in America—that sovereign power resides in the people—is not, as James Wilson said, "a principle of discord, rancor or war; it is a principle of melioration, contentment and peace." [59] We have never had a real revolution in the changes wrought, nothing comparable to the upheavals attending the French and Russian Revolutions. Seventeen seventy-six did not sweep the slate clean, did not cut us off from our heritage.[60] The Constitution of 1789 has been

[57] Since 1937 a short but increasing list of congressional acts (eleven to date) has been set aside.

[58] H. F. Stone to his sister, June 2, 1936, quoted in my *Harlan Fiske Stone*, 426.

[59] Quoted in Charles Page Smith, *James Wilson: Founding Father* (Chapel Hill, 1956), 312.

[60] Edmund Burke compared 1776 to the Glorious Revolution of 1688—"a revolution not made, but prevented." Quoted by Russell Kirk in Introduction to Frederick Gentz, *The French and American Revolutions Compared*, translated by John Quincy Adams (Chicago, 1955). Said Gentz: "The revolution of America was, therefore, in every sense of the word, a revolution of necessity. England, alone,

considered a revolutionary departure from the Declaration of Independence. Not so, John Quincy Adams insisted. These were parts of "one consistent whole," a logical sequence in one continuous effort, laying the foundations of government in reason and consent.[61] When Anti-Federalists, fearful of consolidated power, argued for a bill of rights, Hamilton explained: "The constitution is itself, in every rational sense, and to every useful purpose, *A Bill of Rights*." [62] Besides specific provisions limiting state power in behalf of individual rights, such as Article 1, Section 10,[63] (itself a bill of rights for Chief Justice Marshall), the Constitution embodies certain freedom-protecting principles—notably separation of power, federalism, and judicial review.

Anti-Federalists were unconvinced; they wanted a bill of rights. When they got it, Jefferson and Madison recognized that the strongest argument in favor of the Bill of Rights was the not unnatural assumption that its provisions would be enforced by courts. Needed were specific criteria fixing the limits of national power in relation to the rights of individuals. Madison hesitated; Jefferson spurred him on, pointing out that the argument in fa-

---

had by violence effected it: America had contended ten years long, not against England, but against the revolution: America sought not a revolution; she yielded to it, compelled by necessity, not because she wished to extort a better condition than she had before enjoyed, but because she wished to avert a worse one prepared for her" (p. 56).

[61] J. Q. Adams, *Jubilee of the Constitution: A Discourse Delivered at the Request of the New York Historical Society, April 30, 1839* (New York, 1839), 15–18.

[62] *The Federalist*, No. 84, pp. 440–41. See also James Wilson, State House Speech in Philadelphia, Oct. 10, 1787, in my *The States Rights Debate: Antifederalism and the Constitution* (Englewood Cliffs, N.J., 1964), 125–29.

[63] "No state shall . . . pass any bill of attainder, *ex post facto* law, or law impairing the obligation of contracts."

vor of a declaration of rights of "great weight with me" is "the legal check which it puts into the hands of the judiciary." [64] In submitting the proposed amendments to the first Congress, Madison, now Jefferson's convert, predicted that the Justices "will be naturally led to resist every encroachment upon rights expressly stipulated for in the constitution by the declaration of rights." [65]

In 1789, the Bill of Rights was an almost forgotten appendage. For Chief Justice Warren its provisions constitute "the heart of any constitution." [66] In the beginning, as now, its chief worth lay in judicial responsibility for its enforcement.

The Anti-Federalist campaign was both a great success and an enduring disappointment. Gained were constitutional safeguards for speech, press, religion, right of assembly, and procedural guarantees for persons accused of crime. Lost was the primary objective—constitutional protection for the states, a line or marker specifically safeguarding local authority against federal encroachments. Achieved was a constitutional redundancy—the Tenth Amendment—"the powers not delegated to the United States by the Constitution, nor prohibited by it to the States, are reserved to the states respectively, or to the people." In effect its purpose, Chief Justice Marshall explained, was that of a tranquilizer to quiet "the excessive jealousies which had been excited." [67] Despite the Tenth Amendment, the national government is supreme in the exercise of its delegated and implied powers.

As the Constitution left the hands of the framers and as

[64] Thomas Jefferson to James Madison, March 15, 1789, in Boyd (ed.), *The Papers of Thomas Jefferson*, XIV, 659–61.

[65] U.S. Congress, *Annals of Congress*, I, 1st Congress, 1st Session, June 8, 1789 (Washington, D.C., 1834), 457.

[66] Henry M. Christman (ed.), *The Public Papers of Chief Justice Earl Warren* (New York, 1959), 7.

[67] *McCulloch v. Maryland*, 406.

amended by the Bill of Rights, despite persistent effort to achieve it, no precise line was drawn delineating national power in the interest of the states. The powers of the national government, though enumerated, were "undefined" and "indefinite." Alert to possible inroads on the states, Hugh Williamson of North Carolina objected that the effect might be to "restrain the States from regulating their internal" affairs. Indefinite power in the central authority would, Elbridge Gerry objected, "enslave the States." Hamilton, Madison, and Wilson stood firm, the latter explaining that it was impossible to draw a line dividing state and national powers. "[W]hen we come near the line," he explained, "it cannot be found. . . . [A] discretion must be left on one side or the other. . . . Will it not be most safely lodged on the side of the National Government? . . . What danger is there that the whole will unnecessarily sacrifice a part? But reverse the case, and leave the whole at the mercy of each part, and will not the general interest be continually sacrificed to local interests?" Even Hamilton denied any intention to create a consolidated system. When it was suggested that he wished to "swallow up" the States, he protested, declaring that he "had not been understood. . . . By an abolition of the States, he meant that no boundary could be drawn between the National & State legislatures; that the former must therefore have *indefinite* authority. If it [national authority] were limited at all, the rivalship of the States would gradually subvert it." [68]

The states were to be retained in so far as they could be "subordinately useful." "It was impossible," Madison told the first Congress, "to confine a government to the exercise of express powers; there must necessarily be admitted powers by implication, unless the constitution descended

[68] Farrand (ed.), *Records of the Federal Convention of 1787*, I, 165, 166–67, 170, 323. Italics added.

to recount every minutia." [69] The Tenth Amendment had left federal-state relations unchanged.

With good reason, advocates of a Bill of Rights were profoundly disappointed. Instead of "substantial provisions," Pierce Butler complained, Madison had proposed "a few *milk-and-water* amendments, . . . such as liberty of conscience, a free press, and one or two general things already well secured." "I suppose it was done," Butler speculated as to Madison's strategy, "to keep his promise with his constituents, to move for alterations, but if I am not greatly mistaken, he is not hearty in the cause of amendments." [70] In 1790, the Tenth Amendment was recognized for what it was—a gold brick.

The states'-rights failure of 1790 was compounded in 1868 by the adoption of the Fourteenth Amendment, providing safeguards against state power broad enough to cover the restrictions Madison sought vainly to win in 1790 —"No state shall violate the equal rights of conscience, or the freedom of the press, or the trial by jury in criminal cases." [71] At the outset, however, a sharply divided Court, refusing "to fetter and degrade the state governments," declined to become, under the Fourteenth Amendment's sweeping provisions, "a perpetual censor" of state activities. To do so, a 5 to 4 majority argued, would radically change "the whole theory of the relations of the State and Federal Governments," [72] a relationship apparently immune even to the amending process. In a vehement dissent, Justice Field declared that the effect was to make the Fourteenth Amendment "a vain and idle enactment." State grants of "exclusive privileges" to entre-

[69] *Annals of Congress,* I, 790.

[70] Pierce Butler to James Iredell, Aug. 11, 1789, in Griffith McRee, *Life and Correspondence of James Iredell* (New York, 1857), II, 265.

[71] *Annals of Congress,* I, 452.

[72] Justice Miller in *Slaughter-House Cases,* 16 Wallace 36, 78 (1873).

preneurs, as in this case, he argued, "are opposed to the whole theory of free government, and it requires no aid from any bill of rights to render them void. That only is a free government, in the American sense of the term, under which the inalienable right of every citizen to pursue his happiness is unrestrained, except by just, equal, and impartial laws." [73]

For dissenting Justice Field, judicial protection of property and contract rights was a judicial duty, imposed not only by the Fourteenth Amendment but also by "the fundamental idea of free government." A decade later, John M. Harlan, grandfather of the present Justice Harlan, affirmed congressional recognition of another category of freedoms—"full and equal enjoyment," under the Fourteenth Amendment, of "the accommodations, advantages, facilities, and privileges of inns, public conveyances, and theatres." [74] In the *Civil Rights Cases* of 1883, Justice Field dissenting, Harlan foreshadowed the School Desegregation decisions of the nineteen fifties and the constitutionality of the 1964 Civil Rights Act. [75] In his *Hurtado* dissent of 1884, [76] Justice Harlan (Field not participating) anticipated Justice Black's increasingly successful campaign to bring the entire Bill of Rights under the broad umbrella of the Fourteenth Amendment. [77] Nor was the elder Justice Harlan content merely to rely on provisions of the Constitution. Like Chief Justice Marshall in 1810 and Justice Field in 1873, he cited a supporting theory— "the great and essential principles of free government." [78]

In the 1890's when the judiciary finally became, under

[73] *Ibid.,* 111.

[74] Dissenting in *Civil Rights Cases,* 109 U.S. 3, 27 (1883).

[75] *Heart of Atlanta Motel, Inc.* v. *U.S.,* 379 U.S. 241 (1964).

[76] *Hurtado* v. *California,* 110 U.S. 516 (1884).

[77] This effort was launched in *Adamson* v. *California,* 332 U.S. 46 (1947).

[78] *Hurtado* v. *California,* 557.

the Fourteenth Amendment, what a majority of five in 1873 insisted it must not be, "a perpetual censor," when it became, as President Arthur Twining Hadley of Yale put it in 1908, "an arbiter" between "the voters on the one hand and the property owners on the other," [79] the change seemed revolutionary. Indeed, that is what dissenting Justices, including the elder Justice Harlan, called it. But this judicial "revolution" was not unlimited. Thereafter judicial activists were subjected to the unremitting barbs of Holmes, Brandeis, and Stone, all reiterating James Bradley Thayer's argument of 1893, that "the judicial function is merely that of fixing the outside border of reasonable legislative action. . . . The Constitution does not impose upon the legislature any one specific opinion, but leaves open this range of choice; . . . whatever choice is rational is constitutional." For Thayer, godfather of the modern self-restraint doctrine, the judicial function involves "taking a part, a secondary part, in the political conduct of government." In an essay, singled out by Justice Frankfurter as "the great guide for judges and therefore, the great guide for understanding by non-judges of what the place of the judiciary is in relation to constitutional questions," [80] Thayer warned that the Supreme Court would "imperil" its entire jurisdiction "if it is sought to give them more. . . ." [81]

III

Until 1937, Thayer's sober counsel was to no avail. America then witnessed what some considered a real revolution —the famous "switch in time," a sudden judicial about-face. Endorsing Thayer's principle of self-restraint, the Court then upheld the National Labor Relations Act and

[79] *The Independent*, LXIV (1908), 837.
[80] *Felix Frankfurter Reminisces* (New York, 1960), 300.
[81] Thayer, "Doctrine of Constitutional Law," 129–56 *passim*.

a state minimum wage law, overturning freshly established precedents. The piercing wails of Justices recently dethroned suggested catastrophe, revolution. "The Constitution is gone," [82] Justice McReynolds clamored, and so it was—*his* Constitution.

The intransigent ghost of Rufus W. Peckham, Justice Holmes's major target in 1905,[83] still haunted judicial interpretation. In 1922, Professor Felix Frankfurter asked Justice Holmes about Peckham. "I used to say," Holmes responded, "his major premise was God damn it. Meaning thereby that emotional predilections somewhat governed him on social themes." [84] Repudiating the economic penumbra Justice Peckham fashioned around the "due process" clause of the Fourteenth Amendment, Holmes insisted that the Constitution did not enact any particular economic dogma; it was not "the partisan of a particular set of ethical or economical opinions, which by no means are held *semper ubique et ab omnibus.*" [85]

Holmes's views, long in minority, are now triumphant. Speaking in 1963 for a unanimous Court, Justice Black declared:

We refuse to sit as a "superlegislature to weigh the wisdom of legislation," and we emphatically refuse to go back to the time when the courts used the "Due Process Clause" to strike down state laws regulatory of business and industrial conditions because they may be unwise, improvident, or out of harmony with a particular school of thought. . . . Whether the legislature takes for its text book Adam Smith, Herbert Spencer, Lord Keynes, or some other is no concern of ours.[86]

By 1937 the Court had become the primary, rather than an auxiliary, check on government. It had come to think

[82] Quoted in my *Harlan Fiske Stone,* 391.
[83] *Lochner* v. *New York,* 198 U.S. 45 (1905).
[84] Quoted in Bickel, *Unpublished Opinions of Mr. Justice Brandeis,* 164.
[85] *Otis* v. *Parker,* 187 U.S. 606, 609 (1903).
[86] *Ferguson* v. *Skrupa,* 372 U.S. 93, 98 (1963).

of itself, Justice Stone complained, as "the only agency of government that must be assumed to have capacity to govern." [87] Under fire the justices relinquished what they had usurped. The Court did not abdicate.

Professor Corwin called the ignominious judicial somersault of 1937 *Constitutional Revolution, Ltd.*[88] Hereafter, he predicted, the Court would pay greater deference to the policy-forming organs of government and be less concerned with the wisdom of social and economic legislation. Corwin suggested that the Court, having abandoned guardianship of property, would still have plenty to do if it intervened "on behalf of the helpless and oppressed";[89] it would then "be free, as it has not in many years, to support the humane values of free thought, free utterance, and fair play." [90] Surrender of its self-acquired role as protector of economic privilege would allow the Court "to give voice to the conscience of the country." [91] These prophetic words, reminiscent of Jefferson's argument of 1789 in favor of a bill of rights—the "legal check" it places in the hands of the judiciary—were written in 1940. Looking back as well as ahead, Corwin noted in 1941: "Constitutional law has always a central interest to guard." [92]

The Warren Court's remarkable fulfillment of Corwin's prognostications has provoked fierce attack, from within as well as from without the Court. At issue among

[87] Justice Stone, dissenting in *United States* v. *Butler,* 297 U.S. 1, 87 (1936).

[88] E. S. Corwin, *Constitutional Revolution, Ltd.* (Claremont, Calif., 1941).

[89] E. S. Corwin, "Some Probable Repercussions of 'NIRA' on Our Constitutional System," *Annals of the American Academy of Political and Social Science,* CLXXII (1934), 142.

[90] E. S. Corwin, "Statesmanship on the Supreme Court," *American Scholar,* IX (1940), 159, 163.

[91] Corwin, *Constitutional Revolution, Ltd.,* 110–12.

[92] E. S. Corwin, *The Constitution and What It Means Today* (7th ed.; Princeton, 1941), Preface, viii.

the Justices are basic constitutional verities—federalism and the Bill of Rights—and the Court's responsibility toward them. Upholding values long identified with the late Justice Frankfurter, and in the face of his grandfather's assertion of judicial duty in the *Civil Rights* and *Hurtado* cases, Justice Harlan deplores what he considers the majority's mad rush to bring an ever-increasing number of Bill of Rights provisions under the equal protection and due process clauses of the Fourteenth Amendment at the expense of federalism and separation of powers, values which, he insists, "lie at the root of our constitutional system." [93]

"We are accustomed," Justice Harlan observes, "to speak of the Bill of Rights and the Fourteenth Amendment as the principal guarantees of personal liberty. Yet it would surely be shallow not to recognize that the structure of our political system accounts no less for the free society we have." The Founding Fathers "staked their faith that liberty would prosper in the new nation not primarily upon declarations of individual rights but upon the kind of government the Union was to have." "No view of the Bill of Rights or interpretation of any of its provisions," the Justice warns, "which fails to take due account of [federalism and separation of powers] can be considered constitutionally sound." [94]

For Justice Harlan, the decisions asserting judicial responsibility for "one man, one vote" "cut deeply into the fabric of our Federalism," representing entry into an area "profoundly ill-advised and constitutionally impermissible." [95] Echoing the concern voiced in 1873, when the Court refused to become, under the sweeping provisions

[93] Address at the American Bar Center, Chicago, Aug. 13, 1963.

[94] John M. Harlan, "The Bill of Rights and the Constitution," address at the dedication of the Bill of Rights Room, U.S. Subtreasury Building, New York City, Aug. 9, 1964.

[95] *Reynolds* v. *Sims,* 624.

of the Fourteenth Amendment, "a perpetual censor upon all legislation of the states," [96] Harlan believes that the end achieved would be "at the cost of a radical alteration in the relationship between the States and the Federal Government, more particularly the federal judiciary." [97] Extending to accused persons in state courts the safeguards available to them in the federal courts is denounced as "historically and constitutionally unsound and incompatible with the maintenance of our federal system. . . ." [98]

It is "the very essence of American federalism," Justice Harlan wrote in 1958, "that the States should have the widest latitude in the administration of their own system of criminal justice." [99] Such diversity, he insists, is inherent in federalism. Judicial censorship of obscene and indecent literature trenches on the "prerogative of the states to differ on their ideas of morality," denying both nation and states the advantage of having fifty laboratories of experimentation for trying out "different attitudes toward the same work of literature." [100]

IV

Two basic issues divide the Warren Court: first, the relative claims of the Bill of Rights on the one hand, and federalism and separation of powers, on the other, to judicial guardianship as safeguards of freedom; second, whether economic dogma, such as laissez faire, has any greater claim to judicial consideration than political ideology—"one man, one vote," "unrestrained egalitarianism." In 1873, and for many years thereafter, Justice Field, disregarding the claims of federalism, took up the

[96] Justice Miller, speaking for a 5 to 4 majority in *Slaughter-House Cases,* 78.
[97] *Reynolds* v. *Sims,* 624.
[98] *Pointer* v. *Texas,* 380 U.S. 400, 409 (1965).
[99] *Hoag* v. *New Jersey,* 356 U.S. 464, 468 (1958).
[100] *Roth* v. *United States,* 354 U.S. 476, 505 (1957).

cudgels in favor of economic dogma as a bulwark for economic enterprise. The elder Justice Harlan, on the other hand, invoked political ideology, the principles of free government, as justifying judicial protection of civil liberties. At the moment the Bill of Rights and political ideology are in the ascendancy, but Justice Harlan has, as we shall see, recently annexed fresh support.

Justice Harlan's wide-flung strictures revive the eighteenth-century debate between Federalists and Anti-Federalists as to whether a bill of rights was a necessary supplement to the protection afforded by federalism and separation of powers. Rejuvenated also is a variant of "dual federalism," the doctrine that certain subject matter, notably the administration of criminal justice, is peculiarly within the domain of the states. Justice Harlan's indictment also recalls the charges dissenters Holmes and Stone hurled against the Court when, in deference to economic theory, a majority vetoed government regulation of the economy. In 1905, Holmes insisted that the Constitution must not be equated with any particular *economic* theory;[101] in 1966 Justice Harlan insisted that the Constitution embodies no particular *political* theory. "One man, one vote" is, he declared, a judicial creation, a "political theory," "a piece of political ideology," reflecting "the Court's view of what is constitutionally permissible." [102] Yet "a particular theory" of federalism and separation of powers has his strong endorsement.

On April 5, 1965, shortly before he doffed judicial robes to become Ambassador to the United Nations, Justice Goldberg made a point-by-point reply to "Brother Harlan." Goldberg noted that Harlan's bugaboo, his grandfather's and Justice Black's "incorporation" theory, had made notable progress. Now included among the Four-

[101] *Lochner* v. *New York,* 74.
[102] *Reynolds* v. *Sims,* 555.

teenth Amendment's guarantees against infringement by the states are the liberties of the First, Fourth, Fifth, Sixth, and Eighth amendments. Goldberg did not accept Justice Harlan's easy transition from Brandeis' claims for the advantages of federalism in the field of economics to the area of civil rights. "While I agree with Justice Brandeis," Goldberg observed tartly, "that it is one of the happy incidents of the federal system that . . . a state may . . . serve as a laboratory, and try novel social and economic experiments, . . . I do not believe that this includes the power to experiment with the fundamental liberties of citizens safeguarded by the Bill of Rights." [103]

Nor did Justice Goldberg believe that Harlan's restrictive view of judicial duty would advance any legitimate state interest. Said Goldberg: "to deny to the states the power to impair a fundamental constitutional right is not to increase federal power, but, rather, to limit the power of both federal and state governments in favor of safeguarding the fundamental rights and liberties of the individual." [104] Since *Gideon* v. *Wainwright*,[105] guaranteeing a Florida indigent his constitutional right to counsel, twenty-six states have instituted vital reforms in their criminal procedure. "I didn't start out," the triumphant Clarence Gideon observes, "to do anything for anybody but myself, but this decision has done a helluva lot of good. . . ." [106]

The day when law enforcement officers could do pretty much as they pleased is past. *Mapp* (1961) holds that evidence obtained by search and seizure in violation of the Fourth Amendment is inadmissible in a state court, as in a federal court; *Escobedo*[107] (1964) guarantees the right

[103] *Pointer* v. *Texas,* 410–13.
[104] *Ibid.,* 414.
[105] 372 U.S. 335 (1963).
[106] *Time,* Dec. 17, 1965, 39.
[107] *Escobedo* v. *Illinois,* 378 U.S. 478 (1964).

to counsel under the Sixth and Fourteenth Amendments; *Miranda et al.*[108] (1966) extends the Fifth Amendment's privilege against self-incrimination to the police station. Justice Harlan dissented in all these cases. Pleading the necessity of preserving "a proper balance between state and federal responsibility in the administration of criminal justice," [109] he denounces the new rules as "hazardous experimentation." [110] "The Court," Harlan warns, "is taking a real risk with society's welfare in imposing its new regime on the country." [111] The new rules, he believes, are "most ill-conceived and seriously and unjustifiably fetter perfectly legitimate methods of criminal law enforcement." [112]

Goldberg was unconvinced. In answer to complaints that police chiefs and district attorneys are being handcuffed in the performance of their duties, he retorted: "No system worth preserving should have to *fear* that if an accused is permitted to consult with a lawyer, he will become aware of, and exercise these rights. If the exercise of constitutional rights will thwart the effectiveness of a system of law enforcement, then there is something very wrong with that system." [113] In an opinion for a unanimous court, Justice Black declared that the "Sixth Amendment's right of an accused to confront the witnesses against him is . . . a fundamental right and is made obligatory on the states by the Fourteenth Amendment. . . . [This is] an essential and fundamental requirement for the kind of fair trial which is this country's constitutional goal." [114]

Nor has more equitable representation, in response to

[108] *Miranda* v. *Arizona,* 384 U.S. 436 (1966).
[109] *Mapp* v. *Ohio,* 680.
[110] *Miranda* v. *Arizona,* 748.
[111] *Ibid.*
[112] *Escobedo* v. *Illinois,* 492.
[113] *Ibid.,* 490.
[114] *Pointer* v. *Texas,* 403, 405.

judicial command, weakened the states, or encouraged, as Justice Harlan anticipated, "inertia in efforts for political reform through the political process." In May 1966, the Council of State Government reported that thirty-seven states, under court orders, had reapportioned one or more houses of their legislatures.[115] In time, reapportionment, in progress on a broad front, may better equip the states to meet twentieth-century needs, revitalizing rather than disabling these essential units of local government.

In June, 1965, Justice Harlan's campaign for judicial self-restraint won significant, though qualified, support from Justice Black. theretofore a fierce antagonist. Speaking for the Court in *Griswold* v. *Connecticut*,[116] Justice Douglas invoked amendments 1, 3, 4, 5, 6, 9, and 14. In none, however, was there a specific bar against Connecticut's anti-contraceptive statute. Douglas found the constitutional killer in the right of privacy, in "penumbras, formed by emanations from those guarantees that give them life and substance." The right of privacy, the majority's spokesman declared, is "older than our political parties, older than our school system." [117] This was too much for Justice Black. In dissent, he recalled the danger of falling into the judicial trap from which the Court had narrowly extricated itself in 1937—the ever-seductive snare of judicial pre-eminence. "Subjective considerations of 'natural' justice," Black warned, are "no less dangerous when used to enforce this Court's views about personal rights than those about economic rights." "I get nowhere in this case," the Justice went on, "by talk about a constitutional 'right of privacy' as an emanation of one or more constitutional provisions. . . . I like my privacy as well as the next one," the eighty-year-old Jus-

[115] *U.S. News and World Report,* June 20, 1966, p. 50.
[116] *Griswold* v. *Connecticut,* 479.
[117] *Ibid.,* 486.

tice commented feelingly, "but I am nevertheless compelled to admit that government has a right to invade it unless prohibited by some specific constitutional provision." Black cautioned against reinstating *Lochner* "and other cases from which this Court recoiled in 1937. . . ." Apparently, the dissenting Justice noted, "my Brethren have less quarrel with economic regulations than former Justices of their persuasion had." [118] For Justice Black, "penumbra" of whatever orientation permits judges to enforce their predilections as law.

Justices Black and Harlan dissented again in the 6 to 3 decision of March 24, 1966, declaring unconstitutional the poll tax as a voting qualification. In protest against reading current political theory into the Constitution, Justice Harlan wrote:

Property and poll-tax qualifications, very simply, are not in accord with current egalitarian notions of how a modern democracy should be organized. It is of course entirely fitting that legislatures should modify the law to reflect such changes in popular attitudes. However, it is all wrong, in my view, for the Court to adopt the political doctrines popularly accepted at a particular moment of our history and to declare all others to be irrational and invidious, barring them from the range of choice by reasonably minded people acting through the political process. It was not too long ago that Mr. Justice Holmes felt impelled to remind the Court that the Due Process Clause of the Fourteenth Amendment does not enact the laissez-faire theory of society. . . . The times have changed, and perhaps it is appropriate to observe that neither does the Equal Protection Clause of that Amendment rigidly impose upon America an ideology of unrestrained egalitarianism.[119]

Like Harlan, Justice Black objected to the Court's use of the equal protection clause "to write into the Consti-

[118] *Ibid.*, 530–31, 538–39.
[119] *Harper* v. *Virginia State Board of Elections*, 383 U.S. 663 (1966), 183–84.

tution its notions of what it thinks is good governmental policy." The majority had found adherence to the original meaning of the Constitution "an intolerable and debilitating evil." It believed "that our Constitution should not be 'shackled to the political theory of a particular era,' and that to save the country from the original Constitution the Court must have constant power to renew it and keep it abreast with this Court's more enlightened theories of what is best for our society." Echoing Justice Sutherland's sentiments of an earlier era, Black declared war on this approach: "When a political theory embodied in our Constitution becomes outdated . . . a majority of the nine members of this Court are not only without constitutional power but are far less qualified to choose a new constitutional political theory than the people of this country proceeding in the manner provided by Article V." [120]

Justice Black's dissenting opinion in the poll tax case continues the campaign he launched in 1947 against the "natural justice formula" [121] (which he had himself endorsed in *Palko*[122] and of which Justice Harlan approves) permitting Supreme Court Justices to pick and choose what provisions of the Bill of Rights are incorporated into the Fourteenth Amendment. Under this formula, the Court was licensed, Black declares, "to roam at large in the broad expanses of policy and morals and to trespass, all too freely, on the legislative domain of the States as well as the Federal Government." Black would narrow the range of judicial discretion by extending "to all the people of the Nation the complete protection of the Bill of Rights." [123] Justice Black, resting apparently under the comfortable illusion that the provisions of the Bill of

[120] *Ibid.*, 178–79.
[121] *Adamson* v. *California.*
[122] *Palko* v. *Connecticut*, 302 U.S. 319 (1937).
[123] *Adamson* v. *California*, 89–90.

Rights are mathematically precise, seems to believe that their incorporation into the Fourteenth Amendment would leave no room for theorizing or judicial choice.

At issue within the Court and in the country is the role of the judiciary in a free society; rehearsed is the age-old dichotomy concerning judicial restraint and judicial duty. The late Justice Frankfurter, an Anglophile much impressed with the virtues of the British system of free government, held that "judicial review is itself a limitation on popular government." [124] Of course it is, and that is precisely what the framers intended it to be. But any implication that judicial review is, therefore, suspect as an alien intruder is mistaken. An informed student of the American political tradition might rewrite Frankfurter's statement: "Judicial review is but one among several auxiliary precautions the framers considered essential to the functioning of the American system of *free government*." [125] "Those who won our independence," Justice Brandeis noted in 1927, "recognizing the occasional tyrannies of governing majorities, . . . amended the Constitution so that free speech and assembly should be guaranteed." [126]

The shift from constitutional limitations, featuring federalism and separation of powers, and applied, prior to 1937, to economic regulations, to constitutional limitations and affirmations grounded in the Bill of Rights, is reflected in a host of Warren Court rulings. Cases dealing with civil liberties now claim the lion's share of the Court's work load. In its 1935–36 term, there were 160 decisions in which opinions were written. Of these, only two were in the area of civil rights and liberties. In 1960–

[124] *Minersville School District* v. *Gobitis,* 310 U.S. 586 (1940). See note 141, below.
[125] Compare E. S. Corwin's review of B. F. Wright, *Growth of American Constitutional Law,* in *Harvard Law Review,* LVI (1942), 487.
[126] *Whitney* v. *California,* 274 U.S. 357, 376 (1927).

61, fifty-four of the 120 decisions in which opinions were prepared concerned civil rights and liberties. There were twenty-eight such cases in 1961–62, forty-two in 1962–63, thirty-nine in 1964–65.[127] These figures afford a measure of the Warren Court's dynamic role in giving reality to the Bill of Rights. Fulfilled are Jefferson's and Madison's forecast of 1789, that enforcement of the Bill of Rights would become the special concern of the judiciary.

The paralyzing action of the Hughes Court, preventing social and economic experimentation, is now recognized as indefensible and self-defeating. Has the Warren Court's activism as guardian of civil liberties any higher claims to justify it? [128]

In the simple context of the early 1900's, resolution of the liberty versus restraint paradox involved, as Justice Peckham put it, "a question of which two powers or rights shall prevail—the power of the state to legislate or the right of the individual to liberty of person and freedom of contract." [129] Underlying constitutional interpretation in the 1920's was Chief Justice Taft's conviction that "the Constitution was intended, its very purpose was to prevent experimentation with the fundamental rights [property and contracts] of the individual." [130] Encroachments on "liberty of contract" were then accorded "searching judicial scrutiny." Though the expression had not yet been coined, it was the "preferred freedom." A Federal District Court judge struck a deep vein in our culture in 1922 when he declared: "Of the three fundamental principles which underlie government, and for which government

---

[127] For these calculations, I am indebted to The Commission on Law and Social Action of the American Jewish Congress. Summary and Analysis of the U.S. Supreme Court, 1964–65 Term.

[128] Commentators have tended to shy away from this question. It is, of course, the one with which this chapter is primarily concerned.

[129] *Lochner* v. *New York*, 57.

[130] *Truax* v. *Corrigan*, 257 U.S. 312, 338 (1921).

exists, the protection of life, liberty and property, the chief of these is property." [131]

The dramatic shift under Chief Justice Warren to a new category of preferred freedoms reflects his conception of law as a living process, responsive to human needs. For the present Chief Justice, "the issue . . . is not the individual against society; it is, rather, the wise accommodation of the necessities of physical survival with the requirements of spiritual survival." [132] "I am one," the Chief Justice declared, February 1, 1962, "who believes firmly that the Court must be vigilant against neglect of the requirement of our Bill of Rights and the personal rights that document was intended to guarantee for all time." [133]

Prior to 1937, the Justices fashioned around the due process clauses and other constitutional provisions the economic theory of laissez-faire to prevent government regulation of economic affairs. In recent years the Court has woven about the Constitution a cloak of political theory to protect and promote human dignity. Justices Black and Harlan protest vigorously, contending that judicial adornment of the Constitution by a rationalizing penumbra, of whatever description, is unjustified. But Justice Stone, who wrote the historic Carolene Products footnote,[134] from which the new dispensation of preferred freedoms flowered, reasoned otherwise.

In 1937, when the judicially created barriers crumbled, Stone, leader of the drive for judicial self-restraint, had been concerned lest the guarantees of civil liberties might thereafter be wanting as effective safeguards. What should

[131] Judge Van Orsdel in *Children's Hospital* v. *Adkins,* 284 F. 613, 622 (1922).
[132] Earl Warren, "The Bill of Rights and the Military," *New York University Law Review,* XXXVII (1962), 200.
[133] *Ibid.,* 201–202.
[134] *United States* v. *Carolene Products Co.,* 304 U.S. 144, 151–54 (1938).

be the new interest of judicial guardianship? Of course the baby must not be thrown out with the bath. The upshot was the famous footnote of three paragraphs. Stone did not go so far as to hold that no economic legislation would thereafter violate constitutional restraints, but he did suggest confining the Court's role narrowly in this area. Attached to this self-denying caveat were three adumbrations, indicating new fields of judicial action on behalf of what was later dubbed "preferred freedoms." [135] The first suggests that in cases involving First Amendment freedoms, already absorbed into the Fourteenth Amendment, the usual presumption of constitutionality might not be in order. The second declares that legislation restricting those political processes that might be available to bring about repeal of undesirable legislation might be given special judicial scrutiny. The third intimates that legislation affecting the rights of discrete and insular minorities—racial, religious, or national—may call for more "searching judicial inquiry."

Disavowing originality, Stone found support for these propositions in the opinions of Marshall, Holmes, Brandeis, Hughes, and Cardozo. Justice Stone did not document what he had in mind, but he could easily have done so. All the eminent jurists he mentioned had, from time to time, invoked political theory—a theory of the Constitution—to bolster their position. "The whole American fabric has been erected," Chief Justice Marshall declared, on the proposition "that the people have an original right to establish for their future government such principles as in their opinion, shall most conduce to their own hap-

[135] Chief Justice Stone introduced this expression in *Jones* v. *Opelika,* 316 U.S. 584, 600, 608 (1942); Justice Douglas invoked it for the majority in *Murdock* v. *Pennsylvania,* 319 U.S. 105, 115 (1943). For a critical review of the career of the Carolene Products footnote and a vicious attack on the idea of preferred freedoms, see Justice Frankfurter in *Kovacs* v. *Cooper,* 336 U.S. 77, 90–97 (1949).

piness." [136] Popular consent was, he held, the foundation of free government. When the correction of governmental abuses is not forthcoming from the political process, Marshall claimed heightened responsibility for the judiciary.[137]

Justice Holmes, expressing the conviction that "the ultimate good desired is better reached by free trade in ideas," called this "the theory of our Constitution." [138] Convinced that the Bill of Rights "could not be kept unless we were willing to fight for them," he was inclined to "stand by them." "We forget that they [the Bill of Rights] had to be fought for and may have to be fought for again." [139] Stone recalled that Justice Holmes believed that judges "should not be too rigidly bound to the tenet of judicial self-restraint in cases involving civil liberties." [140]

Brandeis cited "a fundamental principle of the American Government" to justify the wide range accorded "freedom to think as you will and to speak as you think," tracing this priority to those "who won our independence," to men "who were not cowards," who "did not fear change."

---

[136] *Marbury* v. *Madison*, 176.

[137] *McCulloch* v. *Maryland*, 435.

[138] Dissenting in *Abrams* v. *United States*, 250 U.S. 616, 630 (1919).

[139] Holmes, *Holmes-Laski Letters*, I, 203, 529–30.

[140] Stone to Clinton Rossiter, April 12, 1941, in my *Harlan Fiske Stone*, 516. Felix Frankfurter noted that "Justice Holmes attributed very different legal significance to those liberties of the individual which history has attested as the indispensable conditions of a free society from that which he attached to liberties which derived merely from shifting economic arrangements. These enduring liberties of the subject, in the noble English phrase, were, so far as the national government is concerned, specifically enshrined in the Bill of Rights. . . . Because these civil liberties were explicitly safeguarded in the Constitution, or conceived to be basic to any notion of the liberty guaranteed by the Fourteenth Amendment, Mr. Justice Holmes was far more ready to find legislative invasion in this field than in the area of debatable economic reform." Frankfurter, *Mr. Justice Holmes and the Supreme Court*, 51, 49–63, 76 *passim*.

They [the framers] recognized the risks to which all human institutions are subject. But they knew that order cannot be secured merely through fear of punishment for its infraction; that it is hazardous to discourage thought, hope, and imagination; that fear breeds repression; that repression breeds hate; that hate menaces stable government; that the path of safety lies in the opportunity to discuss freely supposed grievances and proposed remedies; and that the fitting remedy for evil councils is good ones.[141]

Brandeis discovered protection against police use of wire tapping not only in the Fourth Amendment's ban on unreasonable searches and seizures, but also in a "fundamental principle of the American government," the right to privacy—the right to be alone, the "most comprehensive of rights and the rights most valued by civilized men." [142]

Ardent exponent of civil liberties both on and off the Court, Chief Justice Hughes referred to the Bill of Rights as a barrier against "gusts of passion and prejudice which in misguided zeal would destroy the basic interests of democracy. We protect the fundamental rights of minorities in order to save democratic government from destroying itself by the excess of its own power." [143] As Chief Justice, Hughes led in restoring the belief that certain rights— freedom of speech, press, and religion—must be preserved "in order to maintain the opportunity for free discussion, to the end that government may be responsive to the people and that changes, if desired, may be obtained by peaceful means." "Therein," he declared, "lies the security of the Republic, the very foundation of Constitutional Government." [144]

[141] *Whitney* v. *California,* 376–77.
[142] Dissenting in *Olmstead* v. *United States,* 277 U.S. 438, 478 (1928).
[143] Proceedings in Commemoration of the 150th Anniversary of the First Congress, House Document No. 212, 76th Congress, First Session, March 4, 1939, p. 32.
[144] *De Jonge* v. *Oregon,* 299 U.S. 353, 365 (1937).

In 1937, with the concurrence, ironically, of Justice Black, only Justice Butler dissenting, Cardozo suggested criteria for deciding which provisions of the Bill of Rights are incorporated into the Fourteenth Amendment. "We reach a different plane of social and moral values," Cardozo wrote, "when we pass to the privileges and immunities that have been taken over from the earlier articles of the Federal Bill of Rights and brought within the Fourteenth Amendment by a process of absorption." To be included the right must constitute "the matrix, the indispensable condition of nearly every other form of freedom"; the right must be prerequisite to a system of "ordered liberty." [145] Under this vague rubric, the Court held that "double jeopardy" does not violate those "fundamental principles of liberty and justice which lie at the base of all our civil and political institutions." [146]

In a dramatic confrontation with Justice Frankfurter concerning the meaning and requirements of judicial self-restraint, Justice Stone, in the forefront of opposition to judicial activists who used vague clauses of the Constitution to prevent regulation of economics, insisted that the self-restraint doctrine must not be employed to uphold the flag salute requirement in violation of religious scruples: "The very terms of the Bill of Rights preclude, it seems to me, any reconciliation of such compulsions with the constitutional guaranties by a legislative declaration that they are more important to the public welfare than the Bill of Rights. . . ." [147]

The divergence between Stone and Frankfurter indicates disagreement as to the kind of government the framers established and the relation of the Court thereto.

[145] *Palko* v. *Connecticut,* 326–27.

[146] *Ibid.,* 328, quoting *Hebert* v. *Louisiana,* 272 U.S. 312, 316 (1926).

[147] *Minersville School District* v. *Gobitis,* 605–607. Italics added.

Frankfurter thought of the American system as "popular"; Stone referred to it as "free government." For Frankfurter legislative supremacy and majority rule were well-nigh inexorable commands. He was accustomed to draw British analogies and cite British decisions. But in America, unlike Britain, legislation cannot be equated with the popular will. When legislation comes to the Court for interpretation, it represents a popular will already deflected by various constitutional devices. Judicial review does limit popular government. In this sense, it is oligarchal. But, in this respect, it is not distinguishable from other undemocratic devices, including the Presidential veto and the bicameral legislature. To impugn judicial review as oligarchal, as inconsistent with popular government, therefore requiring niggardliness in its legitimate use, is to cast a shadow on all those features supporting Madison's considered boast in *Federalist* No. 14 that America "accomplished a revolution which has no parallel in the annals of human society. They reared the fabrics of government which have no models on the face of the globe."

V

"The idea of a Constitution, limiting and superintending the operations of legislative authority," James Wilson commented in the Pennsylvania Ratifying Convention of 1787, "seems not to have been accurately understood in Britain. . . . To control the power and conduct of the legislature by an overruling Constitution was an improvement in the science and practice of government reserved to the American States." [148] The record of the Constitu-

[148] James DeWitt Andrews (ed.), *The Works of James Wilson* (Chicago, 1896), I, 542–43. In this connection, see the illuminating colloquy between Justice Frankfurter and Justice Douglas in *Perez* v. *Brownell*, 356 U.S. 44, 79 (1958), and *Kingsley Corp.* v. *Regents of New York*, 360 U.S. 684, 698 (1959). Of Justice Frankfurter's opin-

tion's framing and ratification clearly reveals an intention to establish *free government*. It was recognized, as Hamilton said in *Federalist* No. 22, that "the fabric of American empire ought to rest on the solid basis of the Consent of the People." But a complex of principles and devices— federalism, separation of powers, bills of rights, judicial review—restrains popular power and limits majority rule. The electorate, through its chosen representatives, can make government conform to its will. But the Constitution sets bounds, enforceable by nine politically non-responsible men. The resulting dilemma was once resolved by recourse to the patent fiction that the Court has no power; it merely applies the Constitution which, in some miraculous way, is always the highest expression of the people's will. In the middle 1930's, when nine men, sometimes only five or six, defeated the power to govern at all levels, very nearly the last vestige of judicial mysticism vanished. Before the astonished eyes of critics and friends, the judicial veil was lifted. Government was allowed to govern.

Control of our economic life, unprecedented in scope,

---

ion for the majority in *Perez*, Justice Douglas wrote: "The philosophy of the opinion that sustains this statute is foreign to our constitutional system. It gives supremacy to the Legislature in a way that is incompatible with the scheme of our written constitution. A decision such as this could be expected in England where there is no written constitution, and where the House of Commons has the final say. But with all deference, this philosophy has no place here. By proclaiming it we forsake much of our constitutional heritage and move closer to the British scheme. That may be better than ours or it may be worse. Certainly it is not ours" (p. 625). In *Kingsley* Justice Douglas repeated his views on the fundamentals of the American scheme of free government: "Reference is made to British law and British practice. [No one except Justice Frankfurter had made any such reference.] But they have little relevance to our problem, since we live under a written Constitution. What is entrusted to the keeping of the legislature in England is protected from legislative interference or regulation here" (p. 698).

made the equitable and unimpeded functioning of the political process more important than ever before. The right to vote, "a fundamental political right," because it is "preservative of all rights," [149] is only the last step in a long development. Informed political action would be impossible if the climate of opinion discouraged free exchange of ideas. Without equal opportunity to utilize the crucial preliminaries—speech, press, assembly, petition—government by consent becomes an empty declamation. By protecting the integrity and unobstructed operation of the process by which majorities are formed, judicial review becomes a surrogate for revolution, contributing positively to government resting on consent.

The contradiction Judge Learned Hand thought he detected in the position of the new activists—tolerance toward experimental legislation in economics,[150] closer judicial scrutiny when First Amendment and other Bill of Rights freedoms are involved—is not that at all. More exacting supervision of the political process follows logically from the Court's greater reliance, after 1937, on political controls in the economic realm. This rationale derives strength not only from the Constitution's framers (not excluding Jefferson) but also from a host of judicial luminaries in our own time.

It is often said that the Supreme Court reflects the social conscience of a nation. In the desegregation decisions and others, including the rulings on reapportionment and right to counsel, the Warren Court has not only interpreted and enforced the social conscience, it has quickened it. In the abstract, it would have been better, perhaps, if encroachment on individual freedom, such as

[149] *Yick Wo* v. *Hopkins*, 118 U.S. 356, 370 (1886). Quoted by Justice Douglas in *Harper* v. *Virginia State Board of Elections*, 383 U.S. 663 (1966).

[150] Learned Hand, "Chief Justice Stone's Conception of the Judicial Function," *Columbia Law Review*, XLVI (1946), 698.

Connecticut's anti-contraceptive statute, Virginia's poll tax, and the police-state methods used in law enforcement, could have been remedied by the state legislature. But this was not done; the prospects were dim. As in school desegregation, reapportionment, and administration of criminal justice, failure of the states to protect individual liberties or undertake corrective measures drove the Court, in the face of delimiting precedents, into untrod fields. The justices faced an untoward condition, not a theory. Judge Cardozo, noting that *stare decisis* is not in the Constitution, expressed willingness "to put it there, . . . if only it were true that legislation is a sufficient agency of growth." [151]

American constitutionalism's continuing theme remains unchanged—that the individual and his freedom are basic. Altered is the content of these values. Formerly the Court assumed special guardianship of property and contract rights. Now the judiciary seems content to leave these to the mercy of political controls. Accorded more exacting scrutiny today are speech, press, and religion, the right to vote, the rights of the criminally accused, the rights of discrete and insular racial, religious, and national minorities, helpless in the face of a majority (or a minority) bent on curbing their freedom. Just as the Court formerly claimed pre-eminence as protector of tangible rights, so today it asserts special responsibility toward moral and spiritual values that lie at the base of our culture. Judicial concern for human values was not previously forthcoming. Reflecting on the constitutional jurisprudence of the 1920's, Professor Frankfurter explained: "That a majority of the Court which frequently disallowed restraints on economic power should so consistently have sanctioned restraints of the mind is perhaps only a surface paradox. There is an underlying unity between

[151] B. N. Cardozo, *Growth of the Law*, 132–33.

fear of ample experimentation in economics and fear of expression of heretical ideas." [152] Not least among the distinctive accomplishments of the Warren Court is its alertness to a subtlety to which Justice Frankfurter, ignoring the commanding lessons of his mentors Holmes and Brandeis, seemed insensitive. Our fourteenth Chief Justice has made "vocal and audible ideals that might otherwise be silenced."

For correction of "great mistakes in the ruling part," John Locke observed, "the appeal lies nowhere but to Heaven"—apparently a euphemism for force, revolution. In providing a mediator between state and nation and between legislature and people, judicial review furnishes a practical alternative to revolution. Without the advantage of hindsight, the framers understood that "those who make peaceful revolution impossible will make violent revolution inevitable." [153] In their *Federalist* essays, Hamilton and Madison freely endorsed the *moral* right of revolution but, dreading the unsettling consequences[154]

[152] Frankfurter, *Holmes and the Supreme Court*, 62.

[153] Attributed to John F. Kennedy, in Theodore Sorensen, *Kennedy* (New York, 1965), 535. See also W. S. Carpenter, *The Development of American Political Thought* (Princeton, 1930), 166–67: "The framers of the United States Constitution vastly improved upon the theory of Locke by regarding their instrument as a fundamental law in subordination to which the law-making body must act. Thus they were able to mark out as constitutional limitations the natural rights which Locke had been unable to define. Furthermore, through the power of judicial control they set up an intermediate defense between the legislature and the reserve power of revolution in the hands of the people." For this reference I am indebted to my friend Dr. Harris Mirkin.

[154] Adams, Hamilton, Madison, Washington, all revolutionaries, distrusted the feelings revolution unleashed. Hamilton put it this way: "In times of such commotion as the present, while the passions of man are worked up to an uncommon pitch, there is great danger of fatal extremes. The same state of the passion which fits the multitude, who have not a sufficient stock of reason and knowledge to guide them, for opposition to tyranny and oppression, very naturally leads

of the very forces 1776 unleashed, they were at great pains to demonstrate that the proposed Constitution reduced the occasions for revolution to a minimum. Jefferson, in later years the Court's bitter critic, advocated binding up "the several branches of government by certain laws, which, when they transgress, their acts become nullities," suggesting that this would "render unnecessary an appeal to the people, or in other words a rebellion, on every infraction of their rights. . . ." [155]

Thanks to judicial review, "revolution" has been domesticated, brought within the four corners of the Constitution. Hamilton spelled it out in *The Federalist*:

> Though I trust the friends of the proposed constitution will never concur with its enemies, in questioning that fundamental principle of republican government, which admits the right of the people to alter or abolish, the established constitution whenever they find it inconsistent with their happiness; yet it is not to be inferred from this principle that the representatives of the people, whenever a momentary inclination happens to lay hold of a majority of their constituents incompatible with the provisions of the existing Constitution, would, on that account, be justifiable in a violation of those principles, or that the courts would be under greater obligation to connive at infractions in this shape, than when they had proceeded wholly from the cabals of the representative body. Until the people have, by some solemn and authoritative act, annulled or changed the established form, it is binding upon themselves collectively, as well as individually; and no presumption, or even knowledge of their sentiments, can warrant

---

them to a contempt and disregard of all authority. The due medium is hardly to be found among the more intelligent; it is almost impossible among the unthinking populace. When the minds of these are loosened from their attachment to ancient establishments and courses, they seem to grow giddy and are apt more or less to run into anarchy." To John Jay, Nov. 26, 1775. Harold Syrett (ed.), *The Papers of Alexander Hamilton* (New York, 1961), I, 176.

[155] "Notes on Virginia" in H. A. Washington (ed.), *The Writings of Thomas Jefferson* (Washington, D.C., 1853–55), VIII, 371–72.

their representatives in a departure from it, prior to such an act.[156]

Brought into juxtaposition are three essential buttresses of freedom: Right of Revolution, Bill of Rights, Judicial Review. Oppression of individuals and minorities may encourage resort to the moral right of revolution, a right no American can gracefully query; an independent judiciary, by courageously interposing its judgment against majorities bent on infractions of the Constitution, advances the cause of peaceful change.

Professor Louis Lusky of the Columbia Law School, who as Justice Stone's law clerk helped to write the Carolene Products footnote, stresses the close connection between the discharge of judicial duty and the right of revolution. The second and third paragraphs of the footnote are "frank recognition" of the important part the Court performs "in the maintenance of the basic conditions of just legislation. By preserving the hope that bad laws can and will be changed, the Court preserves the basis for the technique of political obligation, minimizing extra-legal opposition to government by making it unnecessary." [157]

[156] No. 78, p. 400.

[157] Louis Lusky, "Minority Rights and the Public Interest," *Yale Law Journal*, LII (1942), 20–21. Professor Lusky's point is amply supported by the record. In the Virginia ratifying convention, John Marshall, later Chief Justice, asked: "What is the service or purpose of a Judiciary, but to execute the laws in a peaceable, orderly manner, without shedding blood, or creating a contest, or availing yourselves of force? . . . To what quarter will you look for protection from an infringement on the Constitution, if you will not give the power to the Judiciary? There is no other body that can afford such a protection." J. Elliot (ed.), *The Debates at the Several State Conventions* (Washington, D.C., 1836), III, 503. Gouverneur Morris, in 1802, considered the Courts infinitely valuable to domestic tranquility, peace, and to individual protection against governmental oppression. "The framers of this Constitution had seen much, read much, and deeply reflected. They knew by experience the violence of popular bodies, and let it be remembered, that since that day

In America "vibrations of power" (the "genius" of our system for Hamilton)[158] are institutionalized. The pendulum may swing freely, reflecting alternating moods and responses about man and society. The availability of peaceful remedies for the correction of abuses renders it unnecessary to lop off political heads with the sword of revolution.

VI

Elevated considerations such as these, deeply rooted in our heritage, apparently inspire the Warren Court's activism. Yet Justice Harlan, and perhaps Justice Black, seem convinced that the majority is headed toward the same precipice from which the Hughes Court, under pressure from Congress, the President, and the country, narrowly saved itself in 1937. But, surely, the interests and values concerned, and the Court's responsibility toward them, differ significantly. In 1935–36, a narrow, headstrong majority, flouting persistent pleas for judicial self-restraint voiced by a highly esteemed minority, blocked regulation of the economy; in the hands of an obtuse majority, the Constitution became a strait jacket, not a vehicle of life. Confessing the error of their way, the same justices, almost overnight, breached the Maginot line they had themselves built. The Warren Court, on the other hand, in expanding the limits of freedom, in buttressing the moral foundations of society, in keeping open con-

---

many of the States, taught by experience, have found it necessary to change their forms of government to avoid the effects of that violence. . . . I beg gentlemen to hear and remember what I say: It is this department [the Judiciary] alone, and it is the independence of this department, which can save you from civil war." In U.S. Senate, Jan. 14, 1802, quoted in Farrand (ed.), *The Records of the Federal Convention of 1787*, III, 391–93.

[158] To Rufus King, June 3, 1802, in Henry Cabot Lodge (ed.), *The Works of Alexander Hamilton* (New York, 1904), X, 439.

stitutional alternatives to violent change, brings us closer to the ideals we have long professed.

In Supreme Court opinions, as nowhere else, it is recognized that, though freedom may be a dangerous way of life, it is ours.[159] The Constitution articulates the faith Jefferson voiced in the Declaration of Independence: government can rest securely on reason and consent, rather than on coercion and force. Governments, Jefferson wrote, "derive their just powers from the consent of the governed." The judicial mandate, "one man, one vote"—a judicial venture even bolder than racial desegregation—echoes these sentiments. In making government more responsive to the people, the Warren Court has become a creative force unequalled since the long regime of Chief Justice Marshall.

Jefferson's dubious wager of 1801, challenged as never before, is still to be fully tested. Yet certain Supreme Court Justices continue to proclaim it: "If there be any among us who would wish to dissolve this Union or to change its republican form, let them stand undisturbed as monuments of the safety with which error of opinion may be tolerated where reason is left free to combat it." [160] Presented is a remarkable irony—the Supreme Court, in structure and organization the most oligarchal branch of our government, in the vanguard of democracy.

The story, of course, does not end on this note, happy or otherwise, depending on one's point of view. In certain of the most crucial civil liberties cases, the Justices have

[159] A most eloquent example is from the late Justice Jackson: "If there is any fixed star in our constitutional constellation, it is that no official, high or petty, can prescribe what shall be orthodox in politics, nationalism, religion, or other matters of opinion or force citizens to confess by word or act their faith therein. If there are any circumstances which permit an exception, they do not occur to us." *West Virginia State Board of Education* v. *Barnette*, 638, 642.

[160] In J. D. Richardson (ed.), *A Compilation of the Messages and Papers of the Presidents, 1789–1908* (Washington, D.C., 1909), I, 322.

split five to four or six to three. Still facing the Court are issues of the greatest complexity. A living organism, its values, attitudes, and personnel change. Though the Warren Court, on the whole, seems to have achieved the golden mean Chief Justice Marshall thought he had attained, history affords no justification for believing that it will not yet go too far. Justice Harlan, among others, believes that the majority has already exceeded its authority.[161] If so, one may find comfort in the knowledge that our system provides various corrective devices for judicial usurpation. The dramatic repudiation of its own ill-founded precedents, on the heels of Franklin Roosevelt's Court-packing threat, contradicts Justice Stone's strangely unrealistic dictum that "the only check upon our own exercise of power is our own sense of self-restraint." [162] Dissenters and malcontents, now as always, alert us to Free Government's most distinctive aspect—dialogue, conflict, opposition. No opposition means no democracy, no freedom. The Supreme Court is our final arbiter only in a particular case. Its decision must remain, as Lincoln said, in a never-ending dialogue.[163] We are not dedicated to absolute rule from Mount Sinai; we are dedicated to self-government, rule by the people.

[161] Protesting the new rules imposed on police officers, Justice Harlan observed: "The foray which the Court takes today brings to mind the wise and foresighted words of Mr. Justice Jackson in *Douglas* v. *Jeannette,* 319 U.S. 157 . . . : 'This Court is forever adding new stories to the temples of constitutional law, and the temples have a way of collapsing when one story too many is added.' " *Miranda* v. *Arizona,* 753.

[162] Justice Stone's observation (dissenting in *United States* v. *Butler,* 79) is almost a match for one of the most fantastic descriptions of constitutional interpretation in the annals of the judiciary —Justice Roberts' portrayal of it as a squaring operation, laying the article of the Constitution which is invoked beside the statute which is challenged.

[163] Abraham Lincoln, Speech in Springfield, Illinois, June 26, 1857, in my *Free Government in the Making* (3rd ed.; New York, 1965), 533–37.

CHAPTER 8

Whence and Whither the Burger Court?

T HE SUPREME COURT has always consisted largely of
politicians, appointed by politicians and confirmed
by politicians, in furtherance of controversial political objectives. From John Marshall to Warren Burger, the
Court has been the guardian of some particular interest
and the promoter of preferred values. "Judicial self-
restraint," the exception rather than the rule, is often a
thin disguise for judicial advocacy. On the ninety-fifth anniversary of Justice Frankfurter's birth, Philip Elman, the
Justice's law clerk when the first flag salute case was decided, commented: "For a guy who preached judicial dis-
interestedness, his violation of that principle was the most
extreme on the Court."[1]

The present court, headed by Chief Justice Burger,
joined by two Nixon appointees, presumably "strict constructionists," decided the most emotionally explosive issue
in modern times. Dissenting in the abortion case of 1973,
Justice Rehnquist charged that the decision outlawing numerous anti-abortion statutes "partakes more of judicial
legislation than it does of a determination of the interest of
the drafters of the Fourteenth Amendment."[2]

Strictures against judicial activism come with poor grace

---

[1] *New York Times,* October 23, 1977, p. 34, col. 5.
[2] *Roe* v. *Wade,* 410 U.S. 113 (1973), 174.

from Justice Rehnquist. In 1976 he voted to strike down Fair Labor Standards Act amendments extending the minimum and maximum hour provisions to state employees, substituting judicial control for "political restraints."[3] For the first time in nearly forty years, the Supreme Court blocked congressional power to regulate commerce, disregarding a principle dating from Chief Justice Marshall, and re-established in 1937, that the primary control is political.[4] Justice Brennan, joined by Marshall and White, was aghast: "The reliance of my Brethren upon the Tenth Amendment as 'an express declaration of [a state sovereignty] limitation' . . . not only suggests that they overrule governing decisions of this Court . . . but must astound scholars of the Constitution."[5] These were not idle speculations. In 1941, Justice Jackson called the Supreme Court "almost a continuous constitutional convention."[6]

The decade since the appearance of a revised edition of this book in 1968 witnessed some of the most dramatic events in the Court's history, all exhibiting political overtones. A Chief Justice resigned, a rare event; the Senate refused to confirm the President's nomination of his successor, also unusual. For the first time a Supreme Court Justice quit under political pressure involving the issues of ethics and propriety. In rapid succession two Supreme Court

---

[3] In 1824, Marshall declared: "The wisdom and the discretion of Congress, their identity with the people, and the influence which their constituents possess at election, are . . . the sole restraints on which they have relied, to secure them from its abuse. They are the restraints on which the people must often rely solely, in all representative governments." *Gibbons* v. *Ogden,* 9 Wheaton 1 (1821), 197. Marshall's approach was confirmed by Chief Justice Taft in *Stafford* v. *Wallace,* 258 U.S. 495 (1922), 521, and by Justice Stone in *U.S.* v. *Darby Lumber Co.,* 312 U.S. 100 (1941), 114–15.

[4] *National League of Cities* v. *Usery,* 426 U.S. 833 (1976), 861–62.
[5] *Ibid.*
[6] Robert H. Jackson, *The Struggle for Judicial Supremacy: A Study of a Crisis in American Power Politics* (New York, 1941), x.

nominees failed to receive Senate endorsement. Only one other such nomination had failed confirmation in this century—President Hoover's selection of Fourth Circuit Judge John J. Parker in 1930. Impeachment proceedings were initiated against a Supreme Court Justice, the first since the abortive effort in 1805 to impeach Justice Samuel Chase. As a result of President Nixon's unsuccessful attempt to fulfill his campaign promise to "balance" the judiciary with "strict constructionists," the Court functioned during its 1969–70 term without a full bench, for the first time since the Civil War. These six remarkable episodes illustrate partisan effort to shape and direct the Court toward preferred goals.

I

On June 26, 1968, President Lyndon Johnson announced Chief Justice Earl Warren's intention to resign. The next day the President nominated Associate Justice Abe Fortas to succeed the controversial Chief Justice. With the exception of President Washington's recess appointee, John Rutledge, whom the Senate refused to confirm in 1795, only two Associate Justices had been advanced to the center chair—Edward Douglass White in 1910 and Harlan Fiske Stone in 1941. Accusing President Johnson of "cronyism," opposition formed immediately.

Fortas was charged with various improprieties, including participation in White House strategy conferences on the Vietnam War and acceptance of high lecture fees raised by wealthy business executives who happened to be clients of Fortas' former law partner, Paul Porter. After four days, the Senate voted 45 to 43 to cut off debate, 14 votes short of the two thirds necessary to end the anti-Fortas filibuster. Two days later the ill-fated Justice withdrew his name. For the first time, nomination of a Supreme Court Justice had been blocked by a Senate filibuster.

It was a Pyrrhic victory. Critics of the Warren Court had to reconcile themselves to the continued presence of Chief Justice Warren. "If they don't confirm Abe," the Chief Justice commented cheerfully, while Fortas' fate hung in the balance, "they will have me."[7] So they did for one more year.

When the Senate blocked Fortas' nomination, President Johnson refused to submit another name. L.B.J., a lame duck President, left this high level appointment to President Richard M. Nixon. Finding himself in precisely the same situation in 1801, President John Adams, much to Thomas Jefferson's chagrin, followed an altogether different course. A few weeks before he left the White House, Adams named Secretary of State John Marshall Chief Justice of the United States. If Adams had taken President Johnson's route, Chief Justice Ellsworth's successor probably would have been the ardent defender of states' rights, Spencer Roane. In that event, history during the nation's crucial formative years might have been drastically altered, perhaps for the worse.

Appointment of a Chief Justice is a rare occurrence. There have been thirty-eight Presidents, only fifteen Chief Justices. John Marshall sat in the Court's center chair thirty-four years, from 1801 to 1835. During that time there were six presidents. The contrast is significant substantively as well as statistically, a fact that prompted John Quincy Adams to rate the office of Chief Justice as "more important than that of President." William Howard Taft preferred the Chief Justiceship over the Presidency because it conferred "power without worry." The most impressive recent illustration of the comparatively greater impact of the Chief Justiceship is the regime of Earl Warren (1953–69). His Court initiated a revolution.

[7] Mason, "Pyrrhic Victory: The Defeat of Abe Fortas," *Virginia Quarterly Review*, XLV (Winter, 1969), 19–28.

President Nixon's first step toward fulfilling his 1968 campaign promise to strengthen the "peace forces as against the criminal forces of the country" and thus block the Warren Court's judicial activism, was to select as Chief Justice Warren Earl Burger, sixty-one, Chief Judge, U.S. Circuit Court of Appeals, District of Columbia. Burger's confirmation, June 9, 1969, by a vote of 74 to 3, was hasty—almost pro forma. Earl Warren waited five months for the Senate vote, Burger only eighteen days.

II

In the spring of 1969, *Life* magazine revealed that Justice Fortas had received a yearly twenty thousand dollar fee from the family foundation of Louis Wolfson, then serving a prison term for selling unregistered stock. Fortas' resignation, May 16, 1969, opened the way for President Nixon's nomination of Clement F. Haynesworth, Jr., Chief Judge, U.S. Circuit Court of Appeals. Critics charged that Haynesworth had taken a restrictive view of school desegregation and exhibited insensitivity toward proprieties involving finance and conflict of interests. After weeks of heated debate the Senate, voting 55 to 45, refused to confirm the President's nominee.

The Senate's rejection of Haynesworth stiffened President Nixon's determination to "pack" the Court with "strict constructionists." His next nominee, G. Harrold Carswell, had served seven years as a Federal District Court judge in Tallahassee, and six months on the U.S. Court of Appeals, Fifth Circuit. In 1948, he had said: "I yield to no man as a fellow candidate [he was then running for political office] or as a fellow citizen in the firm, vigorous belief in the principles of White Supremacy, and I shall always be so governed."

Apart from Judge Carswell's avowed racism (which he now disavowed), critics charged that President Nixon's nominee was in fact mediocre. Accepting the criticism, Nebraska Senator Hruska tried to convert it into an asset: "Even if he is mediocre, there are a lot of mediocre judges and people and lawyers. They are entitled to a little representation, aren't they, and a little chance? We can't have all Brandeises, Cardozos and Frankfurters and stuff like that there." Judge Carswell was rejected 51 to 45. Even prominent members of the President's own party voted against him.

The Senate's rejection, in rapid succession, of two Supreme Court nominees evoked Nixon's angry reaction:

With the Senate as presently constituted—I cannot successfully nominate to the Supreme Court any federal appellate judge from the South who believes as I do in the strict construction of the Constitution. Judges Carswell and Haynesworth have endured with admirable dignity vicious assaults on their intelligence, their honesty and their character.

When all the hypocrisy is stripped away, the real issue was their philosophy of strict construction of the Constitution—a philosophy that I share.

To fill the place vacated by Justice Fortas, President Nixon turned to Chief Justice Burger's longtime Minnesota friend, Harry A. Blackmun, Judge, Eighth Circuit, U.S. Court of Appeals, 1959–70. Blackmun was promptly confirmed and sworn in, June 22, 1970, too late to participate in any of the term's decisions.

III

Defenders of Judges Haynesworth and Carswell, piqued by defeat, launched a counteroffensive, calling for the impeachment of libertarian Justice William O. Douglas. When Congressman Gerald Ford, spearhead of the drive, was asked to define "impeachable offense," he replied: "The only honest answer is that an impeachable offense is whatever a majority of the House of Representatives con-

siders it to be at a given moment in history; conviction results from whatever offense or offenses two-thirds of the
other body considers to be sufficiently serious to require
removal of the accused from office." Ford's bluntly realistic
definition was not unprecedented. When, with President
Jefferson's support, impeachment proceedings were insti-
gated against Justice Samuel Chase, Senator Giles explained: "Removal by impeachment was nothing more
than a declaration of Congress to this effect: You hold dangerous opinions, and if you are suffered to carry them into
effect you will work the destruction of the nation. *We want
your offices,* for the purpose of giving them to men who
will fill them better."[8]

Applied to Justice Douglas, this open-ended approach
failed.

IV

The 1969–70 term, with a new Chief Justice and without
a full complement of Justices, ended indecisively. However,
statistics indicated that civil rights and liberties would not
be accorded the priorities enjoyed under Warren. During
Chief Justice Warren's last term (1968–69), the Court
heard and decided twenty-six appeals listed by *United
States Law Week* under "criminal law and procedure." The
prosecution won only eight. During the 1969–70 term, the
first headed by Chief Justice Burger, there were twenty-nine
"criminal law and procedure" appeals. The prosecution
won eighteen.

The 1970–71 term, with a second Nixon appointee, Harry A. Blackmun, in former Justice Fortas' seat, was hardly
launched before the Court dramatically illustrated that in
constitutional law, as in all else, everything turns on men.

[8] Charles Warren, *The Supreme Court in United States History*
(3 vols.; Boston, 1922), I, 294.

A telltale case, decided on December 15, 1970,[9] involving the use of certain kinds of hearsay evidence in criminal trials, indicated a shift in the judicial winds. The Sixth Amendment, ruling out such evidence, gives defendants in criminal cases the right to confront witnesses against them. But, like several other provisions of the Bill of Rights, this guarantee was not applicable in state cases until the judicial mandate of 1965.[10] In the face of this five-year-old precedent and contrary to the decision of the Court of Appeals, Fifth Circuit, the Burger Court ruled that hearsay evidence is admissible.

Other setbacks were just around the corner. In the *Miranda* case of 1966, Chief Justice Warren had formulated new rules of criminal procedure for state courts, replacing what dissenting Justice Harlan called "perfectly legitimate methods of criminal law enforcement."[11] In *Miranda*, Harlan had commented hopefully: "This Court is forever adding new stories to the temples of constitutional law, and the temples have a way of collapsing when one story too many is added."[12] Justice Harlan's prediction of the judicially constructed temple's collapse was partially fulfilled when, on February 24, 1971, by a vote of 5 to 4, the Court ruled that illegally obtained statements, unusable as evidence against a defendant, can be used to attack his credibility. Conflicting statements a defendant gives to police

[9] *Dutton* v. *Evans,* 400 U.S. 74 (1970).

[10] *Pointer* v. *Texas,* 380 U.S. 400 (1965).

[11] *Miranda* v. *Arizona,* 384 U.S. 436 (1966). Not content with operating within the narrow confines that might have been used in deciding the case, the Chief Justice promulgated a new charter of rights for criminal suspects. They were to be advised of their right to be silent, that any statement made might be used against them, and that they had the right to consult a lawyer, who would be provided for them if they could not afford one.

[12] *Ibid.,* 753, quoting Justice Jackson in *Douglas* v. *Jeannette,* 319 U.S. 157, 181 (1942).

officers—despite their failure to inform the defendant of his constitutional rights—were now judged admissible.[13] For dissenters, the *Miranda* temple had been shattered.

The highlight of the 1970–71 term occurred on June 30, 1971, when the Supreme Court voted 6 to 3 to uphold the New York *Times* and the Washington *Post* against the federal government's effort to halt publication of articles and documents based on the McNamara-inspired Pentagon study of the Vietnam War.[14] The Pentagon Papers case tested the Constitution's ideological foundations. Could a political system based on reason and consent endure? On an issue so crucial, unanimity such as had been achieved in the path-breaking *Brown* decision of 1954 was eminently desirable. At that time an initially divided Court ultimately became of one mind. Not so in the Pentagon Papers case. Chief Justice Burger, joined by Justices Blackmun and Harlan, dissented. As if to blunt possible adverse reaction, the Chief Justice declared. "So clear are the constitutional limitations on prior restraint that from the time of *Near* v. *Minnesota,* we have had little occasion to be concerned with cases involving prior restraint against news reporters on matters of public interest."[15] Although the vote was 6 to 3, the Chief Justice told an interviewer that on the substantive issue the Justices were "actually unanimous."[16]

V

In the fall of 1970, the New York *Times* reported that President Nixon was still determined to appoint a Southerner to the Supreme Court. The most likely spot to be

[13] *Harris* v. *New York,* 401 U.S. 22 (1971).
[14] *New York Times* v. *United States,* 403 U.S. 713 (1971).
[15] *Ibid.,* 844.
[16] *New York Times,* July 6, 1971, p. 15, col. 2.

vacated was that occupied by eighty-four-year-old Justice
Black. Asked for his reaction to the President's unswerving
determination, Justice Black replied: "I think it would be
nice to have *another* Southerner up here."

In June, 1971, Justice Black selected his law clerks for
the 1971–72 term, indicating that he intended to carry on.
The Justice had moved into third place in length of service,
but though the longevity goal was in sight, fate defeated its
realization. In September, 1971, Justices Black and Harlan,
both ailing, resigned within days of each other. Hugo Black
died on September 25, 1971. If Black could have remained
on the bench eight months longer, he would have exceeded
John Marshall's and Stephen J. Field's record, having
served thirty-four years, six months, and thirteen days.

In October, 1971, Richard Nixon enjoyed an opportunity no President had experienced since 1940—that of si-
multaneously filling two Supreme Court vacancies. The
President (or his Attorney-General) sent the names of six
candidates to the American Bar Association's twelve-man
screening committee. The list was singularly undistin-
guished, prompting the Washington *Post* to cite it as proof
of Mr. Nixon's "relentless pursuit of mediocrity" for the
high bench.

Abandoning his alleged quest for mediocrity, the President then nominated Lewis F. Powell, Jr., sixty-four, a
distinguished Richmond lawyer, and William H. Rehnquist, forty-seven, law clerk, 1952–53, to the late Justice
Robert H. Jackson, and the Nixon administration's Assis-
tant Attorney-General in charge of the Office of Legal
Counsel. Powell, arousing little or no objections, was confirmed, 89 to 1, emphatically disproving Nixon's widely
publicized lament of 1969 that the Senate, as then constituted, would not confirm a Southerner. Rehnquist ran into
stormy waters. Among other things, critics charged that he
had supported curtailment of defendants' rights in criminal

cases, use of electronic surveillance, preventive detention, and "no knock" police entry. He had proclaimed the President's practically unlimited war power and sanctioned mass arrest of demonstrators. Confronted with these barbed attacks, Rehnquist told the Judiciary Committee: "My fundamental commitment, if I am confirmed, will be to totally disregard my own personal belief." Rehnquist received Senate approval on December 10, 1971, 68 to 26. With the confirmation of Powell and Rehnquist, the Court had a full complement of Justices—four of them Nixon appointees.

The Court's personnel remained unchanged until November, 1975, when President Ford nominated John Paul Stevens, a fifty-five-year-old Federal Appeals Court judge, seventh district, to fill the vacancy created by the retirement of William O. Douglas. The previous New Year's Eve Douglas had suffered a stroke. He had served thirty-six years on the high bench, surpassing the record long held by John Marshall and Stephen J. Field.

Justice Douglas' reluctance to retire raised again the thorny question of how to remove an incapacitated Supreme Court Justice. The Constitution supplies no answer, but history does. On more than one occasion, the power of persuasion exerted on a faltering Justice by the Court itself has proved effective.

In 1869, Associate Justice Field convinced Justice Grier that he was too ill to continue. Later, when Field himself became incapacitated, Justice Harlan asked his colleague whether he remembered urging Grier to retire. "Yes," Field snapped, "and a dirtier day's work I never did in my life."[17] After Justice McKenna's all too obvious demonstration of mental slowdown, Chief Justice Taft reluctantly persuaded him to retire. Justice Holmes, older than Mc-

[17] Charles Evans Hughes, *The Supreme Court of the United States* (New York, 1928), 75–76.

Kenna, then a bystander, was sure he would be "intellec-
tually honest in judging my condition and my product."[18]
But the ninety-one-year-old Justice gave up only after Chief
Justice Hughes requested him to do so. Ignoring or eluding
pressure from whatever source, Justice Douglas reached his
own decision, on November 12, 1975, to leave the Court,
almost a year after he was stricken.

Douglas' successor, though relatively unknown, seemed
eminently qualified. He had established a brilliant academic record. After graduating first in his class at the
Northwestern University Law School, he served two years
as Supreme Court Justice Rutledge's law clerk. The customary labels did not seem to fit. "He's a first-rate lawyer,
a first-rate judge, and a first-rate man. What more can you
ask?" constitutional law professor Philip Kurland commented. The Senate quickly concurred; on December 19,
1975, Stevens was sworn in.

VI

In reconciling the age-old conflict between liberty and restraint, values sometimes antagonistic, sometimes complementary, the Warren Court's tendency was to strike the
balance in favor of liberty. In light of President Nixon's
commitment to "law and order," at times a euphemism for
lawlessness and repression, Court watchers, generally, assumed his appointees would halt, if not reverse the trend.
As a circuit court judge, Burger had commented: "The nature of our system, which seems to have escaped notice occasionally, must make manifest to judges that we are neither
gods nor godlike, but judicial officers with narrow and
limited authority. Our entire system of government would
suffer incalculable mischief should judges attempt to op-

[18] M. D. Howe (ed.), *Holmes-Laski Letters* (2 vols.; New York,
1963), I, 336.

pose the judicial will above that of the Congress and the President, even were we so bold as to assume we can make better decisions on such issues."[19]

Yet Chief Justice Burger's early pronouncements and decisions did not support the belief that the Warren Court's jurisprudence was in serious jeopardy. On May 19, 1970, Burger told the prestigious American Law Institute:

> There are some voices saying that we should "crack down," that we should "smash" the challengers and restore tight discipline. In periods of stress there . . . are always some voices raised urging that we suspend fundamental guarantees, take short cuts, and do other things as a matter of self-preservation and protection. But this is not our way of doing things in this country, short of a genuine national emergency. . . . In those few periods of our history where we suspended basic guarantees of the individual in times of great national stress, we often found in retrospect that we over-reacted.

The Chief Justice conceded that "it would be foolhardy not to be concerned about the turmoil and strife and violence that is going on," but he warned: "We must never and will never give way to panic. . . . I am optimistic. I believe our institutions are durable. They are capable of surmounting any attack."[20]

VII

The three major pillars in the Warren Court's constitutional edifice—race relations, reapportionment, and rules of criminal procedure—though somewhat eroded, have not been erased. Within a few weeks after taking the Court's center chair, Chief Justice Burger announced, in the face of Attorney-General Mitchell's foot-dragging, that "continued

[19] Quoted in Alpheus T. Mason and William M. Beaney, *American Constitutional Law* (5th ed.; Englewood Cliffs, N.J., 1972), xi.
[20] *Proceedings, American Law Institute*, 47th Annual Meeting (Washington, D.C., 1970), 26–27.

operation of segregated schools under a standard of allowing deliberate speed for desegregation is no longer permissible."[21] A break in the solid judicial dike erected in 1954
against the "separate but equal" formula occurred in 1972
when four Nixon appointees, voting as a bloc and speaking
through the Chief Justice, declared that the goal was to dis-
mantle the dual system. "Judicial power ends when a dual
system has ceased to exist."[22]

Certain decisions, such as the Detroit school desegregation case, though deplored by dissenters as a "giant step
backward," underscore continuing complexities.[23] In a case
involving the touchy reverse discrimination issue, Justice
Brennan, expressing the view of seven members, held that
the only way to "make whole" the victims of illegal job
discrimination was to let them skip past fellow workers on
the seniority ladder to the level they would have attained
had they never been subject to discrimination.[24] Chief
Justice Burger, concurring in part, likened the majority
opinion to "robbing Peter to pay Paul." Instead of automatically retroactive seniority, it would be "more equitable" for courts to compel a discriminatory employer to
remunerate those persons victimized.

Washington v. *Davis*[25] upheld a verbal test for police
force applicants even though it excluded a disproportion-
ate number of blacks. The Justices were unanimous on
June 25, 1976, when the Court, speaking through Justice
Marshall, held that the Civil Rights Act of 1866, according
"all persons" the same contractual rights as are enjoyed by
white citizens, prohibits racial discrimination in private

[21] *Alexander* v. *Holmes County Board of Education,* 396 U.S. 19
(1969); *Swann* v. *Charlotte-Mecklenburg Board of Education,* 402
U.S. 1 (1971).
[22] *Wright* v. *Emporia,* 407 U.S. 451 (1972), dissenting at p. 479.
[23] *Milliken* v. *Bradley,* 418 U.S. 717 (1974), 782.
[24] *Franks* v. *Bowman Transportation Co.,* 427 U.S. 273 (1976), 281.
[25] 426 U.S. 229 (1976).

employment against whites as well as nonwhites.[26] Stricken down in 1977 was an ordinance banning "for sale" signs in front of houses, even though the aim was to prevent the flight of homeowners for racial reasons.[27] Significantly, the Court was unanimous, Justice Marshall being its spokesman.

Having been remanded to the district court, *Milliken,* the Detroit school desegregation case, was again before the Justices, June 27, 1977, evoking significant implications for affirmative action programs. By unanimous vote the Court held that remedial action—reading, in-service training, testing, and counseling—compensating for past acts of *de jure* segregation, could be borne by the District School Board and the state.[28] *Regents of California* v. *Bakke,* destined to become the most important race-relations case since Brown, squarely presented the affirmative action issue.

In a class of one hundred, the University of California Medical School at Davis set aside sixteen places for "economically and educationally disadvantaged minority applicants" and rejected white applicant Allan Bakke who ranked higher under the school's multiple admissions standards, including undergraduate grades, Medical College Admissions Test, community involvement, character, and other factors measured by recommendations and personal interview. Bakke filed suit and the California Supreme Court ordered admission. The U.S. Supreme Court granted certiorari. Argued October, 1977, this historic decision came down on June 28, 1978 (57 L Ed 750).

Computer analysis had led Dr. Harold Spaeth to predict that the nine Justices would decide unanimously in favor of Bakke. The Court did so by vote of 5 to 4, in the nar-

[26] *McDonald* v. *Santa Fe Trail Transportation Co.,* 424 U.S. 952 (1976).
[27] *Lindmark Associates Inc.* v. *Willingboro,* 431 U.S. 85 (1977).
[28] *Milliken* v. *Bradley,* 433 U.S. 267 (1977).

rowest possible lineup, 4–1–4. Four Justices (Burger, Stevens, Stewart, and Rehnquist) upheld Bakke under the Civil Rights Act of 1964 which forbids discrimination on grounds of race. Four others (Brennan, Marshall, White, and Blackmun), invoking both the 1964 act and the Fourteenth Amendment's equal protection clause, ruled that affirmative action, including the Davis arrangement, is constitutionally permissible. Justice Powell, though agreeing that the Constitution does not invalidate all affirmative action programs, held that Bakke's constitutional rights had been violated. Powell thus contributed the ninth vote, tipping the balance in favor of Bakke's admission.

Both sides won; both lost. Bakke was admitted and the medical school's quota system was disallowed. The Justices thus escaped bombshells from all sides, except from critics who complained about "loss of candor" and "lack of judicial leadership." Perhaps recalling the tragic consequences of *Dred Scott,* the Court left wide latitude to nonjudicial forums for determining the future of affirmative action. Said dissenting Justice Blackmun: "The administration and management of educational institutions are beyond the competence of judges and are within the special competence of educators, provided always that the educator performs within legal and constitutional bounds." Justice Powell, casting the deciding vote, bore down on this point: "The concepts of 'majority' and 'minority' necessarily reflect temporary arrangements and political judgments. . . . The white 'majority' itself is composed of various minority groups, most of which can lay claim to a history of prior discrimination at the hands of the state and private individuals. . . . There is no principled basis for deciding which group would merit 'heightened judicial solicitude' and which would not. . . . The kind of variable sociological and political analysis necessary to produce such rankings simply does not lie within judicial competence."

Citing Harvard's admission plan as "an illuminating example," Justice Powell ruled that universities could consider race a factor in flexible admissions programs. At the same time, he warned against broadly gauged objectives designed to remedy societal discrimination. "Hence, the purpose of helping certain groups whom the faculty of the Davis Medical School perceived as victims of 'societal discrimination' does not justify a classification that imposes disadvantages upon persons like respondent (Bakke), who bear no responsibility for whatever harm the beneficiaries of the special admissions program are thought to have suffered." Recalled is Edmund Burke's provocative caveat: "Believe me, Sir, those who attempt to level, never equalize."

The Bakke case shattered the so-called Nixon bloc of Justices. During the Burger Court's early years, the four Nixon appointees voted together 70 percent of the time. In 1977–78 their solidarity dropped to 36 percent. On May 31, 1978, one month before Bakke came down, the four Nixon Justices voted as a unit, as we shall see, in the most controversial decision of the 1977–78 term—the Stanford *Daily* case. The reaction was explosive. Editorially, the New York *Times* denounced it as "a double blow," jeopardizing both privacy and freedom of the press. Herblock drew one of his most devastatingly critical cartoons, featuring the vicious likeness of Richard Nixon hovering over the heads of the Justices he appointed.

Bakke puts the record in fairer focus. Predictably, Burger and Rehnquist voted for Bakke. Nixon appointees Blackmun and Powell each went his own way. The "Minnesota twins," Burger and Blackmun, are no longer ideologically Siamese. Like their predecessors, members of the Burger Court are not computers but fallible human beings, motivated by passions, desires, and beliefs common to all people.

The emergence of Justice Powell as the Court's spokesman in Bakke is not surprising. During his first six full terms, he stood with the majority more frequently than any of his colleagues, amassing a record of only sixteen dissenting votes in 852 cases. An intriguing question is thus raised: Does this mild-mannered Justice follow or lead? The question may not be well taken. Edmund Burke reminds us that "in all bodies, those who will lead, must also in a considerable degree, follow. They must conform to the taste, talent, and disposition of those whom they wish to conduct." It is interesting to note that in a recent poll of legal scholars and practitioners (cited by R. G. Zimmerman in the July 30, 1978, issue of the *New Orleans Times-Picayune*) Powell was voted "the best justice."

The Bakke case evidences judicial determination to make haste slowly on an infinitely complex issue, with us since the nation's birth. Justice Stevens would have moved even more cautiously. Invoking the well-established tradition of avoiding constitutional issues wherever possible, he would have decided the case in Bakke's favor as a violation of the Civil Rights Act of 1964.

From the side of the precarious majority endorsing racial classification, Blackmun took a more aggressive stand: "In order to get beyond racism, we must first take account of race. . . . And in order to treat some persons equally, we must treat them differently. . . . The ultimate question is: Among the qualified how does one choose?"

The answer in 1978 was not found in Justice Harlan's famous aphorism of 1896: "The Constitution is color blind." In Bakke five Justices were mindful of Chief Justice Marshall's arresting caveat: "We must never forget that it is a Constitution we are expounding."

Another pillar in the Warren Court constitutional edifice is reapportionment. Supported by a six to three margin, it shows least disintegration. Despite decisions endorsing deviations in congressional and state redistricting that departed from the one man one vote formula, judicially mandated reapportionment is still the success story of the Warren court.[29] Understandably, the Chief Justice rated it his "greatest achievement."

New rules of criminal procedure, the Warren Court's most venturesome and controversial innovation, have been whittled down but not eliminated. The record is mixed; the rules have been both qualified and extended. Inroads on the rights of the accused occurred in an area where tradition had become almost sacrosanct—trial by a jury of twelve. Arguing that the unanimous vote of twelve jurors was an historical accident, the Nixon-appointed Justices, joined by swing-man Byron White, struck a blow for "law and order," upholding a 9 to 3 jury conviction in Louisiana and a 10 to 2 vote in Oregon.[30] In a biting dissent, Justice Douglas deplored the Burger Court's activism. The majority had discarded two centuries of American history, "restructuring American law . . . for political, not for judicial action." The activist shoe was then on the other foot.

The rights of defendants apparently suffered another setback on December 1, 1973, when the Court upheld two unrelated convictions, one for a traffic violation, the other for possession of narcotics. Rejecting the defendants' contention that their Fourth Amendment guarantees against "unreasonable searches and seizure" had been violated, the majority ruled that after "custodial arrest," no additional justification was necessary to search for further incriminat-

[29] *Connor* v. *Williams,* 404 U.S. 549 (1972); *Mahan* v. *Howell,* 404 U.S. 1201 (1971); *Gaffney* v. *Cummings,* 412 U.S. 735 (1973); *White* v. *Weiser,* 412 U.S. 183 (1972).

In *Connor* v. *Finch,* decided May 31, 1977, the Justices, voting 7 to 1, demonstrated continuing sensitivity to the "one man, one vote" principle. Justice Rehnquist did not participate.

[30] *Johnson* v. *Louisiana,* 406 U.S. 356 (1972); *Apodaca* v. *Oregon,* 406 U.S. 404 (1972).

ing evidence. Justices Marshall, Douglas, and Brennan dissented. Denouncing the decision as "a clear and marked departure from our long tradition," they were concerned lest "a police officer, lacking probable cause to obtain a search warrant, will use a traffic arrest as a pretext to conduct a search."[31]

In the 1975–76 term, the Court ruled that warrants are not needed for arrest in public places. A heroin suspect, standing in the doorway of her house, had no reasonable expectation of privacy and was therefore subject to warrantless arrest.[32] In another case it was held that a person may be convicted of selling drugs, even when undercover agents supplied him or her with them and other agents were the purchasers.[33]

On December 9, 1975, Justice Stewart, expressing the view of five Justices, held that incriminating statements made after a suspect received the Miranda warning were admissible in a murder case, even though the accused had exercised the right to silence at earlier interrogations concerning robberies. Dissenting vigorously, Justice Brennan, joined by Marshall, declared that the decision "virtually empties Miranda of principle. . . . Today's decision signals rejection of Miranda's basic premise that the techniques of police questioning and the nature of custodial surroundings produce an inherently coercive situation."[34]

In *Oregon* v. *Haas*,[35] the suspect, although given the Miranda warnings, was told he could not see a lawyer until he reached police headquarters. Yet the Court approved admission of inculpatory statements he made on the way to the

---

[31] *U.S.* v. *Robinson*, 414 U.S. 218, 239, 248 (1973).
[32] *U.S.* v. *Santanta*, 427 U.S. 38 (1976).
[33] *Hampton* v. *U.S.*, 425 U.S. 484 (1976).
[34] *Michigan* v. *Mosley*, 423 U.S. 96 (1975), 118.
[35] 420 U.S. 714 (1975).

police station. Denying state power to interpret the federal Constitution more strictly than the Supreme Court, the Justices left "a State, free *as a matter of its own law* to impose greater restrictions on police activity than the Court holds to be necessary under federal constitutional standards." [36] In dissent, Justice Marshall noted "the increasingly common practice of reviewing state court decisions upholding constitutional claims in criminal cases." [37]

Another setback for the revised rules of criminal procedure occurred the last day of the 1975–76 term. The Court ruled, 5 to 3 (Justice Stevens did not participate), that federal judges may no longer set aside conviction in a state court, even if the evidence has been obtained illegally and in violation of the Fourth Amendment's ban against unreasonable searches and seizures. Justice Brennan, dissenting, noted that this case marked the continuance of the "Court's business of slow strangulation" of the exclusionary rule. Justice Stewart wrote a separate dissenting opinion. [38]

During the Warren Court years, review of conviction in state courts through habeas corpus jurisdiction was easily available. Not so in the Burger Court. Concurring in *Schneckloth* v. *Bustamonte*, [39] Justice Powell indicated that search and seizure claims under collateral review should be cut back. Three years later, speaking for the Court and converting dictum into law, Powell ruled that when the state has provided opportunity for full litigation a state prisoner need not be granted federal habeas corpus relief on the ground that the evidence produced at the state level constituted an unconstitutional search and seizure in violation of the Fourth Amendment. Justices Brennan and Marshall

[36] *Ibid.*, 719.
[37] *Ibid.*, 726.
[38] *U.S.* v. *Janis*, 428 U.S. 433 (1976), 460.
[39] 412 U.S. 218 (1973).

dissented; Justice White wrote a separate dissenting opinion.[40]

Fearing elimination of constitutional protections established in earlier cases, Brennan and Marshall escalated their dissents into a crescendo of bitterness. In a case involving border patrol checkpoints, Justice Brennan noted: "Today's decision is the ninth this term marking the continuing evisceration of Fourth Amendment protections against unreasonable searches and seizures."[41] But, on March 23, 1977,[42] the Court rejected the request of twenty-one states that *Miranda,* the symbol of the Warren Court's prodefendant stance, be overruled.

Although the trend favors the prosecution, there are deviations from this tendency. The Burger Court requires a hearing before a parolee may have his parole canceled.[43] On occasion the rights of criminal defendants have been extended. In the 1963 landmark *Gideon* v. *Wainright* case,[44] the Warren Court had ruled that an indigent convicted of a felony must be furnished counsel. In an opinion by Justice Douglas, the Burger Court went further, holding that no person can be jailed for a petty offense unless he has been furnished free counsel or has waived that right. Chief Justice Burger, exponent of efficiency equaled only by Chief Justice Taft, was relaxed in the face of a more crowded docket certain to result from the ruling. Calmly reassuring his colleagues and the bar, he declared: "The dynamics of

[40] *Stone* v. *Powell,* 428 U.S. 465 (1976). See Donald E. Wilkes, Jr., "The New Federalism in Criminal Procedure: State Court Evasion of the Burger Court," 62 *Ky. L. J.* 465 (1974); Wilkes, "More on the New Federalism in Criminal Procedure," 63 *Ky. L. J.* 873 (1975); Stanley Mosk, "The New States Rights," 10 *Calif. L. Enforcement* 81 (1976).

[41] *U.S.* v. *Martinez,* 428 U.S. 543 (1976), 467.

[42] *Brewer* v. *Williams,* 430 U.S. 387 (1977).

[43] *Morrissey* v. *Brewer,* 408 U.S. 471 (1972).

[44] 372 U.S. 335 (1963).

the profession had a way of rising to the burdens placed on it."[45]

In 1972, it was held that a capriciously imposed death penalty violates the Eighth Amendment provision against "cruel and unusual punishment," because juries and judges could, and did, apply the punishment in an arbitrary and capricious manner.[46] On July 2, 1976, it was decided (Justices Brennan and Marshall dissenting) that capital punishment does not inherently run counter to the Eighth and Fourteenth Amendments and can be used as a penalty for certain offenses, including murder.[47] In 1977, the Court barred the death penalty for rape of an adult woman.[48] A widely publicized ruling, April 19, 1977, held that paddling public school students as a disciplinary measure does not constitute "cruel and unusual punishment," since the Eighth Amendment was designed to protect those convicted of crime. Justices White, Brennan, and Stevens dissented.[49]

The Court came no closer in the 1977–78 term to a definition of the death penalty, agreeing only that it could not be automatically imposed for a particular crime. Before sentencing, the judge or jury must consider mitigating factors such as the prisoner's character, record, and circumstances of the crime. Once again the Court's mandate required more than a score of states to rewrite capital punishment laws. Understandably, Chief Justice Burger acknowledged that its latest ruling had not simplified the constitutional status of capital punishment, adding that the Court still "has an obligation to reconcile previously conflicting views."

[45] *Argersinger* v. *Hamlin,* 407 U.S. 25 (1972).
[46] *Furman* v. *Georgia,* 408 U.S. 238, (1972).
[47] *Gregg* v. *Georgia,* 433 U.S. 584 (1976).
[48] *Coker* v. *Georgia,* 433 U.S. 584 (1977).
[49] *Ingraham* v. *Wright,* 430 U.S. 651 (1977).

In freedom of speech and press cases the record wavers. Except for its ruling outlawing state abortion laws, no decision of the Burger Court has aroused deeper concern among citizens and dissenting Justices than *Branzburg* v. *Hayes.*[50] Voting 5 to 4, the Court held that the First Amendment accords a journalist no privilege against appearing before a grand jury and answering questions as to either the identity of his/her news source or information he or she has received in confidence. Justice Stewart, no card-carrying liberal, joined Brennan and Marshall in dissenting. For Stewart, "The Court's crabbed view of the First Amendment reflects a disturbing insensitivity to the critical role of an independent press in our society."[51]

Justice White, for the majority, recognized a constitutional status for news gathering: "Without some protection for seeking out the news, freedom of the press could be eviscerated."[52] But the Court indicated that for protection the press must rely not on law, but on its own social influence. If the issue were ultimately drawn in law, the press would have to yield to the crucial role of the grand jury and the obligation of every citizen to testify. Significantly, concurring Justice Powell emphatically denied the dissenters' charge that this decision left state and federal authorities "free to 'annex' the news media as 'an investigative arm of the government.' "[53] Justice Powell's reassurance seems to have been well taken. "Open and public discourse" was upheld in the Nebraska press case of June 30, 1976, in which the Court voted unanimously that judges generally may not gag the press in criminal trials.[54]

The Justices struck down parts of the campaign financing

[50] 408 U.S. 665 (1972).
[51] *Ibid.*, 725.
[52] *Ibid.*, 681.
[53] *Ibid.*, 709.
[54] *Nebraska Press Association* v. *Stuart,* 427 U.S. 539 (1976). For a perceptive commentary on this major ruling, see D. Grier Stephenson,

law on the ground that the regulations restricted First Amendment rights. Disallowed was the provision that puts a fifty thousand dollar limit on the use by a Presidential candidate of his own or his immediate family's money. The Justices found this a violation of the First Amendment. But the Court endorsed ceilings on contributions of one thousand dollars to candidates seeking federal office as a less "direct and substantial" restraint on expression.[55]

The New Hampshire requirement that noncommercial vehicle licenses bear the motto "Live Free or Die" was set aside by a strangely divided Court (Burger, Brennan, Stewart, Marshall, Powell, and Stevens) as violative of the First Amendment.[56] Rehnquist and Blackmun dissented.

In outlawing legislation barring price advertising of prescription drugs, the Court ruled for the first time that "commercial speech" is protected by the First Amendment.[57] From *Pharmacy* it seemed but a short step to the Court's June 22, 1977, 5 to 4 decision to outlaw as a violation of the First Amendment Arizona's bar against advertising the fees lawyers charged clients for routine legal services.[58] Earlier the Justices had ruled 7 to 2 that it is unconstitutional for states to insist that nonprescription contraceptives be sold by drug stores or by doctors.[59]

Cutting back on the right of privacy, the Justices sustained a Georgia statute sanctioning publication of a seventeen-year-old deceased rape victim's name, obtained from official court records.[60] On April 21, 1976, the Court voted

---

Jr., "The Mild Magistracy of the Law: *U.S.* v. *Richard Nixon,*" *Intellect,* CIII (December, 1976), 288–92.

[55] *Buckley* v. *Valeo,* 424 U.S. 1 (1976).

[56] *Wooley* v. *Maynard,* 430 U.S. 705 (1977).

[57] *Virginia State Board of Pharmacy* v. *Virginia Citizens Council,* 425 U.S. 748 (1976).

[58] *Bates* v. *State of Arizona,* 433 U.S. 350 (1977).

[59] *Carey* v. *Population Services International,* 431 U.S. 678 (1977).

[60] *Cox Broadcasting Corp.* v. *Cohn,* 420 U.S. 469 (1975).

7 to 2 that in a federal prosecution, the accused has no defensible Fourth Amendment rights in subpoenaed bank records.[61] *Time Inc.* v. *Firestone*,[62] decided on March 2, 1976, gave limited protection to the press against libel suits. The Justices refused even to hear arguments in a lower court case upholding state prosecution of homosexual acts.[63] Yet a sharply divided Court upheld Detroit's zoning ordinances restricting proliferation of movie theaters that show sexually explicit movies.[64]

VIII

The most bitterly criticized decision in the 1977–78 term (*Zurcher* v. *The Stanford Daily*, decided May 31, 1978), upheld police search for evidence of a crime on the *Daily*'s premises of persons not themselves involved. Suspecting that the newspaper possessed unpublished photographs of campus violence, the police had obtained a search warrant enabling them to rummage through files, desk drawers, and wastepaper baskets. Nothing prevented them from uncovering private and confidential information not related to their original search. Involved were the Fourth Amendment's protection of the people's right to be secure in their persons, houses, papers, and effects against unreasonable searches and seizure, and the First Amendment's freedom-of-the-press provision. The latter was of special concern since such a sweeping search opened to the police information they had no right to see.

In a 5 to 3 decision, the Court, speaking through Justice White, joined by the four Nixon appointees, ruled that there was no requirement that the evidence be secured

[61] *U.S.* v. *Miller*, 425 U.S. 435 (1976).
[62] 424 U.S. 448 (1976).
[63] *Doe* v. *Commonwealth's Attorney*, 403 F. Supp. 1199, 96 Sup. Ct. 1489 (1976).
[64] *Young* v. *American Mini Theatres, Inc.*, 427 U.S. 50 (1976).

through a subpoena duces tecum rather than a search warrant. Dissenting Justices Stewart and Marshall argued that unannounced police search of newspaper offices unconstitutionally hampered news gathering and reporting, and that a search warrant should be issued only if the magistrate found probable cause to believe a subpoena would be impractical.

Reaction was explosive. Critics widely denounced the decision as a severe judicial blow, taking small comfort in the fact that the Court itself acknowledged the freedom of legislatures to supply additional protection for the press and individual freedom. Quick to respond, Kansas Republican Senator Robert Dole, certainly no liberal, proposed a bill to limit the judicially conferred power. It is hard to reconcile this decision with certain other Burger Court rulings in this area, including *Pentagon Papers, United States* v. *U.S. District Court,* and the Nebraska press case.

IX

Court reporters and commentators are almost united in believing that the Warren Court's constitutional jurisprudence had been substantially altered, perhaps reversed. "What the Warren Court Hath Given, the Burger Court Taketh Away"; "Now, Clearly, It Is a Burger Court," are typical headlines. "I have a feeling I'm seeing an old movie played backward," University of Michigan Law School's Yale Kamisar commented.

The main focus of attack is on decisions involving criminal justice and procedure. The tide that ran strongly in the direction of the accused during Warren's Chief Justiceship has ebbed. In this area Justices Brennan's and Marshall's dissenting opinions have been stridently outspoken. Speaking for six members of the Court, Justice Rehnquist ruled that an informer's tip carried enough reliability to justify the police in forcibly stopping a suspect, in reaching for the spot where the gun was supposed to be hidden, and searching his person and car. For the dissenters (Brennan, Marshall, and Douglas), the "decision invokes the specter of a society in which innocent citizens may be stopped, searched, and arrested at the whim of police officers who have only the slightest suspicion of improper conduct." [65]

Rehnquist was again the Court's spokesman in *Paul* v. *Davis,* where it was held that a private citizen demeaned by the police as an "active shoplifter" has no recourse in federal courts. "Reputation alone," the Court ruled, "apart from some more tangible interests such as employment is not sufficient by itself to invoke the procedural protection of the due process clause." For Rehnquist the complaint involved merely " a classical claim for defamation actionable in the courts of virtually every state." [66] In a dissenting opinion of unusual vehemence, Justice Brennan, joined by Justices Marshall and White, warned that under the majority opinion, "police officials, acting in their official capacities as law enforcers could condemn innocent individuals as criminals and thereby brand them with one of the most stigmatizing and debilitating labels in our society." The dissenters called the decision a "regrettable abdication," and "a saddening denigration of our majestic Bill of Rights." [67]

By the end of Warren's Chief Justiceship uniformity in state and federal criminal procedural rights had been carried to unprecedented lengths. Federalization of such rights had not occurred without protest. The most compelling ammunition for retrenchment in deference to states' rights has been the dissenting opinions of Harlan, White, and Stewart, especially Harlan's. The wonder is not that *Miranda* should still be in relatively good standing, but that it should

[65] *Adams* v. *Williams,* 407 U.S. 143 (1972).
[66] 424 U.S. 693 (1976), 697, 702.
[67] *Ibid.,* 735.

have retained so much vitality. The warning Justice Rehnquist sounded in 1976 echoed Justice Harlan's of a decade earlier: "Federal courts must be constantly mindful of the 'special delicacy of the adjustments to be preserved between federal equitable power and state administration of its own law.' "[68]

In an interview on April 8, 1976, Chief Justice Burger, reacting to mounting criticism, declared that there had been "no significant change in the Court's attitude toward the rights of criminal defendants in either four years or eight years or 12 years."[69] On the contrary, during "the last four or five years, the Court has opened up the area of prisoners' rights that were never previously accorded inmates." Dissenting opinions that give vent to opposing viewpoints, the Chief Justice declared, should not always be read literally because "they sometimes overstate the case." On May 17, 1977, the Chief Justice again portrayed his Court as defender of a wide range of rights, including those of racial minorities, welfare recipients, women, prisoners, illegitimate children, and the media.[70]

Burger himself may have been guilty of overstatement. On August 11, 1976, Justice Powell had noted a "leveling off" of judicial activism, due in part to changes in the Court's membership. Justice Powell, unlike the Chief Justice, conceded that "in recent years the Court had decided a number of criminal cases differently from what might have been expected during the decade of the 60s. But it is alarmist to suggest any significant weakening of the basic rights of persons accused of crime." Less categorical than Burger, Justice Powell contends that "a more traditional, and, in my view, a sounder balance is evolving between the

[68] *Rizzo v. Good,* 423 U.S. 362 (1976), 378.
[69] *New York Times,* April 9, 1976, p. 1, col. 8.
[70] *Ibid.,* May 18, 1977, Sec. N, p. 18, col. 3.

rights of accused persons and the right of a civilized society
to have a criminal justice system that is effective as well as
fair."[71]

In the January, 1977, issue of the *Harvard Law Review,*
Justice Brennan presents a solemn picture of judicial trends.
Brennan recalls that during the 1960's civil rights were increasingly federalized. State courts then saw no reason to
consider protections secured by state constitutions. The
Justice notes with approval that "more and more state
courts are construing state constitutional counterparts of
the Bill of Rights as guaranteeing citizens of their states
even more protection than the federal provisions, even
those identically phrased." Although Justice Brennan applauds this stopgap as a happy tribute to federalism, it over-
looks "one of the strengths of our federal system [which]
provides a double source of protection for the rights of our
citizens. Federalism is not served when the federal help of
that protection is crippled."[72]

Yet certain commentators, deploring the Warren Court's
alleged lawmaking and Constitution amending, charge that
Burger and his strict constructionist colleagues are "clinging as firmly to judicial government as its predecessor."[73]
Largely ignored is a record of judicial statesmanship hard
to match. Two major decisions, both unanimous, contributed incalculably to the downfall of the man who appointed
four of the Court's members.

[71] *Ibid.,* August 12, 1976, p. 18, col. 3.

[72] William J. Brennan, Jr., "State Constitutions and the Protection
of Individual Rights," 90 *Harvard Law Review* (January, 1977), 489,
495, 503.

[73] Raoul Berger, quoted by Warren Weaver, Jr., in the *New York
Times,* October 31, 1977, p. 19, col. 1. For balanced analyses of the
Burger Court's constitutional jurisprudence, see A. E. Dick Howard,
"State Courts and Constitutional Rights in the Day of the Burger
Court," *The George Mason Lectures* (Williamsburg, Va., 1977); Rob-
ert J. Steamer, "Contemporary Supreme Court Directions in Civil
Liberties," *Political Science Quarterly,* 92 (Fall, 1977), 425–42.

In June, 1972, the Court adjudicated a hotly contested issue at the heart of the Nixon administration's "law and order" campaign. Involved was the government's contention that electronic surveillance approved by the Attorney-General, but without prior judicial sanction, was a lawful exercise of the President's power to protect "domestic security." After two lower courts had rejected the government's claim, the case was appealed to the Supreme Court. Framing the Court's opinion in the idiom of basic principles, Justice Powell wrote:

> There is, understandably, a deep-seated uneasiness and apprehension that [electronic surveillance] will be used to intrude upon cherished privacy of law-abiding citizens. Those charged with investigative and prosecutorial duty should not be the sole judge of when to utilize constitutionally sensitive means in pursuing their tasks. . . . Official surveillance, whether its purpose be criminal investigation or on-going intelligence gathering, risks infringement of constitutionally protected privacy of speech. . . .
>
> History abundantly documents the tendency of government —however benevolent and benign its motives—to view with suspicion those who most fervently dispute its policies. The danger to political dissent is acute where the government attempts to act under so vague a concept as the power to protect "domestic security". . . . The price of lawful public dissent must not be a dread of subjection to an unchecked surveillance power. Nor must the fear of unauthorized official eavesdropping deter vigorous citizen dissent and discussion of Government action in private conversation. For private dissent, no less than open public discourse, is essential to our free society.[74]

Upheld was the people's right to know. Protected were rights deemed fundamental in both the Declaration of Independence and the Constitution—the right to consent, to criticize and oppose. As to these values, Justice Powell expressed sentiments worthy of Jefferson, of Oliver Wendell

[74] *United States* v. *United States District Court*, 407 U.S. 297 (1972), 312, 314, 317, 320.

Holmes, Louis D. Brandeis, Harlan Fiske Stone, and Earl Warren.

In 1973, President Nixon challenged Judge Sirica's order commanding the President to turn over sixty-four taped conversations for use as evidence in the trial of seven Watergate defendants. By the time the Court granted certiorari, Nixon had defied congressional subpoenas. Stalemate was a disturbing possibility. The circumstances amid which the Court took jurisdiction are reminiscent of *Marbury* v. *Madison* and the ill-fated Dred Scott decision.

Appearing for the President was James St. Clair, who argued that executive privilege is absolute, lacking constitutional perimeters, except those fixed by the President. In opposition was Special Prosecutor Leon Jaworski, whom Nixon himself had appointed. Chief Justice Burger met St. Clair's argument head on: "The President's Counsel . . . reads the Constitution as providing an absolute privilege of confidentiality for all presidential communications." While recognizing that "confidentiality of presidential communications has constitutional underpinnings" calling "for great deference from Courts," the claim of public interest in the confidentiality of such conversation must be squared with other values. Unqualified executive privilege would encroach on the primary constitutional function of the judicial branch to do justice in criminal proceedings and "plainly conflicts with the function of Courts under Article 111." So, although conceding that interest in preserving confidentiality is weighty, the Court concluded: "Without access to specific facts, a criminal prosecution may be totally frustrated. The President's broad interest in communication will not be vitiated by disclosure of a limited number of conversations preliminarily shown to have some bearing on the pending criminal causes."[75]

[75] *United States* v. *Nixon,* 418 U.S. 683 (1974), 703, 706, 712–13. Judicial independence may also be observed in the Pentagon Papers

The most significant aspect of the tapes case was President Nixon's challenge of judicial review itself. This basic adjunct to separation of powers and the rule of law was emphatically reaffirmed. In almost consecutive paragraphs, the Court quotes Chief Justice Marshall: "Many decisions of this Court have unequivocally reaffirmed the holding in *Marbury* v. *Madison.* . . . We therefore reaffirm that it is 'emphatically the province and duty' of this Court 'to say what the law is' with respect to the claim of privilege presented in this case."[76] Three Nixon appointees sat in the tapes case, yet the decision was unanimous. "A putative rebel leader . . . against constitutional government itself" was foiled with the support of Justices whom the discredited President had appointed.[77]

X

In terms of voting, the judicial alignment is reminiscent of the 1930's. Only at the extremes is any particular decision predictable. Justices Brennan and Marshall are solidly on the so-called liberal side, whereas Chief Justice Burger and Justice Rehnquist usually maintain a conservative stance. Blackmun and Powell do not fit into any neat category. The former spoke for the Court in the abortion case, evoking Justice Rehnquist's charge of judicial law making. Powell wrote the opinion in *United States* v. *U.S. District Court,* a pronouncement worthy of the Court at its best. Counterparts of the 1930's swing men, Hughes and Roberts, are Stewart and White. But none of the categories is frozen. The Burger Court demonstrates that judicial lawmaking can travel several ideological paths. It is no longer

---

and impoundment cases. See *Train* v. *City of New York,* 420 U.S. 35 (1975).

[76] *U.S.* v. *Nixon,* 703.

[77] Judge Noel Fox in *Murphy* v. *Ford,* 390 F.Supp. (1975), 1372–73 (W.D. Michigan, 1975).

safe to predict how the Justices will vote either as a bloc or as individuals. On occasion, even Rehnquist is aligned with the liberals! Blessed with rare judicial temperament, Stevens is a balancing influence.

For various reasons Presidents Nixon and Ford might not have been able drastically to alter the course of judicial decisions even with a Court of their own making. No Court, however recent its composition, is completely new. Only two Presidents, Washington and Franklin Roosevelt, have named a full bench. From 1969 to November, 1975, five carry-over Justices—Brennan, Douglas, Marshall, Stewart, and White—were still on the bench. In addition, the Warren Court's constitutional jurisprudence seems to have been grounded in American ideological and constitutional taproots. In his Northwestern University Lectures of 1971, former Justice Goldberg argued that change in judicial personnel would not end judicial activism on behalf of fundamental liberties:

I believe that a proper view of judicial restraint applies with far greater force to laws that regulate economic and social matters than to laws that inhibit the exercise of basic personal liberty. . . . "Judicial restraint" has only limited applicability when the treatment of minorities, the fundamental liberties of individuals, or the health of the political process are at issue. . . . Once fundamental rights have been recognized, there has never been a general reversal of direction by the Court, a going back against the trend of history.

"There is an enormous difference," Goldberg concludes, "between not opening new frontiers of human liberty and closing ones formerly open, between declining to move forward and legitimatizing repression."[78] The Burger Court has yet to demonstrate the error of Goldberg's forecast.

[78] Arthur J. Goldberg, *Equal Justice: The Supreme Court in the Warren Era* (Evanston, Ill., 1971), 41-42, 61, 90, 93. For elaboration of Goldberg's thesis, see Mason, *The Supreme Court: Palladium of*

Freedom (Ann Arbor, 1962), chap. 6. For contrasting views, see Alexander Bickel, *The Supreme Court and the Idea of Progress* (New York, 1970); Philip Kurland, *Politics, the Constitution and the Warren Court* (Chicago, 1970); Robert G. McCloskey, "Economic Due Process and the Supreme Court," reprinted in L. W. Levy (ed.), *American Constitutional Law* (New York, 1966), 155–87; and Nathan Glazer, "Toward an Imperial Judiciary," *The Public Interest*, No. 41 (Fall, 1975).

In rejecting the so-called double standard, Bickel and Kurland overlook the fact that Felix Frankfurter, their mentor, inspired by Holmes, had embraced the concept of "preferred freedoms" at the beginning of his judicial career. In 1939, Archibald MacLeish and E. F. Pritchard, Jr., both friends and close students of Frankfurter's pre-Court writing, declared:

"The question which history presents to us is the question whether our present industrial and economic system can be changed over to an efficient, workable and socially effective system without the substitution of authoritarian forms of government for the democratic forms of government to which we are devoted. Translated into constitutional terms that question becomes the question whether the Court can and will permit the legislatures the widest latitude in framing economic measures altering property relations while sharply rejecting all attempts to curtail or restrict civil liberties. On that issue the position of Mr. Frankfurter is clear. He has stated his views on both halves of the question separately. And, in writing of Mr. Justice Holmes, he has by inference stated his view of the two together. In the case of economic measures, as Mr. Frankfurter puts it, Holmes was 'hesitant to oppose his own opinion to the economic views of the legislature.' The legislatures clearly having power to interfere with property rights in certain cases, Mr. Justice Holmes was willing, in cases involving economic and social legislation alleged to violate the Due Process clauses, to make the legislative discretion as broad as possible. But not so in cases where laws and other acts encroached on guaranteed rights and liberties such, for first example, as freedom of speech. There he was far more ready to declare acts of legislation unconstitutional because history had taught him that 'since social development is a process of trial and error, the fullest possible opportunity for the free play of the human mind was an indefeasible prerequisite. . . .' It is difficult to avoid the conclusion that Mr. Frankfurter will take his stand upon the same distinction." (MacLeish and Pritchard [eds.], *Law and Politics* [New York, 1939], xxiii.)

David F. Forte (ed.), *The Supreme Court in American Politics: Judicial Activism* vs. *Judicial Self-Restraint* (Lexington, Mass., 1972),

Another deterrent to a President's power to mold the Court is the force wielded by stare decisis. Decisions are sometimes avowedly overruled, but not often. Because of judicial sensitivity to departures from this principle, the Court is more likely to distinguish shaky precedents than to uproot them. "Respect for continuity alone," Justice Frankfurter wrote in 1950, requires adherence to precedent. The Court should not give "fair ground for the belief that Law is the expression of chance—for instance, of unexpected changes in the Court's composition and the contingencies in the choice of successors." [79]

The Warren Court's most audacious law-making foray was *Miranda*. Although passage of time did not make that case any more palatable to Justice Harlan than when it was decided, he felt obliged to adhere to it "purely out of respect for stare decisis." [80] Justice Stewart was concerned in 1974 lest a basic change in constitutional interpretation be regarded as resting on no firmer ground than "a change in our membership," inviting "the popular misconception that this institution is little different from the two political branches of the government." [81]

On June 25, 1976, the Court ruled 7 to 2 that the 1866 federal law prohibiting "all racial discrimination, private as well as public, interfering with the making and enforcement of contracts" bars private schools from excluding black children. [82] Justices Powell and Stevens concurred, not because they considered this the correct decision but be-

---

provides a wide range of views on this controversial subject.

"Judicial restraint is but another form of judicial activism." Laurence Tribe, *American Constitutional Law* (New York, 1978), iv.

[79] Dissenting in *U.S.* v. *Rabinowitz,* 339 U.S. 56 (1950), 86.

[80] *Orozo* v. *Texas,* 394 U.S. 311 (1969), 315.

[81] *Mitchell* v. *W. T. Grant,* 416 U.S. 600 (1974), 636.

[82] *Runyon* v. *McCrary,* 427 U.S. 160 (1976).

cause the Court was not writing on a "clean slate." Speaking through Justice Stewart, the majority relied on *Jones* v. *Mayer.*[83] The concurring Justices believed that *Jones* had been wrongly decided. Yet, in the interest of stability and orderly development of the law, they concurred. Said Justice Stevens:

> Even if *Jones* did not accurately reflect the sentiments of Congress (that drafted the Fourteenth Amendment), it surely accords with the prevailing sense of justice today. . . . The policy of the nation as formulated by the Congress in recent years had moved constantly in the direction of eliminating racial segregation in all sectors of society. This Court has given a sympathetic and liberal construction to such legislation. For the Court now to overrule *Jones* would be a significant step backward, with effects that would not have arisen from the correct decision in the first instance. Such a step would be so clearly contrary to my understanding of the *mores* of today that I think the Court is entirely correct in adhering to *Jones.*[84]

Finally, the psychological effect of the robe should not be underestimated. "There is a good deal of shallow talk," Justice Frankfurter noted in 1952, "that the judicial robe does not change the man within it. The fact is that on the whole judges do lay aside private views in discharging their judicial function."[85] After donning the robe of Chief Justice, Burger commented to a friend: "Six months ago if you had asked me what the Supreme Court should and should not do, I probably could have given you a quick answer. But now, I am not so sure. New problems arise that the authors of the Constitution did not anticipate. But the answers to the problems ought to be made to fit an existing

[83] 392 U.S. 409 (1968).

[84] *Runyon* v. *McCrary,* 191.

[85] Felix Frankfurter, *Of Law and Men: Papers and Addresses, 1939–1956,* 133. Certain other judges hold that the robe works no changes at all. See above, 218.

pattern; a new pattern should not be made." The Chief
Justice concluded soberly, "The hardest question is when
the Court should step in."[86]

Chief Justice Burger's identification of one of the central
complexities of constitutional interpretation did not encourage the belief that a complete about-face would occur under his leadership. Nor has this happened. Justice
Holmes reminds us of an inescapable imperative binding
the Burger Court no less than any other: "Historic continuity with the past is not a duty; it is only a necessity."[87]

EPILOGUE

One of the ironies of Supreme Court history is that the
Court itself is still sharply divided as to its role under the
rubric of judicial review. Certain Justices and commentators interpret the judicial function narrowly, arguing that
it requires no more than policing the barriers between the
national government and the states, and among the three
organs of national authority, and enforcing the constitutional line that safeguards individual rights against government invasion at all levels. Justices of this persuasion march
under the "self-restraint" banner.

Other Justices hold with Edmond Cahn that "judicial review is always more than pure and simple enforcement of
the Constitution; in addition, it always comprises express
or tacit interpretation of the Constitution, or—in other
words—a continual process of adjusting and adapting the
fundamental fabric."[88] Judicial "activism" identifies Supreme Court Justices of this persuasion.

During the past century, judicial activism has manifested

[86] Quoted in Mason and Beaney, *American Constitutional Law,*
xxv–xxvi.

[87] O. W. Holmes, *Collected Legal Papers* (New York, 1920), 139.

[88] Edmond Cahn (ed.), *Supreme Court and the Supreme Law*
(Bloomington, 1954), 19.

itself in two areas. From 1890 to 1937, the Court vetoed state and national legislation designed to regulate the economy. Judicial power, invoked negatively, blocked the march of social democracy. Under Presidential siege, as if to confess error, the Justices surrendered this self-acquired role. Since 1937, particularly under the Chief Justiceship of Earl Warren and continuing under Chief Justice Burger, the Court has used judicial power positively to achieve presumably socially desirable goals. Reflecting on the judicial blockage of 1935–36 against government power to regulate the economy, Archibald Cox writes: "There was a sense that the Justices made a mess of things when they attempted to enlarge their orbit, as they did in resisting government regulation of the economy."[89]

Another orientation toward judicial activism emerged after 1937. Of this, Anthony Lewis observes: "The 15 years since Warren became Chief Justice have been years of legal revolution. In that time the Supreme Court has brought about more social change than most Congresses and most Presidents."[90] On the same phenomenon, Fred Rodell comments: "Not since the Nine Old Men of unhallowed memory struck down the first New Deal almost 30 years ago . . . has any Supreme Court used its politico-legal power so broadly and boldly as did Earl Warren."[91]

Although four of the present members (Burger, Powell, Rehnquist, and Blackmun) were appointed to end the Warren Court revolution, the Court headed by Warren Burger has involved itself in more social, political, and cultural areas than ever. Among recent and current constitutional issues are homosexuals, sex discrimination, environment,

[89] Archibald Cox, *The Role of the Supreme Court in American Government* (New York, 1976), 34.

[90] Anthony Lewis, "A Man Born to Act, Not to Muse," *New York Times Magazine,* June 30, 1968.

[91] Fred Rodell, "The Warren Court Stands Its Ground," *New York Times Magazine,* September 27, 1964.

privacy, nuclear power, paddling public school children, and the hair style of policemen. The pre-1937 Court blocked legislative initiative; the Warren and Burger Courts have taken policy-making initiatives on their own.

Certain of the Burger Court's rulings demonstrate statesmanship of a high order. Three Nixon appointees sat in *United States* v. *Richard Nixon,* yet the decision was unanimous. Justice Powell's opinion in *United States* v. *United States District Court* rivals historic pronouncements by Holmes, Brandeis, and Stone. The Court was unanimous in the Nebraska Gag Law ruling. Even in the Pentagon Papers case, charged with political overtones at the highest level, the Justices were agreed on the substantive issue.

With few exceptions, Supreme Court Justices have been sensitive to the baffling public interest-private rights dichotomy. Woodrow Wilson's faith did not waver even after Justice Holmes accused his colleagues of enacting Herbert Spencer's *Social Statics:* "Whether by force of circumstance or deliberate design, we have married legislation with adjudication and look for statesmanship in our courts."[92] By and large, the Supreme Court, including that headed by Warren Burger, has fulfilled Wilson's expectations.

Whither the Burger Court? Are we headed for another showdown with the Judiciary? Certain commentators, alleging judicial usurpation, seem inclined toward an affirmative answer. Raoul Berger, for example, asks how long the public can continue to respect a Court that condemns others' acts as unconstitutional yet itself acts unconstitutionally.[93] Louis Lusky, who as a law clerk in 1938 helped

[92] Quoted in Mason, *William Howard Taft: Chief Justice* (New York, 1964).

[93] Raoul Berger, *New York Times,* October 31, 1977, p. 19, col. 1. See also Berger, *Government by Judiciary: The Transformation of the Fourteenth Amendment* (Cambridge, Mass., 1977). For a brilliant review of Berger, see Walter F. Murphy, "Constitutional Interpreta-

Justice Stone lay constitutional foundations for the Warren Court's judicial activism, pointedly asks *By What Right?*[94] Other observers, sharing Woodrow Wilson's belief that the Constitution is not "a mere lawyers' document" but a "vehicle of a nation's life,"[95] do not anticipate a Court crisis similar to that which rocked the country in 1937. "A written document," Wilson commented, "makes lawyers of us all, and our duty as citizens should make us conscientious lawyers . . . but life is always your last and most authoritative critic."[96]

---

tion: The Art of Historian, Magician, or Statesman?" *Yale Law Journal*, 87 (1978), 1752.

[94] Louis Lusky, *By What Right? A Commentary on the Supreme Court's Power to Revise the Constitution* (Charlottesville, Va., 1975).

[95] Woodrow Wilson, *Constitutional Government in the United States* (New York, 1917), 69–70, 157, 192.

[96] *Ibid.*, 70.

Index